Gateway to Japan

Gateway to Japan

Hakata in War and Peace, 500–1300

Bruce L. Batten

University of Hawai'i Press
Honolulu

Printed in the United States of America

11 10 09 08 07 06 6 5 4 3 2 1

Library of Congress Cataloging-in-Publication Data

Batten, Bruce Loyd.
Gateway to Japan : Hakata in war and peace, 500–1300.
p., maps, cm.
Includes bibliographical references and index.
ISBN-13: 978-0-8248-2971-1 (hardcover : alk. paper)
ISBN-10: 0-8248-2971-9 (hardcover : alk. paper)
ISBN-13: 978-0-8248-3029-8 (pbk. : alk. paper)
ISBN-10: 0-8248-3029-6 (pbk. : alk. paper)
1. Japan—Relations—Korea. 2. Korea—Relations—Japan. 3. Japan—Relations—China. 4. China—Relations—Japan. 5. Japan—History—To 1333. 6. Fukuoka-shi (Japan)—History. I. Title.
DS849.K6B36 2006
952'.22—dc22

2005027461

University of Hawai'i Press books are printed on acid-free paper and meet the guidelines for permanence and durability of the Council on Library Resources

Designed by University of Hawai'i Press Production Staff
Printed by the Maple-Vail Book Manufacturing Group

To Eugene, Lisa, and Koji

Contents

Maps, Figures, and Tables

MAPS

FIGURES

Tables

Preface

This book is about Hakata, a bay in western Japan that served as that country's "front door" for many hundreds of years, back in a time when overseas travel was an adventure reserved for few, and the world seemed far larger, and more mysterious, than it does today.

Today if you go to Japan you will probably take a plane and land at Narita's New Tokyo International Airport (which is neither new nor in Tokyo). Not long after the plane touches down, you will disembark, enter the terminal, go through immigration control, pick up your bags and—voila!—find yourself in Japan, surrounded by Japanese people. But fear not. Despite its exotic image, Japan is in many ways similar to other industrialized countries. Its cities look much like their counterparts in other parts of the world, and their inhabitants use the same appliances and wear the same fashions that you do back home. If you speak English, you will be happy to find that most Japanese have some familiarity with that language (they certainly ought to, after studying it for six years in junior and senior high school), and in any case they are almost universally nice to foreigners. As any visitor to Japan can attest, a few minutes on a street corner with a lost expression on your face is a sure ticket to a hands-on tour to your destination by some kind Japanese soul.

A thousand years ago, if you went to Japan you would have arrived not at Narita but in Hakata, and you would have come by ship. Chances are that you would have been Korean or Chinese, since these were almost the only peoples in contact with Japan at the time: East Asia remained virtually a world unto itself. You would have been able to communicate only by passing back and forth notes scrawled in Chinese, which served as a kind of lingua franca in East Asia, at least among the educated few. Communication with ordinary people—most of them farmers—would have been well-nigh impossible, not just because they were illiterate, but because you had few chances to meet them: from the moment you dropped anchor until the moment you set sail for home, you were under strict official supervision (house arrest, not to put too fine a spin on it). And yet, you would have been treated with the utmost courtesy and respect. Like today, your Japanese hosts would have been generally friendly and curious. But also like today, there would have been psychological, as well as linguistic, barriers between you and them. With time and patience, these barriers could certainly be overcome. But they were—and are—real.

I should know. I've lived in Japan now for a quarter of a century, much of that time spent teaching history at a university on the outskirts of Tokyo. By great good fortune, however, my very first experience in Japan was in Fukuoka, a city of (then) a million people situated on the shores of Hakata Bay. I went to Fukuoka in the summer of 1979, immediately after graduating from the University of Oregon. I was supposed to be an English conversation teacher, but my real purpose in going to Japan was to master Japanese and learn as much as possible about the country and its people. And learn I did—particularly about the city of Fukuoka and its unique history. That was when I realized that Hakata was the premodern equivalent to Narita Airport: for much of the country's history it was literally the gateway to Japan.

This knowledge stood me in good stead when I went back to the United States to enter graduate school in 1981, and also later, during my professional career in Japan. I wrote my doctoral dissertation at Stanford on the history of Dazaifu, an old imperial outpost near Hakata, and I also published various articles and a book on the subject in Japanese. The book (which came out in 2001) sold a respectable number of copies and garnered a review in *Nihon keizai shinbun,* Japan's answer to the *Wall Street Journal.* (The reviewer said, in essence, that seeing his country's history through the eyes of a foreigner made him realize how tightly bound Japanese historians were to their own national identity. I think it was intended as a compliment.)

The present volume is neither a belated attempt to fob off my dissertation on an unsuspecting public nor a translation of my Japanese book on Dazaifu. The former, in retrospect, was a narrow exercise in institutional history. The latter, although more wide-ranging in scope, was intended for Japanese readers with a working knowledge of their country's history. The present work assumes no such knowledge, although it does assume some interest in Japan, cross-cultural relations in world history, or both. My goal is to show why Hakata and its history are relevant, not just to our understanding of Japanese society, but also to the broader theme of globalization.

As noted, I have been working, on and off, on this topic for more than twenty-five years, and I dare say that I know more about it than most other non-Japanese (or Japanese, for that matter) researchers. However, much of that knowledge I owe to the help of others, in both Japan and the United States.

My earliest and greatest intellectual debts are to my teachers, particularly my dissertation adviser at Stanford, Jeffrey P. Mass. Jeff, following the teachings of his own mentor, John Whitney Hall, believed that Japanese history was essentially self-propelled—that external relations were frosting on the cake of homegrown institutions. But that didn't stop him from supporting my efforts to prove otherwise. No one could have asked for a better adviser. Jeff's untimely death from cancer in 2001 was a great loss, not just to me, of course, but to the academic community at large.

I did the initial research for my dissertation in Fukuoka, at Kyushu University, during the years 1983–1985. There I was supported financially by grants from the Fulbright Commission, the Social Science Research Council, and the Japan Foundation. (I also later received support from the Whiting Foundation for writing up my dissertation during 1985–1986—my apologies to them for not being able to complete the project until 1989, despite what I said on the grant application!) While in Fukuoka, I received the friendly help of many local researchers, especially Hirano Hiroyuki of Shimonoseki City University, Chō Yōichi of Seinan Gakuin University, and the late Kurazumi Yasuhiko of the Kyushu Historical Museum in Dazaifu.

Of course, all of this was a long time ago. In the intervening years I have received support and advice from so many people that it is difficult to know whom to thank. But I'll do my best.

First, on the academic side, I am grateful to Robert Borgen, Andrew Goble, and Sakayori Masashi for discussing this topic with me ad infinitum, usually over a few (medicinal) Japanese beers; to Sakaue Yasutoshi and Saeki Kōji, for listening to—and constructively criticizing—my ideas every time I visited Fukuoka; to Ōba Kōji for giving me several guided tours of the Kōrokan site and for helping me secure permission to reprint photographs and drawings belonging to the Fukuoka City Board of Education; to Yamauchi Shinji for taking the time to explain to me the finer points of maritime commerce in the Heian era;

to Shigematsu Toshihiko and Ikezaki Jōji, for accompanying me on a strenuous hike to see the ruins of Ōno Fortress on one of the hottest days in recent memory; and to Mikael Adolphson for organizing the 2002 "Centers and Peripheries in Heian Japan" conference at Harvard, which gave me the necessary kick in the pants to commence work on the present project. Other fellow researchers who gave me helpful advice or just listened to me rant and rave about Hakata include Martha Chaiklin, Thomas Conlan, Karl Friday, Lorraine Harrington, Cappy Hurst, Ishigami Eiichi, Lee Sungsi, Kate Nakai, Joan Piggott, Ken Robinson, Ethan Segal, Ronald Toby, Hitomi Tonomura, and Suzuki Yasutami. I also appreciate the constructive comments I received from two anonymous readers for University of Hawai'i Press. I wasn't able to follow all of their suggestions, but I did the best I could.

Speaking of UHP, this is my second book with Hawai'i, and once again I wish to express my appreciation to Patricia Crosby and the other fine people who helped out on the production side, especially Ann Ludeman and Joanne Sandstrom.

On a more personal level, thanks are owed to my family, for putting up with my inexplicable desire to write books, and to various friends who kept me sane during this project, especially Semba Yukari and Holly Whitney. Other friends who contributed materially (although in some cases unwittingly) to the completion of this work include Adam Cardamon, Chūjō Ken, Steve Gershon, Henri Hatayama, Joseph Hicks, Simon Hunter, Ikeda Manami, Kawahara Hiromi, Lee Kwangil, McKenna Mason, Audrey Morrell, Stephen and Carmelita Nussbaum, Eric Rutledge, Sakai Yoshie, Rocco Sorrenti, Mark Stevenson, Clark Taber, and Travis Venters. Also thanks to the Koike family for many great evenings at La Petite Chaise, their restaurant in Shibuya, and to Kondō Seiichi of Japan's Ministry of Foreign Affairs and other members of his bimonthly discussion group, "K Salon," for much stimulating discussion on the topic of cultural exchange.

Needless to say, none of the above are responsible for any errors remaining in the book, which I made all on my own.

A Note on Spelling, Names, and Dates

All Japanese words in the text are romanized according to the standard, modified Hepburn system. (The few Korean and Chinese terms and names are given, respectively, in McCune-Reischauer and pinyin transcription.) Consonants in modern Japanese are generally pronounced as a native English speaker would guess, except for *g*, which is always hard, and *r*, which sounds like a cross between an English *r* and *l*. Vowels are pronounced as in Italian. Long or double vowels are indicated with a macron (e.g., Jōmon), except in the case of place-names that will already be familiar to most readers (e.g., Tokyo, Kyoto).

Regarding place-names, alert readers will notice a few anachronisms. When writing about very early periods of history, I occasionally refer to "Japan," "Korea," or "China" (or to things "Japanese," "Korean," or "Chinese") regardless of whether countries bearing these names (or their cognates) actually existed at the time. The terms should be understood as shorthand for "the geographic region now known as Japan (or Korea, or China)," no more, no less. (By the way, the term "Nihon" or "Nippon," from which our "Japan" is ultimately derived, was invented in the late seventh century C.E.)

Japanese personal names are given in the Japanese order, with the surname preceding the given name. (The same is true for Chinese and Korean names.) Readers familiar with early Japan will probably notice that I have omitted the possessive particle "no" between family and given names, writing, for example, "Fujiwara Nakamaro" instead of the (technically more correct) "Fujiwara no Nakamaro."

Finally, dates are given in the hybrid form standard among historians of Japan. The Japanese calendar is keyed to "era names" *(gengō* or *nengō)* so that 2005, for example, is the seventeenth year of Heisei. Also, in premodern times the Japanese used a lunar calendar (ultimately Chinese in origin), whose months and days were not in synch with the solar Gregorian calendar in use today. In the text I have converted Japanese years to the nearest Gregorian equivalent but have left months and days untouched. To make it clear that these are early Japanese dates, not Western ones, I refer to, for example, the "fifth month," not "May," of a certain year.

Introduction

I get off the subway at Akasaka Station in Fukuoka and wait on the platform. After a few minutes, as planned, fellow historian Sakaue Yasutoshi steps off a train coming from the opposite direction, and we head out the exit and up the stairs into the bright morning light. It is late March 2003, and the temperature is still chilly, but as we reach street level and look around, I can see the cherry trees already in bloom. We walk up the slope into Maizuru Park, past a moat and some impressive ramparts—the remains of a castle built in 1601–1607 by Kuroda Nagamasa, the first lord of Fukuoka domain.

Fukuoka Castle was home to Kuroda's heirs and successors for two and a half centuries—until 1868, when Japan's Meiji Restoration put an end to the old samurai regime. Following the ouster of the Kuroda family, the castle grounds—situated just south of Hakata Bay to the west of Fukuoka's Tenjin district—temporarily housed Fukuoka's new prefectural government. When the prefectural offices moved to Tenjin in 1876, the site was taken over by Japan's new imperial army. Barracks for the 24th Infantry Regiment, which served in several of Japan's subsequent foreign wars, were built on the ruins of the old castle buildings and remained in use until 1945, when Japan was demilitarized at the end of World War II. In the postwar period, Fukuoka city planners—unable to kept their hands off such a prime piece of real estate, and perhaps also conscious of their duty to repudiate Japan's military traditions—built an athletic field and a courthouse atop the ruins of the castle and the army barracks (figure 1). Under the name Heiwadai (Peace Hill) Stadium, the athletic field later became the home ground of a professional baseball team, the legendary Nishitetsu (later Seibu) Lions.

As I mentally review this history, Professor Sakaue and I continue to climb, past more cherry trees, past grassy slopes with picnicking families—and ultimately to an ugly steel fence with a clearly marked

FIGURE 1. Kōrokan site from the air, ca. 2000. The view is from the southeast. The site is visible under the outfield of the old baseball stadium. Note the surrounding castle moat and, in the background, Fukuoka Tower, Fukuoka Dome, and Hakata Bay. *Source:* Fukuoka City Board of Education. Reproduced with permission.

sign: "Archaeological excavation in progress: no trespassing!" Having advance permission, we ignore the sign, pull the (fortunately unlocked) latch on the gate, and walk inside.

In front of us lies a crazy patchwork of pits and trenches. At first glance the angry cuts in the red earth look like nothing so much as a small-scale strip-mining operation. Men and women wearing helmets and work clothes streaked with clay scurry back and forth with wheelbarrows full of rocks and earth. We catch the eye of the nearest excavator and ask for Ōba Kōji, the archaeologist in charge of this site. The worker points him out, and in a moment we are exchanging greetings with Mr. Ōba himself, a dapper man in his fifties with a mustache and a quick, ironic smile.

As Mr. Ōba gives us a brief overview of this year's operations, I look around and confirm with my own eyes what he is telling us. The old baseball stadium is gone—removed by court mandate to excavate the archaeological treasures underneath—although some of the foundations are still evident. Going back centuries in time with each meter of earth, the excavators have removed not just the stadium but also the remains of the earlier army barracks and castle facilities. All of these structures were built atop the ruins of a much older, and much more important, structure—the Tsukushi Lodge (Tsukushi-no-murotsumi), a hostel for foreign visitors built by Japan's imperial government in the late seventh century. For a period of centuries, nearly all of Japan's foreign contacts were routed through this single location. It was, quite literally, the gateway to Japan.

After the Tsukushi Lodge (also known as the Kōrokan, a Chinese-style moniker adopted in the ninth century) was abandoned around 1100 C.E., its very location was forgotten and remained a mystery until modern times. The site was tentatively reidentified in the 1920s by Nakayama Heijirō, an amateur archaeologist and professor of medicine at Kyushu Imperial University. However, final proof did not come until late 1987, when the City of Fukuoka began renovating the outfield bleachers at Heiwadai Stadium. In its haste to improve the facilities of this lucrative sports franchise, the city had begun construction without notifying Japan's Agency for Cultural Affairs, which has jurisdiction over important historical sites. Alerted to the violation, the agency immediately stepped in to halt construction and order a salvage excavation.[1]

Within a few short weeks in late 1987 and early 1988, the site yielded the remains of buildings dating from the late seventh through

FIGURE 2. Early 8th c. stone rampart at Kōrokan site, March 2003. Photograph by author.

ninth centuries, together with vast quantities of Chinese porcelain from the ninth through eleventh—all miraculously preserved under the stadium bleachers. More prosaically, excavators also chanced upon the remains of three eighth-century toilets. An analysis of their contents produced a wealth of seeds, pollen, and parasite eggs, all constituting direct (if unsavory) evidence of the diets of Japanese officials and foreign guests at the Tsukushi Lodge.

As a result of these and further discoveries, the decision was made to tear down the stadium and conduct a full-scale excavation—one that has now been going on for sixteen years. Today I have taken the five-hour train ride from Tokyo to look at the latest discoveries. Aside from the usual postholes and roof tiles, these include two stone walls—one dating from the late seventh century, the other, more impressive one, from the early eighth. Our guide, Mr. Ōba, is currently showing us the latter, displayed in relief in the largest and deepest of the pits. Pointing at the large blocks of stone, Mr. Ōba says, "Who would have guessed that the guesthouse was surrounded by a stone rampart like this? This was built in the early eighth century, when the facility was enlarged. It's not clear why they rebuilt it at this time. Perhaps it had something to do with the reopening of diplomatic relations with Tang China" (figure 2).

Admittedly, the remains of the Kōrokan lack the physical grandeur of other, better-known archaeological sites. Even the stone wall I have come to view today—one of the most significant discoveries here in many years—is a far cry from Stonehenge, the pyramids of Egypt, or the Great Wall of China. Although I have devoted much of my academic career to the early history of Fukuoka, I would have a hard time visualizing the original layout of the Kōrokan without the benefit of expert, hands-on commentary from Mr. Ōba.

With his help, this is what I see. Two fenced, gravelled compounds, one to the north, the other to the south, face each other across a narrow ravine spanned by a footbridge. The northern slope of the ravine is buttressed by the stone wall that we are now viewing. Within each compound stands a large one-story building in post-and-lintel style, painted red and white and with a gray tile roof. All in all, the design is fairly typical of Japanese government facilities in the eighth century, though the buildings lack the large foundation stones used at some other sites, such as the palace at Heijō-kyō (Nara) or, closer at hand, the Dazaifu (Kyushu government-general) headquarters.

Turning now to the larger context, we know that the Kōrokan was much closer to the shoreline of Hakata Bay than at present. This is not, of course, to say that the site itself has moved. Rather, the bay has shrunken considerably over the centuries as the result of sedimentation and landfill. During the Nara period (710–784), chances are good that an inlet of the sea came all the way to the guest lodge, probably to a harbor near the outlet of the ravine before us.

Unlike today, there would have been few if any other man-made structures in the vicinity. Now the site is conveniently near downtown Fukuoka, but originally it seems to have been chosen for its proximity to the bay—and isolation from everyplace else. There was no city of Fukuoka, and the nearest town was Dazaifu, situated behind a series of natural and man-made fortifications approximately thirteen kilometers to the southeast. Dazaifu, home to several thousand bureaucrats, soldiers, and their families, was the imperial headquarters for western Japan, and the Kōrokan and associated facilities were placed directly under its supervision.

The physical remains of the Kōrokan belie this site's importance—if not to world history, then at least to the history of Japan. For, as noted above, the Kōrokan was Japan's principal gateway to the outside world during the Nara and Heian (794–1185) periods. Even after the abandonment of the facility, other areas in northern Kyushu continued to play the same role throughout the whole of the premodern period, until the arrival of Commodore Perry's "black ships" in the mid-nineteenth century forced Japan to open other ports in Honshu and Hokkaido to trade with the West.

To understand the historical significance of northern Kyushu let us take a glance at the map of Japan (map 1). Japan is situated on a volcanic archipelago approximately three thousand kilometers from one end to the other. Of the seven thousand or so islands that make up the archipelago, the four largest, from northeast to southwest, are Hokkaido, Honshu, Shikoku, and Kyushu. Of these four, Honshu is quite literally the "main island"—almost three times the size of its nearest rival (Hokkaido), centrally situated, and home to all of Japan's historical capitals. Today the capital is Tokyo, on Honshu's eastern Pacific coast, but through much of premodern history political power was concentrated at the eastern terminus of the Inland Sea, which lies between Honshu and Shikoku.

Northern Kyushu lies directly on the shortest, most convenient route between these early capitals and the Asian continent—a route traversing the Inland Sea, rounding the Kyushu coast to Hakata, and then heading across the Genkai Sea to the Korean Peninsula. Hakata itself is two hundred kilometers as the crow (or perhaps seagull) flies from Pusan, South Korea, but this distance is significantly ameliorated by the presence of two natural stepping-stones, the islands of Iki and Tsushima. The latter island (actually an archipelago), historically the furthest outpost of Japanese control, lies just over fifty kilometers short of Korea, which is visible from Tsushima on a clear day. Given these geographic facts, it is no surprise to learn that many of Japan's early exchanges with the continent were channeled through the Hakata area.

This fact is not lost on the residents of Fukuoka, who are rightly proud of their city's historical legacy. "Thanks to its geographical proximity to the continent," boasts the city's official Web site, "Fukuoka City has enjoyed a long history as a gateway for Asian culture into Japan, and as a base for trade with our Asian neighbors." The site further describes Fukuoka as "Japan's oldest internationally oriented city."[2]

The Kōrokan site has played a major role in the development of this self-image. Soon after its rediscovery, the site was co-opted to serve as centerpiece for the Asia Pacific Exhibition of 1989.[3] The first area to be excavated was enshrined in situ in a prefabricated structure,

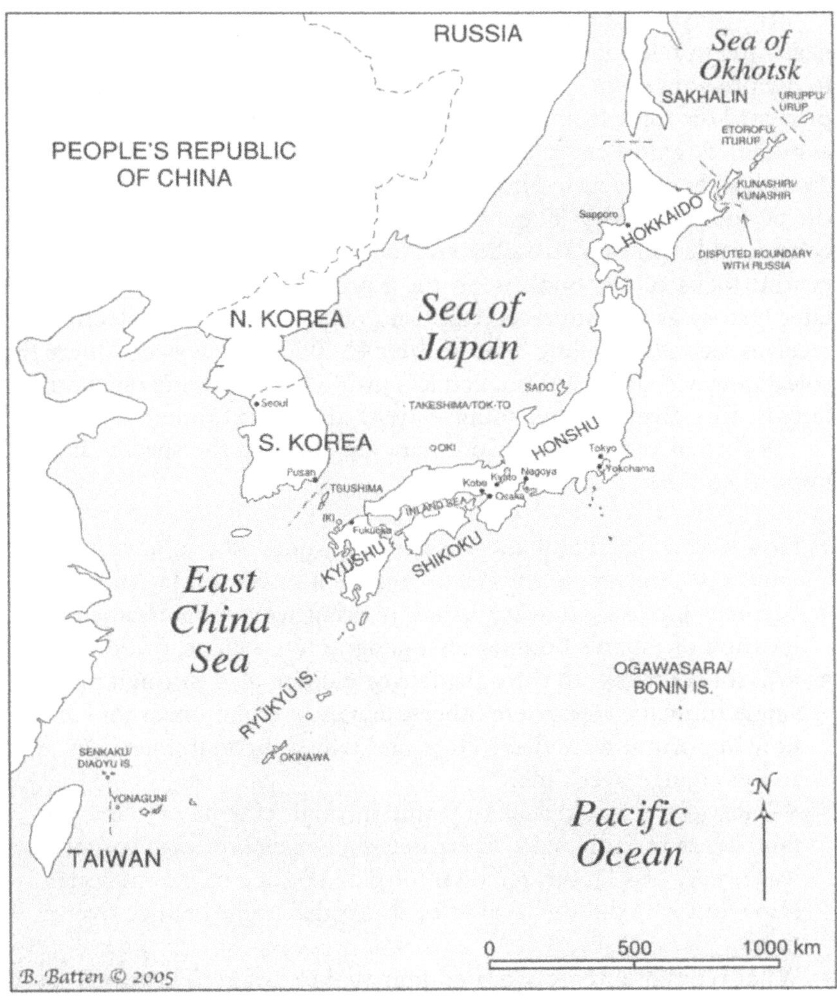

Map 1. Japan today.

complete with explanatory signs—much like Dinosaur National Monument in Colorado and Utah. And many of the early discoveries were put on display in the new Fukuoka City Museum erected within the exhibition grounds two kilometers west of the site. In subsequent years, the Kōrokan has been the focus of numerous city-sponsored symposia and publications. To this day, the Kōrokan remains the prime symbol of Fukuoka's cosmopolitan past—and present.

The purpose of this book is to shed new light on premodern Japanese foreign relations. In that sense it represents a companion volume to my previous work, *To the Ends of Japan*. But whereas that book approached the topic from a macro, theoretical perspective, this one takes a micro, down-to-earth approach. Specifically, it is a case study of cross-border contacts in Hakata, or more broadly northern Kyushu, in the period 500–1300. These dates are somewhat arbitrary, as there is considerable spillover to earlier and later centuries. But in any case, the central focus of the book is on the Kōrokan and Dazaifu. Hakata's later history as a commercial emporium is by no means neglected, but receives secondary billing because after 1300 Hakata was no longer the sole gateway to Japan. (Also, and less justifiably, skimping on Hakata's later history gives me something to write about next time.)

With that brief justification, here are some of the specific issues I hope to address:

- How and why did Hakata—rather than some other point along the "natural" route from the Asian continent to central Japan—becomes Japan's gateway? What, in other words, determined the location of Japan's boundaries—geography, politics, or both?
- Was all contact with the outside world channeled through this single route, or were there other avenues of communication? If so, how important were they? How and why did communication routes change over time?
- What was the actual level of traffic through Hakata or other portals? More broadly, was Japan essentially a closed social system, or was it part of a larger, regional (or global) zone of interactions? How and why did the level of cross-border traffic change over time?
- What types of interaction predominated in different historical periods? Was all interaction peaceful, as Fukuoka's self-image implies, or were there periods of tension or war?
- Finally, and most fundamentally, why did "foreigners" come to Japan, and how did Japanese people deal with them?

Although this is an academic book, the above issues are not of purely academic concern; indeed, they are highly pertinent to Japan's role in the world today. Now, as in the period examined by this book, Japan has one principal gateway—New Tokyo International Airport (although it also has a host of other, lesser entrances, corresponding to other international airports and seaports). Now, as then, Japan's relationship with the outside world is ambivalent. Japanese people are justifiably proud of their unique cultural heritage, but much of that heritage is in fact borrowed from China (or Korea) and the West. Japan is now part of the "West" but at the same time remains a world apart. Its relationships with other countries are now entirely peaceful but were unabashedly aggressive as recently as 1945. Japanese people today are both astonishingly open-minded and frustratingly exclusive in their dealings with outsiders—tolerant of the most divergent attitudes and practices, but forever erecting mental barriers between "us Japanese" and "those foreigners." This is true even when the foreigners in question have lived in Japan for decades and speak the language fluently. "Why did you come?" "How shall we deal with you?" These are questions that even the most cosmopolitan Japanese still find themselves asking vis-à-vis foreigners in their midst.

Viewed in this light, the book represents an attempt to explain present-day Japan by reference to its past. To give a brief preview, here are some of my major conclusions: (1) although relatively infrequent by world standards, cross-border interactions were nonetheless of critical importance to the development of the Japanese state and the Japanese people; (2) natural crossroads or foci of interaction, such as Hakata, have always tended to attract the exercise of political power and the drawing of boundaries; and (3) throughout Japanese history there has been a clear and consistent inverse relationship between the power of Japan's central government (that is, the degree of political centralization) and the volume of cross-border traffic.

The organization of the book is at once thematic and (loosely) chronological, an approach made possible because prevalent forms of interaction changed systematically over time. Chapter 1, "War," focuses on Chinese expansionism and its consequences for Japan and East Asia as a whole. Chapter 2, "Diplomacy," examines the treatment of foreign (mainly Korean) envoys in Kyushu, with an eye to revealing the subtle (and sometimes not-so-subtle) contradictions and obfuscations of the diplomatic process. Chapter 3, "Piracy," provides a close-up view of random attacks on Kyushu by "foreign pirates," many of them from Korea. (Japanese pirates, who were every bit as dangerous, also make a brief cameo appearance.) In chapter 4, "Trade," I examine foreign commerce, which turns out to have been neither fully "foreign" nor truly "commerce" in the modern sense of the word, in and around Hakata. Finally, in chapter 5, I briefly trace the story forward into medieval and early-modern times, an exercise that sets the stage for restating some of my principal conclusions.

This book thus surveys about eight centuries in the life of a major Japanese port. With this brief introduction, let us now return to the Tsukushi Lodge, not as it appears under the excavators' spades today, not as it stood in the eighth century, but as it was being constructed in the late 600s. The builders of the lodge would have been surprised to learn how their creation was later co-opted by the city of Fukuoka to serve as a symbol of peace and international understanding! For the Tsukushi Lodge, like Dazaifu and all other government facilities in this area, was built under the threat of war.

CHAPTER 1

War

Once upon a time, residents of a fishing village in Japan watched with trepidation as a fleet of foreign warships appeared in the offing beyond their little harbor. Their main concern was for their lives. Who knew what strange creatures might be on board or what nefarious plans had brought them to Japan?

The fears of the villagers were in a sense misplaced. No monsters were aboard these vessels, and no Japanese blood would be shed when their occupants cast anchor and rowed ashore. The villagers, and their descendants, would continue to fish, and watch the seas, long after the events of that day became distant memories.

Nonetheless, the arrival of the foreigners would irrevocably alter the course of Japanese history. It touched off panic among common folk and government leaders alike. It led to frantic debates over foreign policy—and domestic policy as well. Before long, Japan found itself in the midst of civil war. When the revolution came to an end, the victors began to rebuild their country in the image of the "evil empire" that had come knocking at the gates.

The year was 1853 and the place was Uraga, situated near the tip of the Miura Peninsula at the mouth of Edo (now Tokyo) Bay. The foreign vessels were under the command of Matthew Calbraith Perry, an American naval officer charged by President Millard Fillmore to induce Japan to establish trade and diplomatic relations with the United States. (Not incidentally, Fillmore wanted Japan to open its ports to American whaling vessels, whaling being one of the great American industries of the era. How many American critics of present-day Japanese whaling practices are aware of this historical irony, I wonder?) Perry's arrival is indelibly impressed upon the Japanese imagination as one of the defining moments in their country's history—the event that

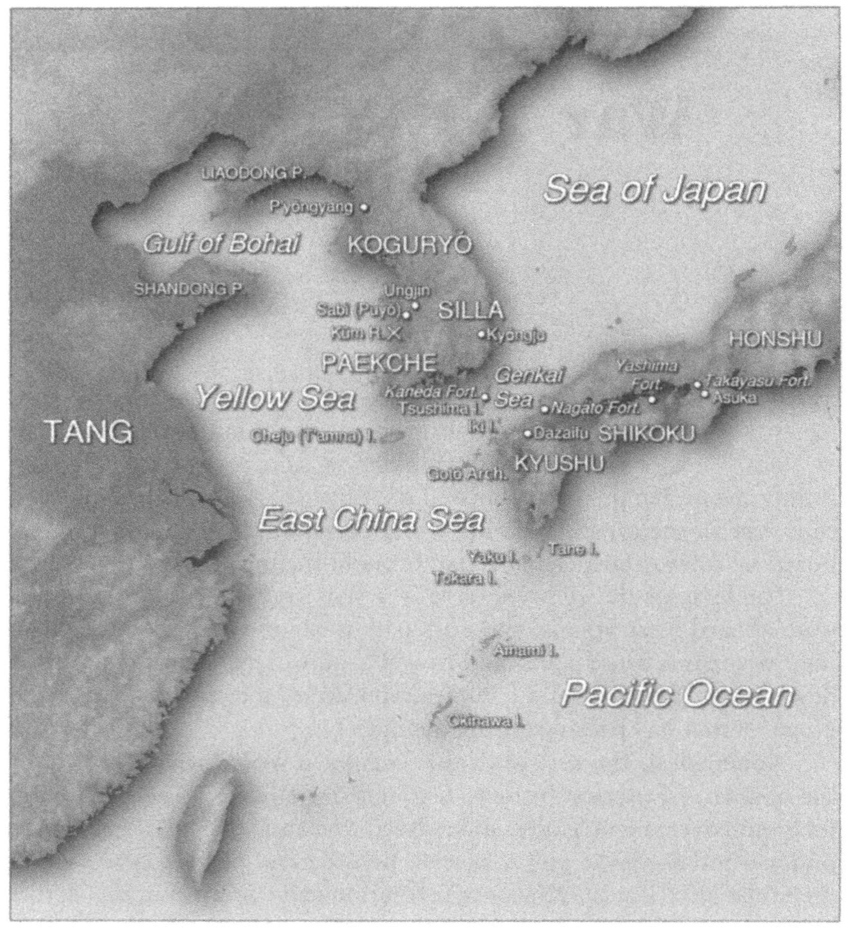

MAP 2. Japan in East Asia, 7th c.

dragged a reluctant Japan into the modern world and turned a hidebound feudal society into a modern nation-state.[1]

Warships on the Horizon

What few people realize is that Perry's arrival was not the first time that such a scenario had played out upon Japanese soil. The events of 1853 were a close replay of an equally momentous occasion some twelve hundred years earlier. The year was 664, and the location was Tsushima, a mountainous isle (actually, two isles separated by a narrow strait) about 50 kilometers south of the Korean port of Pusan and 150 kilometers west of Hakata on the Kyushu mainland (map 2).

On that earlier occasion, the visitors had been Chinese, not American. Their large junks, bearing flags of the Tang empire, had first been sighted on an early summer's day in the fourth month of the Japanese lunar calendar. The ships were slowly approaching Tsushima across the Korea Strait from the general direction of Paekche, a kingdom on the west side of the Korean Peninsula. They seemed to be making directly for the village—or more precisely, for the small harbor below, where the villagers' fishing ships lay at anchor. Those watching the approach were worried—and with good reason.

The Tsushima islanders, of course, were used to seeing foreign vessels—just as they were used to taking their own ships to other nearby islands and even, sometimes, to the Korean coast. Japan in the seventh century was ostensibly an agricultural society, but had the thousand or so residents of Tsushima been forced to rely on the meager produce of their farms, most of them probably would have starved. Tsushima was an island of fisherfolk and petty traders. They harvested laver and abalone along the rocky shoreline and fished for yellowtail and cuttlefish in the nearby seas. They spoke a dialect of Japanese, but many could probably also understand the language of the Koreans on the other side of the strait. Relations between the two groups were friendly, for the most part. They fished together, bartered, and sometimes intermarried. And while such intimate ties were not exactly condoned by their respective governments, they were not actively discouraged, either. The Yamato government (and its counterparts in Korea) hardly had the wherewithal to patrol the seaways or prevent island residents from pursuing their traditional livelihoods. Yamato was situated at the eastern terminus of Japan's Inland Sea—six hundred kilometers east of Tsushima, up to several weeks' journey by ship. While its rulers may have laid theoretical claim to Tsushima, for the most part the islanders lived their own lives, free from central interference.

But the times were rapidly changing—as most of the islanders knew even before they saw the strange new vessels approaching their harbor. Only the previous year—663 by the Western calendar, the second year in the reign of King Tenji (r. 661–671),[2] for those few in Tsushima who cared about such things—a vast fleet had come from Hakata on its way to "rescue Paekche," so they said. Woe be to them! Not long afterward, some of the tattered remnants of Yamato's once-proud navy limped back to Tsushima. Few of the war veterans tarried long; they seemed afraid of who might follow in their wake. The same was true of the many refugees from Paekche—some of them members of the royal family—who accompanied the Japanese survivors. Before long, almost all of the new arrivals had departed for the Kyushu mainland, or for Yamato.

Even the common fisherfolk in Tsushima knew who had inflicted the defeat upon the combined forces of Yamato and Paekche. Paekche's traditional enemy was its neighbor to the east, Silla. But the two kingdoms had been squabbling for centuries, with few major geopolitical consequences. What was new this time was that Silla had somehow managed to enlist the support of the great Tang empire in China. The Japanese forces sent to aid Paekche had been overconfident, ignorant, or both. They had been greeted near the mouth of the Kŭm River not by their friends from Paekche, not even by their enemies from Silla, but by an armada of Chinese warships. Tang was the most powerful country in Asia—indeed in the entire world at this time—and its military machine made quick work of the Japanese fleet. The Yamato leaders had made the mistake of their lives—a mistake that would have profound repercussions for the subsequent development of their country.

Of course, the residents of Tsushima could not read the future. All they knew was that their worst fears were coming true. Paekche was gone, its former territory now occupied by Silla and Tang. But the victors were not satisfied. They had noted Yamato's participation in the final defense of Paekche, and they had not forgotten. Now was the time to settle that score. The Chinese were coming. Neither Tsushima nor Japan as a whole would ever be quite the same.

Early Warfare and Relations with the Continent

What could have possessed Yamato leaders when they sent their best men and ships to fight the Chinese Goliath? Did the ill-fated expedition take place in a fit of madness? Did the kings and queens of Yamato lack information about events on the peninsula, or were they ignorant of the power of Tang? What could possibly have been important enough about far-away events in Korea to justify such a preposterous, risky undertaking? To answer these questions, we must turn back the historical clock to survey the origins of warfare in Japan and the nature of Japanese relations with the Asian mainland.

Whether or not we agree with scientists who say that aggression is in our genes,[3] there is no doubt that violence was endemic to human society from the start. The fossil evidence shows that our extinct "cousins," the Neanderthals, killed (and perhaps even ate) each other on occasion, and the same is true for early *Homo sapiens*.[4] But warfare—organized, large-scale fighting—remained unknown through most of the history of the human species, until the invention of agriculture and the emergence of densely populated, highly stratified societies with land and property worth fighting over.[5]

What was true elsewhere was also true in Japan.[6] The islands were initially settled by foragers from the Asian mainland during the last Ice Age, perhaps around 100,000 B.C.E.[7] Society consisted of small mobile bands of hunters and gatherers during the Paleolithic period of ca. 100,000 to ca. 14,500 B.C.E. Climatic warming made food resources more readily available, and this availability resulted in population growth and the formation of permanent village settlements during the subsequent Jōmon period of ca. 14,500 to ca. 1000 B.C.E.[8] Some Jōmon-era skeletons show evidence of wounds inflicted by stone axes and arrowheads—the contemporary state of the art in weaponry.[9] However, all in all, society seems to have been relatively peaceful (although perhaps not the golden age envisioned by some Japanese authors eager to trace their national origins to happy, well-fed Jōmon villagers living in a spirit of mutual cooperation and harmony with nature[10]).

Starting around 1000 B.C.E., a new wave of immigrants—this time rice farmers with bronze- and iron-working skills—made their way to the archipelago from Northeast Asia via the Korean Peninsula.[11] The newcomers first settled in northern Kyushu, where they intermarried with, or sometimes simply displaced, the Jōmon aborigines. High agricultural productivity led to rapid population growth and the establishment of splinter communities in low-lying areas throughout Kyushu, Honshu, and Shikoku. This period, known to archaeologists as the Yayoi, lasted for more than a millennium and saw the emergence of socially stratified villages and eventually chiefdoms ruling entire river basins or alluvial plains. The Yayoi period also marked the beginning of warfare in the archipelago, attested archaeologically by the presence of fortified villages and frequent wound marks on skeletons.[12]

Violence escalated in the subsequent Kofun period, named for the large tomb mounds characteristic of the four and a half centuries from 200 to 650.[13] The construction of these mausoleums must have required vast inputs of labor, suggestive of increasing concentration of power in the hands of the tombs' occupants. The earliest tombs were built in Yamato, but this type of burial soon spread throughout the three main islands, indicating, at the very least, the emergence of a common political culture. Kofun society was dominated by a militarized, equestrian elite, as attested by the iron swords, armor, helmets, stirrups, and bits found within Kofun burials and by the clay figures of warriors and horses planted around their margins. Fighting was widespread—not between villages or chiefdoms, as in the Yayoi period, but between regional power blocs. Of these, Yamato was clearly the most important, but it did not command anything like a unified state until the late 520s, when Iwai, the lord of Tsukushi in northern Kyushu, was defeated by Yamato in a war known from several eighth-century sources. (Iwai is buried at Iwatoyama Tumulus in Yame, Fukuoka. At 135 meters in length, Iwatoyama is the largest Kofun in northern Kyushu).[14]

On other occasions the fighting spilled outside the boundaries of what we now think of as Japan onto the Asian mainland. The earliest proof of this is a huge (6.4 m) stone stele erected in 414 on the banks of the Yalu River in what is now northeastern China by King Kwanggaet'o of Koguryŏ. The stele commemorates the king's many accomplishments, including military victories against the "Wa" in 400 and 404. According to the stele, Wa forces had been active in the southern part of the peninsula since 391 and had allied themselves with Paekche against Silla and, eventually, Koguryŏ.[15]

Although "Wa" is the old name for the Japanese islands (or vicinity), there is no need to assume that King Kwanggaet'o's opponents were sent by Yamato. Perhaps they were, or perhaps they were not; the answer depends upon what degree of hegemony Yamato had established within the Japanese islands themselves at this time. As late as the 520s, as we have seen, a local warlord in Kyushu could exercise (if only temporarily) a significant degree of independence. Interestingly, Yamato's campaign against Iwai was specifically motivated by the latter's seizure of the sea-lanes between Kyushu and Korea and his unholy alliance with Silla, Yamato's traditional enemy.

Why were residents of the islands, whether from Kyushu or Yamato or elsewhere, interested in Korean politics in the first place? Why send troops to the peninsula? Why form an alliance with Paekche? The answer is simple: goods that Japanese elites coveted were available in the peninsula.

Some of these goods were physical in nature. A prosaic example is iron ingots. As noted above, iron weapons and horse trappings were essential to the Kofun-period elite. And yet, none of this iron came from Japan itself; all of it was imported from southern Korea, particularly the Kaya region near the mouth of the Naktong River. But this was not all. Imports from the peninsula also included prestige goods such as gold earrings and crowns.[16]

Other goods were more ethereal. At this time, Korean civilization was significantly more advanced than its Japanese counterpart. Elites in the islands were naturally eager to learn what they could from their peninsular neighbors. Architecture, sculpture, painting, literature, religion, political philosophy, law, administration, what have you—knowledge about these and other topics was not only desirable in and of itself, but it was also useful in establishing superiority over other claimants to power in the Japanese islands.

Granted that elites in the Japanese islands were desirous of contact with the Korean Peninsula, what accounts for their ability to establish (if only temporarily) a military presence there? After all, if the Koreans were so advanced, should they not have been able to prevent the Wa from gaining any sort of foothold in the peninsula?

The answer to this is simple, if counterintuitive: Wa troops were in Korea by invitation. The peninsula at this time was home to three full-fledged kingdoms (Koguryŏ, Silla, and Paekche) and one regional federation or chiefdom (Kaya), all in a state of perpetual competition. Power politics was the name of the game, and each kingdom sought out whatever allies it could in the struggle to survive and prosper. For Paekche and Kaya, both situated on the southern peninsula just across the Korea Strait from Kyushu, the Wa were a continual source of hope. Wa troops in Paekche or Kaya were there not in spite of Korean wishes but because of them: in short, goods were being traded for military service.[17]

To this admittedly complicated picture we now must add one final element—China, always the center of the East Asian world. China itself was politically fragmented in these centuries, following the collapse of the great Han Empire in 220. Successor dynasties—the Northern and Southern kingdoms—were less powerful than the Han, but nonetheless retained a substantial cachet of prestige as well as undeniable cultural and technological advantages over not just Wa but also the various Korean kingdoms. Accordingly, rulers of these lesser states all vied for the attention and approval of the powers-that-be in China, both to strengthen their own authority vis-à-vis domestic rivals and to gain an advantage over neighboring "peer polities."[18]

An excellent example is provided by an envoy sent by Yamato's "King Bu" to the emperor of Liu Song, a minor Chinese dynasty, in 478. The Wa ambassador carried a letter from Bu describing his ancestors' conquest of "fifty-five countries of hairy men" to the east, "sixty-six countries of various barbarians" to the west, and "ninety-five countries" across the sea to the north. This was followed by an account of a campaign against Koguryŏ and a request for military titles. Apparently taking Bu's account more or less at face value, the Chinese emperor appointed him "King of Wa and Generalissimo Who Maintains Peace in the East Commanding with Battle-Ax All Military Affairs in the Six Countries of Wa, Silla, Imna, Kala, Jinhan and Mok-han."[19]

Bu is generally identified with the "Emperor Yūryaku" described (retrospectively) in eighth-century Japanese chronicles, as well as with a "Great King Wakatakeru" known from late fifth-century sword inscriptions from central Kyushu (Edafunayama Tumulus in Kumamoto) and the Kantō Plain (Inariyama Tumulus in Saitama).[20] The discovery of these swords in areas several hundred kilometers west and east, respectively, of the Yamato homeland, incidentally, gives some credence to Bu's claims of conquest, although it must be recalled that even half a century later, in the 520s, a large portion of Kyushu could temporarily "secede" from the Yamato polity under the leadership of Iwai.

In sum, during the early centuries C.E. both the Japanese islands and the Korean Peninsula were politically fragmented, with state building progressing by fits and starts in a general context of geopolitical competition and competitive emulation. Warfare was commonplace, with the scale of conflict increasing from the purely local to the interregional and international.[21]

An East Asian "World War"

The stakes grew still higher and the competition more fierce with the emergence, for the first time in centuries, of a unified China under the Sui (581–618) and Tang (618–907) dynasties. Sui and Tang expansion had a cascading effect throughout East Asia, forcing local leaders to strengthen their regimes or risk obliteration, either at Chinese hands or at those of their increasingly powerful neighbors. The end result, in the 660s, was a kind of East Asian "world war"—a war that had profound consequences for all states in the region, including Japan.

Koguryŏ, situated on the northern part of the peninsula, was the first of the Korean kingdoms to come into conflict with China. A Koguryŏ foray into northeast China in 598 led to swift Sui retaliation and a pro forma submission by the Koguryŏ king. Suspicions of Koguryŏ collusion with the Turks of central Asia, among other things, led to further Sui invasions in 612, 613, and 614. Only the last succeeded in reaching the Koguryŏ capital of P'yŏngyang, where another nominal submission was accepted. This was obtained at the expense of the Chinese domestic order, however, for the tremendous cost of the invasions led to widespread popular uprisings and the demise of Sui in 617.[22]

The Sui dynasty was replaced by the Tang in 618. Domestic consolidation occupied Chinese attention for several decades, and relations with Koguryŏ improved. By the 640s, however, Tang control of China was secure enough to permit the type of dynastic expansionism that had proved the undoing of Sui. The spark was ignited in 642 when a Koguryŏ general named Yŏn Kaesomun assassinated his king, replacing him with a docile puppet. Yŏn not only halted the flow of Koguryŏ tribute to Tang but also attacked Silla and prevented its embassies from reaching China. When the Chinese emperor sent an envoy to Koguryŏ to try to resolve the issue diplomatically, Yŏn imprisoned him. In response, the Chinese launched an invasion of Koguryŏ in 645, but like the earlier Sui campaigns it ended in failure. Yŏn Kaesomun began to detain more Tang envoys, and in 647 the Chinese mounted yet another expedition, which again had inconclusive results. A third campaign was planned for the following year but was called off on the death of the Tang emperor.[23]

Koguryŏ's aggressive foreign policy continued after the Tang failure, in the form of an attack on the Chinese vassal state of Khitan in 655 and, in league with Paekche, an invasion of Silla in 656. Repeated requests by Silla for aid during this general period were answered by Chinese retaliations against Koguryŏ in 655 and 658–659, the first of which produced the usual pledges of obedience. The minimal success of most of the Sui and Tang invasions resulted primarily from the difficulty of securing the mountainous and well-defended land route to P'yŏngyang.

By 660, however, the Chinese had formulated a new and ultimately successful strategy with their ally Silla. Both would first attack Paekche, Tang by sea and Silla by land. Once Paekche fell, the combined armies would strike north to P'yŏngyang, which would be crushed between them and another Chinese army approaching by the traditional land route. The initial attack on Paekche, which took place in 660, was successful and resulted in the capture of most of the royal house. Following standard practice, Paekche was placed under the supervision of several governments-general, the principal of which was at Ungjin. When the Tang/Silla forces struck north for Koguryŏ, however, a restoration movement broke out under a Paekche general named Poksin. Because of this and other difficulties, P'yŏngyang remained unmolested for several more years.

At this point Yamato came into the picture.[24] According to the official Japanese history of the period, *Chronicles of Japan,* Poksin sent one of his followers to the Japanese court in the tenth month of 660 with a request for military aid and the repatriation of Paekche's Prince P'ung, who had been living in Japan since 631.[25] The court's response was surprisingly vigorous. In the first month of the next year, Queen Saimei (r. 655–661), the reigning queen, left Naniwa Harbor (modern Osaka) in command of an expeditionary navy, which arrived at "Nanotsu" (Hakata) in northern Kyushu two months later.[26] The queen, however, died in the seventh month, before any concrete military measures had been taken.[27] After Saimei's death, her son Naka, long the real power behind the throne, returned to Hakata.[28] The queen's body was sent back to Asuka for interment, and Prince Naka, now assuming the throne as King Tenji, "attended to the organization of the foreign war."[29]

Chronicles of Japan describes the king's prosecution of the war in a series of entries dated 661–663, which tell the following story: In the eighth month of 661, the king dispatched five generals to "aid Paekche." Arms and grain were also sent.[30] In the following month, Prince P'ung was crowned by King Tenji, given a Japanese bride (in some sort of political marriage?), and escorted home by an "army of more than 5,000."[31] Late in the first month of 662, Poksin, leader of the resistance in Paekche, was presented with a gift of arrows, silk thread, silk floss, cloth, tanned hides, and rice.[32] Early in the third month, the "King of Paekche" (P'ung) was sent a gift of cloth.[33] Sometime during the same month, a "general"—presumably one of those already in Korea—was sent to the aid of Koguryŏ.[34] In the fifth month, Prince P'ung is said—contradicting the earlier account—to have been escorted home by a "great general" in charge of "170 warships," and then crowned by order of King Tenji.[35] Sometime during the same year, Tenji had "arms repaired, ships prepared, and army provisions made ready" in order, again, to "aid Paekche."[36] Finally, in the third month of 663, six more generals were sent, in command of "27,500 men," to "smite Silla."[37]

The account in *Chronicles of Japan* leaves us with many questions. As noted, there are several inconsistencies, which may be explained as the result of reliance by the volume's editors on conflicting primary sources.[38] In addition, the text is frustratingly silent about many important aspects of the war. Who, for example, ruled the country while Saimei and Naka/Tenji were in Kyushu? Did the entire court move west with them? (Certainly the generals, whose names we know, were members of the Yamato nobility.) How were the troops recruited? In Kyushu? The few names that survive from later sources suggest that many, perhaps most, of them came from that island. How was the army provisioned? Who made the ships, and where? To these and other questions, we will never know the answers.

At any rate, one thing is clear: even allowing for some exaggeration on the part of *Chronicles of Japan,* the war effort was huge. Yamato not only sent troops and supplies to the aid of Paekche, but also provided its Korean ally with a new sovereign in the form of Prince P'ung. Perhaps the best measure of the strength of the effort, however, is the personal participation of Queen Saimei and Prince Naka. Assisting Paekche clearly took priority over everything else in the minds of these Yamato rulers.

Why? Queen Saimei, according to *Chronicles of Japan,* justified the expedition as follows: "We learn that in ancient times there have been cases of troops being asked for and assistance requested: to render help in emergencies, and to restore that which has been interrupted, is a manifestation of ordinary principles of right."[39] This (possibly apocryphal) speech, while high-sounding, hardly constitutes a satisfying historical explanation.

More to the point, saving Paekche was in Saimei's (and her son's) self-interest. As we have seen, the royal family, and by extension the entire Yamato elite, were heavily dependent on continued access to foreign goods, cultural as well as material. And while, in theory, those goods could come from any of the Korean kingdoms (or China), in fact they had almost always been channeled through Paekche and Kaya. These areas were geographically close to Kyushu, and their rulers had strong historic (as well as cultural) ties with the Yamato sovereigns. Kaya had been absorbed by Silla in the sixth century, rendering Yamato even more dependent on Paekche. So when Paekche stood in danger of falling, Queen Saimei and other Yamato leaders were naturally concerned, to say the least. Of the other two Korean regimes, Silla was historically hostile, Koguryŏ was ambivalent (and farther away, at the northern end of the peninsula), and Saimei and Naka must have been worried to death (literally, in Saimei's case) that without Paekche they would lose their access to iron, prestige goods, and cultural capital. Their motivation in going to Paekche's aid was to forestall this worst-case scenario. In addition, they probably hoped to put Paekche in their debt and turn the country into a Yamato tributary; this would seem to be the implied meaning behind Tenji's "enthronement" of Prince P'ung.[40]

Of course, the whole plan was a house of cards, resting as it did on the assumption that Yamato could actually turn the tide in Paekche's favor. With our twenty-twenty hindsight, of course, we know this assumption to have been false, but this does not mean that the Yamato leaders were necessarily behaving irrationally. Even though there was a good deal of traffic (for ancient times) across the Korea Strait before and during the war, Saimei and Naka/Tenji could hardly have been able to follow the action in anything like real time, and there must have been significant gaps in their knowledge. Possibly they were also misled, intentionally or otherwise, by their Paekche allies, who obviously had a vested interest in the outcome. But based on what they knew or guessed, Saimei and Naka/Tenji presumably calculated the chances of success as high enough to make the gamble worthwhile. Even today, with the Internet, military satellites, and CNN at their fingertips, heads of state have been known to initiate ill-advised campaigns overseas.

King Tenji did not have to wait long to realize his mistake. Not long after the Japanese fleet crossed the Korea Strait, during the eighth month of 663, it was crushed by an armada of 170 Tang warships near the mouth of the Kŭm River, just downstream from Paekche's (newly defunct) capital of Sabi (Puyŏ).[41] According to Chinese sources, approximately four hundred Japanese vessels were sunk in the engagement.[42] The remains of the Japanese fleet limped home in the following month, bringing with them a large number of refugees from Paekche.[43] Not everyone came at once, however; Japanese veterans trickled home, one or two at a time, over a period of decades. The most interesting case on record is that of Ōtomobe Hakama, a soldier from Kamitsuyame in northern Kyushu. Captured by Tang, Hakama later sold himself into slavery to raise funds for two fellow prisoners to return to Japan. Hakama finally returned to his homeland in 690 after spending thirty years in China. As a reward for his selfless behavior, he was awarded court rank, presents of fabric, rice, and land, and a three-generation exemption from taxes by then-empress Jitō (r. 686–697).[44]

After Japan's defeat, the Chinese army quickly mopped up the Paekche restorationists and then turned its attention to Koguryŏ. It had little success, however, until the death of Yŏn Kaesomun in 666. Succession disputes between Yŏn's sons weakened the regime considerably, and in 668 P'yŏngyang fell before a combined Tang/Silla attack. Like Paekche before it, Koguryŏ was occupied by the Chinese army and administered through several governments-general (and in this case, a protectorate as well). By this time, however, the imperialistic ambitions of the Chinese were evident to their Korean allies. Friction between the two camps came to a head when Silla provided open support for a Koguryŏ restoration movement in 670. This was crushed by Tang troops four years later, but the Chinese were able to devote less and less time to Korea because of problems on the Tibetan front. In 676 they withdrew completely, leaving Silla to rule over a newly unified Korean Peninsula.[45]

Aftermath

The war of 663—known in Japanese as Hakusuki-no-e-no-tatakai or the "Battle of Paekchon River," after the old name for the Kŭm River—has long attracted the attention of historians and laymen alike in Japan. However, despite the amount of ink and paper that have been expended on the topic, much remains unclear. We can speculate, but never know for certain, what was in the minds of Queen Saimei and Prince Naka when they made the decision to aid Paekche. Likewise, many logistic details of the war will always be shrouded in mystery. Another unanswered—and in this case, probably answerable—question regards the effects of the war. In the end, how important was the Battle of Paekchon River? To what extent did it influence the later development of Japanese history?

Certainly, the war was important. Most scholars today would agree that its major effect was to hasten political centralization in Japan, putting more power into the hands of the Yamato elite as a whole, and the royal family in particular. The need to mobilize for war put Saimei and Naka/Tenji in the driver's seat as never before. The defeat itself was a terrible shock, but it also made clear the need to build a strong, centralized state that could hold its own against continental powers such as Silla and Tang. King Tenji seized the moment to implement a series of political and administrative reforms that further concentrated power in his own hands and in those of the central government as a whole.

On the other hand, it is possible to read too much into the events of the 660s. I have fallen into this trap myself: in one of my first scholarly papers, I argued that the Battle of Paekchon River was the single most important event in the formation of Japan's "*ritsuryō* state"—the name given by Japanese scholars to the centralized, Chinese-style polity of Nara times.[46] This is an example of tunnel vision. My aim was to debunk the view, then current in American scholarship on Japan, that premodern Japan was essentially a closed social system, where most events and trends could be explained without reference to external inputs—that is, foreign relations. That view was, and is, wrong. But while the war of 663 certainly accelerated the trend toward centralization, it was but one link in a larger chain of events. Most generally, the trend toward centralization—which began around 600 and lasted a full century, culminating in the promulgation of the Taihō Code in 702 and the construction of Heijō-kyō (Nara) in 710—should be understood as the result of competitive emulation between Japan and the various Korean states (especially Silla) in the face of imperial expansion in China.[47]

In Kyushu, however, the effects of the war were immense and long lasting. As I will argue below, it is no exaggeration to say that the events of the 660s and early 670s created an international boundary where none existed before. Prior to the war, there was no clear line between "us" and "them," and traffic between the Korean Peninsula and Kyushu was relatively free (although never tremendously frequent, given the dangers and the distances involved). Within a decade after Japan's defeat, such a line had come into existence (in the Korea Strait between Tsushima and Silla), and Japan had a fortified border with a single designated gateway. The gateway was Hakata, and the gatekeeper was Dazaifu, the command center south of the bay.

Of course, Yamato had long had a significant interest in northern Kyushu, and in particular Hakata, because of the area's strategic location. The most sensible way to get from Yamato to the Korean Peninsula was to go down the Inland Sea, follow the northwest Kyushu coast to Hakata, and then cut across the Genkai Sea via the islands of Iki and Tsushima. To control Hakata was thus to control access to the continent—the key to hegemony in early Japan. This is why the Iwai "rebellion" posed such a threat in the 520s, and why the court moved so swiftly to put it down. After Iwai was killed, his son offered territory near Hakata to the court (in order, according to the chronicles, to save his own skin).[48] Soon afterward, in 536, Yamato established a line of granaries (*miyake,* probably best understood as supply depots) up and down the Inland Sea. Much of Fukuoka Plain was also converted into a granary at this time.[49] In 1984, remains of sixth-century storehouses and office buildings, presumably part of this "Nanotsu

Miyake," were uncovered by archaeologists working on a salvage operation near Japan Railways' Hakata Station in Fukuoka.[50]

Later, at the beginning of the seventh century, a Yamato representative was stationed in or near the Nanotsu Miyake (assuming that it was still functional at this time). The representative bore the title Tsukushi Dazai (Kyushu governor-general) and his duties evidently involved the reception of foreign visitors.[51] It seems likely that this post was created in conjunction with the resumption of official relations with China. The Sui dynasty had reunified China in 581, and Wa sent its first embassy to the ascendant empire in 600. A second embassy, dispatched in 607, returned the following year together with a baker's dozen of Sui diplomats—the first Chinese embassy to have visited Wa in centuries, if not the first ever.

So Yamato had a presence in Hakata. And that presence—the Tsukushi Dazai—was undoubtedly the prototype for the later Dazaifu. But there is no guarantee that the Tsukushi Dazai was a permanent position (quite the opposite, judging from surviving records), and there is no real indication that Hakata was more than a stepping-stone on the way between Japan and Korea (or China). Yes, Hakata was probably more important than other stops along the way, but it was not yet unique. In the early seventh century, Wa had no clear border, and no real gateway. But all of this was to change after the Battle of Paekchon River.

The immediate stimulus for change was the arrival of five separate Chinese embassies from the Chinese government-general in Ungjin between 664 and 671. The first group, led by Guo Wucong, consisted of 30 Chinese and 100 subjugated Paekcheans. These made landfall in 664 at Tsushima, but were reportedly refused permission to enter Japan proper.[52] Guo returned the next year in a party of 254, which stayed in Japan for three months.[53] In 667 a third group arrived in the guise of escorts for Japanese *kentōshi* (envoys to Tang) returning from a visit to Chinese-occupied Korea.[54] The fourth group, under the command of Li Shouzhen, arrived in early 671 and stayed for some six months.[55] The final Chinese embassy arrived at the end of 671 and also stayed for about half a year. It consisted of about 2,000 people (including 1,400 Japanese prisoners of war slated for repatriation) and was led by Guo Wucong, now making his third trip to Japan.[56]

Chinese reasons for sending these "embassies" have been subjected to intense scrutiny by Japanese scholars.[57] The details are too intricate to concern us here, but none of the missions seems to have had overt military objectives. In general, the earlier visits were intended to impress upon Japan its subordinate place in the Tang-centered universe, while the later missions were by and large conciliatory. The change of attitude resulted from Tang's declining fortunes in Korea, where the Chinese army faced increased resistance from Silla.

Be this as it may, few of these visits were welcome from the Japanese point of view, and the earlier ones, at least, were viewed with outright alarm. As described at the beginning of this chapter, the residents of Tsushima were probably scared witless when the first warships sailed into view in 664. Court leaders also seem to have construed the visit as a threat—not surprising given the events of the previous year. As noted, their response was to refuse Guo permission to enter the country (on grounds that he was a private messenger from the Tang commander in Paekche, not an official representative of the Tang emperor).

The best measure of the court's reaction to these early visits, however, is the feverish defense program it pursued between 664 and roughly 670. Consider the following records from *Chronicles of Japan:*[58]

> *Third year of Tenji [664]:*
> In this year, border guards *(sakimori)* and signal fires were emplaced in Tsushima Island, Iki Island, and Tsukushi Province. Also, a great embankment was built in Tsukushi to store water. It was named the Water Fortress *(mizuki).*
>
> *Fourth year of Tenji [665], eighth month:*
> Tappon Ch'unch'o, of *talsol* [second] rank, was sent to Nagato Province to build a fortress. Ŏngnye Pongnyu, of *talsol* rank, and Sabi Pokpu, of *talsol* rank, were sent to Tsukushi Province to build the two fortresses of Ōno and Ki.
>
> *Sixth year of Tenji [667], eleventh month:*
> In this month, Takayasu Fortress in Yamato Province; Yashima Fortress in Sanuki Province, Yamada district; and Kaneda[59] Fortress in Tsushima Province were built.
>
> *Ninth year of Tenji [670], second month:*
> Also, Takayasu Fortress was completed, and rice and salt were stored [there]. Also, one fortress in Nagato and two fortresses in Tsukushi were built.

In short, over a period of about seven years the court put together the "hardware" and "software" necessary to protect Japan from foreign invasion. On the software side, border guards, or *sakimori,* were deployed on Tsushima, Iki, and "Tsukushi," that is, the northern part of the Kyushu mainland. We can see the system in action in late 671, with the arrival of the final Chinese embassy. This was preceded by an advance party of four Japanese men, who reported to the Tsushima governor as follows:

> Two thousand people—600 under the Tang envoy Guo Wucong and 1,400 under the escort Sat'aek Sondŭng—on board 47 ships have anchored at Hichi Island. They are saying to each other, "We now have many men and ships, and if we were to arrive [in Japan] without warning the border guards would probably fire their arrows at us out of surprise." So they sent [us] to declare in advance their intention of presently coming [to Japan].[60]

As for hardware, the text mentions beacons or flares, as well as a number of fortifications. Nothing further is known of the beacons, although presumably they functioned like those seen in *The Return of the King,* the last movie in Peter Jackson's *Lord of the Rings* series. In a spectacularly filmed sequence, news of the impending invasion of Gondor is conveyed to the neighboring country of Rohan by a string of beacons set atop snow-covered peaks. There are no snow-covered peaks in Tsushima or northern Kyushu, but there are plenty of lesser mountains, and an early warning system of beacons would have been easy to implement as well as highly effective.

Better known are the various fortresses. As *Chronicles of Japan* indicates, a line of castles was built from Tsushima through northern Kyushu, Nagato on the western tip of Honshu, Sanuki on the Shikoku coast of the Inland Sea, and finally to Yamato. With one exception (Nagato), all of these castles (and several others not mentioned in *Chronicles of Japan* but evidently built in the same period) have now been identified and excavated. Typically, they consist of a massive stone rampart, up to several kilometers in circumference, girding a strategically situated peak. The wall is broken by one to several gates as well as sluices to allow the passage of streams (figure 3). Inside, scattered around the summit, are several dozen wooden buildings—mostly warehouses for storing grain, salt, and other supplies, but also perhaps barracks. Clearly, the fortresses were designed as places of refuge in the event of foreign invasion.[61]

Japanese archaeologists refer to Ōno Fortress, Ki Fortress, and the rest as Korean-style mountain fortresses *(Chōsen shiki yamajiro)*

FIGURE 3. Stone rampart at Ōno Fortress. *Source:* Kyushu Historical Museum (Kyūshū Rekishi Shiryōkan). Reproduced with permission.

because of their close resemblance to structures built on the peninsula during the same general period. The resemblance is not coincidental. The individuals credited by *Chronicles of Japan* for building the fortresses all bear Korean names and were, in fact, former subjects of Paekche who had fled to Japan after the war.

The front line of defense was clearly Tsushima. Here was Kaneda Fortress, on top of a hill overlooking the narrow strait that separated the two main islands of the Tsushima archipelago. Border guards manned watches at the castle and the top of other peaks, casting their gaze over the Korea Strait. It is evident from the passage cited above (in connection with Guo Wucong's 671 visit) that entering the waters off Tsushima was considered tantamount to entering Japan—that a line had essentially been drawn in the middle of the Korea Strait. At the risk of slight exaggeration, this was Japan's first international boundary, and it came into being as the direct result of the intense military and diplomatic interactions between Japan and the continent during the 660s.

If Tsushima represented the perimeter of state control, the real focus of power in the region was the Kyushu government-general. Dazaifu traced its institutional ancestry to the early seventh-century Tsukushi Dazai, but it was now—or would be soon—a large, permanent office.[62] The main positions were all filled by trusted members of the court aristocracy, and the head of the organization—the governor-general, or viceroy, as he is sometimes called in English[63]—was often, at least in the immediate postwar years, a member of the royal family itself.

An example is Prince Kurikuma, a grandson of King Bidatsu (r. 572–585), who was appointed governor-general in mid-671.[64] Kurikuma had a chance to prove his mettle the very next year, when a bloody succession dispute broke out following the death of King Tenji. The dispute, known to history as the Jinshin War, was between Prince Ōama (Tenji's younger brother) and Prince Ōtomo (Tenji's son). Ōama eventually proved victorious, assuming the throne as Emperor Tenmu (r. 673–686), but during the course of the fighting, his opponent, Ōtomo, sent a messenger to Kyushu to ask Prince Kurikuma for troops. The messenger, Saeki Otoko, was told to kill Kurikuma if he refused to cooperate. When Otoko approached the prince, according to *Chronicles of Japan*, Kurikuma

> took the [written] order and replied, "The land of Tsukushi has always guarded [Japan] from external dangers. It is not because of internal enemies that we mount our guard, facing the sea with fortresses high and moats deep! Were I now to respect this order and call forth warriors, the land would be empty. If something unexpected were to suddenly occur, the country would collapse completely. Even if I were slain a hundred times thereafter, what good would it do? I do not willfully rebel against [Ōtomo's] might! This is why I will not lightly call forth warriors."[65]

At this time, the chronicle continues, "Prince Mino and Prince Takeie, the two sons of Prince Kurikuma, stood at his side with their swords girded and would not retreat. Thereupon, Otoko gripped his sword firmly and advanced; but he feared that conversely he might [himself] be slain. Therefore, unable to accomplish the deed, he returned [to Yamato] empty-handed."[66] (Prince Kurikuma's son Prince Mino also served a stint as Dazaifu governor-general toward the end of the seventh century.[67] Evidently, guarding the country was a family tradition.)

Prince Kurikuma had an eventful tenure as governor-general. Indeed, when Ōtomo's recruitment officer arrived, the prince had just managed to get rid of the final Chinese embassy from Paekche, which spent a full six months in Hakata. As noted, this party included two thousand men in two groups. The larger group, fourteen hundred in number, is thought to have consisted mainly of Japanese prisoners of war slated for repatriation. The other six hundred men were probably Chinese, or their Korean allies.[68] Dealing with such a large group of foreigners can have been no easy task, all the more so because they seem to have demanded a huge payment of military supplies, perhaps in exchange for the POWs. According to *Chronicles of Japan,* unspecified quantities of "armor and bows and arrows," together with "1,673 bolts of pongee, 2,852 bolts of cloth, and 666 bolts of silk floss" were "bestowed" upon Guo Wucong and company just before their departure.[69] The reader is apparently supposed to believe that this was part of a routine exchange of gifts, something that might happen any time a foreign ambassador was in port.[70] But we should not allow ourselves to be fooled; Guo was given enough goods to outfit an army, which was undoubtedly his intent. (At this time Tang was already fighting its erstwhile ally, Silla, for control of the peninsula.) The Chinese meant business, and Kurikuma had to pay up or face the consequences. He must have been under a good deal of stress throughout late 671 and early 672.

He was not alone. Yamato representatives in Kyushu during this general period had to put up with demanding, long-term visitors as a matter of course. Of the five postwar Chinese missions to Japan, only one (that of 665) was invited to Yamato.[71] Excuses can be found in most cases: the first embassy (in 664) was not "official," the third (in 667) was just acting as an escort for returning Japanese diplomats, and the fifth mission (in 671) had the misfortune to arrive just before Tenji's death.[72] But isn't it easiest just to conclude that the Japanese wanted to keep these recent—and perhaps future—adversaries at arm's length? Clearly, they couldn't keep them out of the country altogether, but they could at least try to prevent them from snooping around Yamato itself.

What this meant, however, was that diplomatic facilities—at the very least, lodgings—were urgently required in Kyushu. So were facilities to house the Dazaifu governor-general and his rapidly expanding staff. Archaeological excavations at the Tsukushi Lodge and the Dazaifu office complex indicate that construction at both sites began in the late seventh century.[73] Because archaeological dating techniques are imprecise, investigators are reluctant to be more specific. But given the historical context, there can be no real doubt that the Tsukushi Lodge and the Dazaifu headquarters were built in the 660s—at precisely the same time when the various fortifications mentioned by *Chronicles of Japan* were also under construction.

The task of creating all of these facilities from scratch staggers the imagination. Before building could even begin, it was necessary to come up with blueprints of some kind. The spatial arrangement of the Dazaifu offices and surrounding fortifications suggests that all of these facilities were built according to a master plan. Some scholars suggest that Paekche's last capital, Sabi, served as a model,[74] which could very well be true given the attested role of Korean immigrants in building some of the fortresses. On a more mundane level it was also necessary to clear the ground and procure construction materials. This was no easy matter. Some of the logs used in the Dazaifu office complex and Ōno Fortress were of Japanese cedar *(hinoki; Chamaecyparis obtusa),* which was locally available. But many were of Japanese umbrella pine *(kōyamaki; Sciatopytis verticillata),* which grew only in southern Kyushu, in what is now Miyazaki Prefecture.[75] The logs must have been rafted (or taken by ship) all the way around the island—a tremendous undertaking in and of itself.

The amount of labor needed for construction is also mind-boggling. According to Hirota Itsuo and Wada Hiroshi, the Mizuki, an embankment built across the valley of the Mikasa River in 664, contains a total of 384,000 cubic meters of earth. They calculate that to move this amount of earth in a year would require thirty-five hundred men working eleven-hour days, six days a week.[76] And the Mizuki is only one of the many facilities built in this area during the 660s (figure 4).

Altogether the postwar construction boom must have dwarfed the war effort itself. Probably most of these workers were recruited in Kyushu—unless the court was using decommissioned soldiers for this purpose, which is entirely likely. But remember that most of those troops also probably came from Kyushu. Put together, back-to-back, the war and its aftermath temporarily (and in the case of war dead, of course, permanently) robbed many, perhaps most households in the island of their able-bodied adult males. Quite literally, the events of the 660s emasculated Kyushu. As a direct result, for the first time in history, the island and its inhabitants were now firmly under Yamato's thumb.

A Visual Tour

What did things look like when all of these government installations were up and running? Fast forward to 702, thirty years after the

FIGURE 4. The Mizuki today. The view is from the east, looking down on the now-overgrown embankment from the summit of Shiōjisan. Photograph by author.

departure of the last Tang embassy. During the intervening decades, the kingdom of Wa had been given a new name, Nihon (Japan; literally, "origin of the Sun"), and transformed into a centralized, bureaucratic empire that bore more than a passing resemblance to Tang China.[77] The country was no longer ruled by a "great king" *(ōkimi)* but by a self-styled living god, the emperor.[78] It had a capital city, a sophisticated bureaucracy (staffed largely by aristocrats from the Yamato area), and an effective system of local government that focused on maintaining order and channeling tax receipts to the center. Although these changes were top-down, directed by Tenmu and his successors—his widow Jitō and their grandson Monmu (r. 697–707)—they required the cooperation of political actors both in Yamato and in other parts of the country. Some element of coercion may have been involved. (Tenmu, in particular, was a charismatic military leader, as the Jinshin War made plain to all.) But more generally, building a stronger state was in everyone's interest given the competitive international environment.

Let us take a quick tour of Hakata and Dazaifu at this time (map 3). First, the physical geography. Hakata Bay, one of the finest natural harbors in Kyushu, lies nestled between the arms of the Itoshima Peninsula to the west and Shikanoshima, a semidetached island to the east. To the south lies Fukuoka Plain, a large (230 km^2) expanse of flat land created by the alluvial action of numerous waterways flowing into the bay: from east to west, the Tatara, Umi, Mikasa, Naka, Hii, and Muromi rivers.[79] (Note that the coastline itself lay considerably south of its present location; in the eighth century, unlike today, there was no artificial landfill, and the natural process of sedimentation was also much less advanced.[80]) The plain in turn is surrounded on three sides (to the east, west, and south) by ranges of hills and low mountains. The total effect is of a natural amphitheater, rising gradually from the blue waters of the bay to the verdant rice fields of the plain to the dark forests of the mountains in the distance.

So much for the natural setting; now for the human geography. In the early eighth century, virtually every hill in the area with an ocean view was topped by a lookout staffed by *sakimori,* their eyes trained to the sea twenty-four hours a day, 365 days a year. At dock by the bayside was a fleet of Japanese warships, designed to intercept and attack any enemy craft.[81] Administrative offices and dock facilities were scattered around the perimeter of the bay, but the most imposing structure of all was the Tsukushi Lodge. This facility, which overlooked the bay from a promontory between the Naka and Mikasa rivers, was also fortified and under heavy guard.

We will spend considerably more time in the Tsukushi Lodge in the next chapter, but for now let us move south, onto Fukuoka Plain itself. Today the plain is occupied by the concrete, people, and buildings that make up the city of Fukuoka. In the eighth century, however, there was no city; there were only scattered villages. The plain was a checkerboard of rice fields, each a perfect square measuring 109 meters on a side. This type of land division, known to historians as the *jōri* system, was linked to the centralized scheme of land allocation and taxation introduced in the late seventh and early eighth centuries. Here in Fukuoka Plain, an unusually thorough effort had been made.

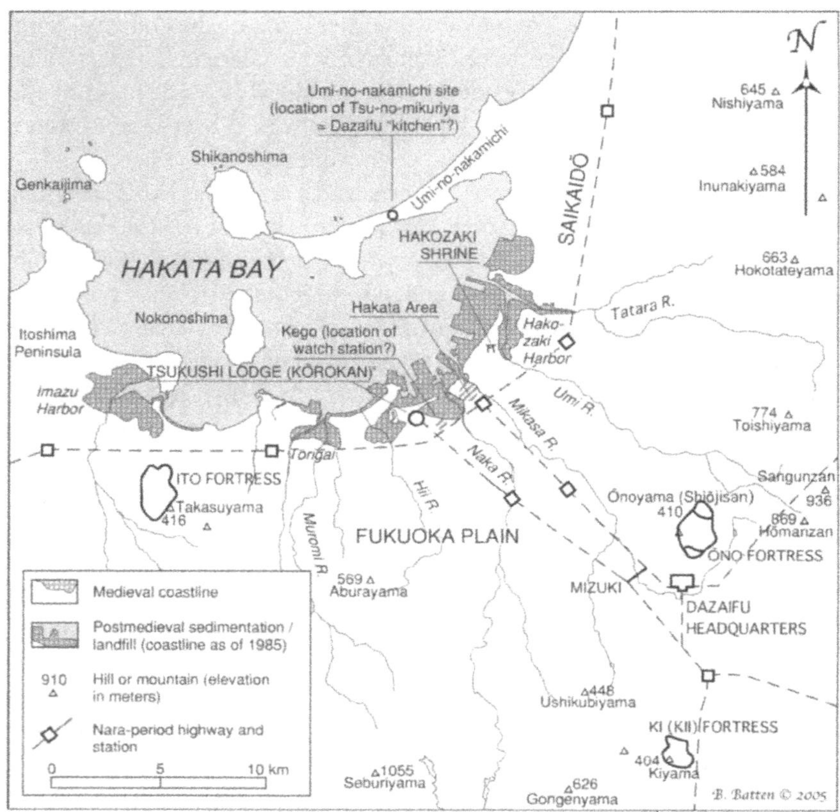

Map 3. Hakata and vicinity. *Sources:* (1) Modern coastline based on 1:200,000 map by Kokudochiriin (1985); (2) medieval coastline from Kawazoe Shōji et al., eds., *Fukuoka ken no rekishi,* map on p. 123; (3) ancient roads and stations from Kinoshita Ryō, ed., *Kodai o kangaeru: Kodai dōro,* map on pp. 274–275.

The symmetry of the checkerboard was marred only by the forested hills between river valleys and by slight regional variations in the orientation of the *jōri* divisions themselves, which in this region usually followed the course of the nearest river. The end result, not surprisingly, was a radial pattern, with the principal axis of field division running west-northwest around the Tatara River on the east side of the bay, more or less northwest around the central Mikasa and Naka rivers, and north-northwest along the Muromi drainage to the west.[82] Despite this slight asymmetry, the net result was a striking display of centrally imposed order.

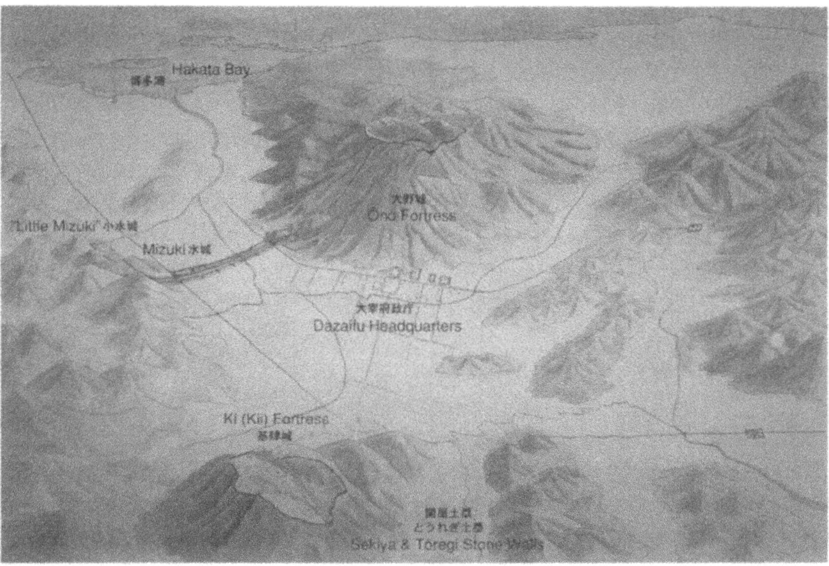

FIGURE 5. Dazaifu and surrounding fortifications, ca. 700. The view is from the southeast, looking toward Hakata Bay. *Source:* Kyushu Historical Museum (Kyūshū Rekishi Shiryōkan). Reproduced with permission.

The plain also contained some government roads and stations (with lodging facilities and horses for official business). The main trunk of the Saikaidō or Western Sea Circuit ran around the shore of the bay. There were also two roads heading south-southeast toward Dazaifu. One branched off from the Saikaidō at Yoshino-no-Umaya, a post station near the Mikasa River mouth. The second began several kilometers farther west from the Tsukushi Lodge.[83]

A visitor heading down either of these roads would eventually have come to a line of fortifications—the defense perimeter of Dazaifu (figures 5, 6).[84] To get to the city, one had to pass under the shadow of Ōno Fortress, which girded the summit of a prominent local peak, Shiōjisan, and directly through the Mizuki. First, there was a narrow bridge spanning the sixty meter boundary moat on the Mizuki's Hakata side. Next, there was a passageway, almost a tunnel, cut through the embankment itself. All of these locations were heavily guarded by *sakimori* and other soldiers.

Once past the Mizuki and within the boundaries of present-day Dazaifu city, the visitor would find several more military installations,

FIGURE 6. Mizuki, ca. 700. The view is from the west. Dazaifu is on the other side of the embankment in the right background. *Source:* Kyushu Historical Museum (Kyūshū Rekishi Shiryōkan). Reproduced with permission.

again bristling with soldiers and guards, and beyond them, a most remarkable sight: here, hundreds of kilometers from central Japan and half a day's journey from the nearest port, tucked away in a small mountain valley in the wilds of Kyushu, was a bustling city of several thousand individuals—high-ranking aristocrats "on loan" from the central government as well as lesser government officials, soldiers, clerics, and family members of most of the above.

An earlier generation of scholars believed that the Dazaifu city was essentially a miniature version of contemporary national capitals such as Fujiwara-kyō (built in 694) and Heijō-kyō (built in 710). These consisted of large, rectangular grids of streets oriented to the cardinal directions, with the imperial palace and government buildings situated at north center.[85] Thirty years of archaeological investigation have made it abundantly clear that Dazaifu never had a fully developed street grid.[86] Nonetheless, there were important points of resemblance to Fujiwara-kyō and Heijō-kyō. A large boulevard, Suzaku Ōji, lined with willows, ran through the exact center of Dazaifu, forming its main north-south axis. Throughout the city area,

FIGURE 7. Dazaifu headquarters, ca. 700. The view is from the southwest. Shōjisan rises behind the headquarters to the left. *Source:* Kyushu Historical Museum (Kyūshū Rekishi Shiryōkan). Reproduced with permission.

but particularly in the vicinity of Suzaku Ōji, were scattered dozens of government offices and temples and hundreds of private dwellings. All of these increased in number and size toward the north, where lay the main focus of the city—the Dazaifu headquarters, whose remains today are seen at Tofurō (figure 7).[87]

The headquarters was sited at the northern terminus of Suzaku Ōji, directly south of Shiōjisan and just west of Kanzeonji, Kyushu's largest Buddhist temple. In terms of location, the headquarters was thus analogous to the imperial palace that dominated the north-central portions of Fujiwara-kyō and Heijō-kyō. Even from a distance, a visitor could trace the symmetrical outline of the walled compound and make out the vermilion-painted pillars and gray-tiled roofs of the individual buildings within. Also visible would have been the figures of minor officials, scurrying from office to office in their characteristic green or blue robes and black caps. Most of these, together with their superiors, also hard at work within the official compound, were field agents of Japan's emperor—bureaucrats assigned to Kyushu for a period of four to five years who would return to the capital for additional assignments when their terms of office expired.

What was the function of the Dazaifu organization? It is clear from surviving historical sources (e.g., national histories such as the *Chronicles of Japan* and *Chronicles of Japan, Continued,*[88] administrative documents, and the inscribed wooden slips known as *mokkan*) that much of the daily work of the Dazaifu officials pertained to local government (particularly tax collection) in Kyushu.[89] This region was known at the time as the Western Sea Circuit (Saikaidō, after the highway of the same name) or, alternatively, the nine provinces and two islands. The nine provinces of mainland Kyushu consisted of Chikuzen (central Fukuoka Prefecture, where Hakata and Dazaifu were); Chikugo (western and southern Fukuoka); Buzen (eastern Fukuoka and northern Ōita); Bungo (the rest of Ōita); Hizen (Saga and most of Nagasaki); Higo (Kumamoto); Hyūga (Miyazaki and part of Kagoshima); Ōsumi (eastern Kagoshima); and Satsuma (western Kagoshima). The two islands were Iki and Tsushima (both Nagasaki), in the Genkai Sea between northern Kyushu and the Korean Peninsula (map 4).

Dazaifu was seemingly intended from the start as a kind of regional capital for the Saikaidō. Just as the city itself was a scaled-down version of the national capital, the administrative organization it housed was organizationally and functionally a miniature version of the central government.[90] Dazaifu's location in the what is called the Futsukaichi Structural Valley is also significant. This area served as a natural passageway between Fukuoka Plain and the much larger Chikushi Plain to the south. Chikushi Plain, in turn, provided convenient overland access to almost any part of Kyushu. Traveling up the Chikugo River to the east led you to the Hita Basin and then an easily negotiated pass across the mountains into eastern Kyushu. Downstream, along the fringes of the half-landlocked Ariake Sea, were routes leading to peninsular western Kyushu and the Hayato-dominated territories to the south. (The Hayato were aboriginal hunter-gatherers known for their fighting skills.) An aerial view of Kyushu would thus have shown Dazaifu at the hub of a network of roads, radiating out from it like spokes on a wheel[91]—perfectly situated, in other words, to exert authority over the entire island.

But although Dazaifu was deeply involved in governing the nine provinces and two islands of Kyushu, this function was secondary to

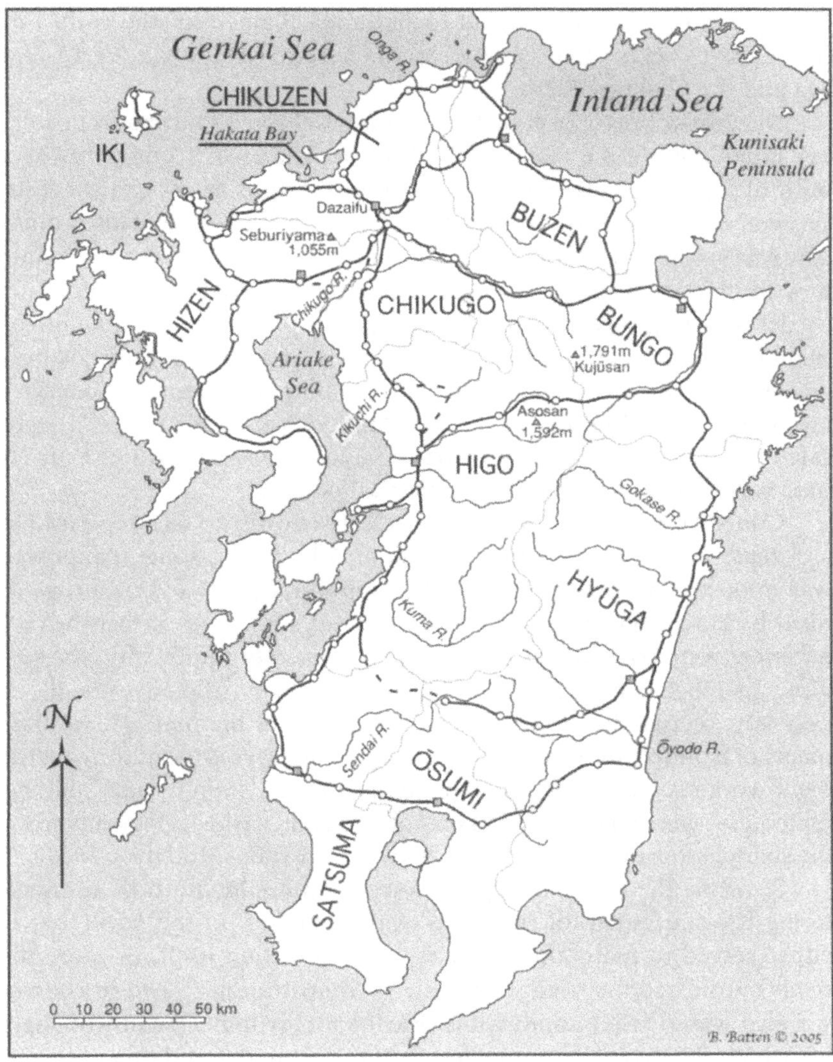

MAP 4. Kyushu in the 8th c. *Source:* Adapted from map in Shimojō Nobuyuki et al., eds., *Shinpan kodai no Nihon 3 Kyūshū, Okinawa,* pp. 590–591.

its role in frontier administration. If the location of Dazaifu was ideal for purposes of governing Kyushu, it was even better for supervising coastal traffic and coordinating maritime defense. Dazaifu was conveniently close (but not too close) to Hakata, the island's largest port and the one most easily reached from the continent. It was also in an ideal position to restrict access to Fukuoka Plain from the south, in the (unlikely) event that enemy forces chose to invade via the Ariake Sea and the Chikugo Plain.

Dazaifu's control of Kyushu was essential to its role in administering Japan's maritime frontier. One of the ironies of frontier history, both in Japan and elsewhere, is that these regions are crucial to state survival but notoriously difficult to rule from the center. States must control their frontiers if they hope to maintain territorial integrity, but they are hindered in the accomplishment of this goal by distance and by destabilizing forces, not only foreign but domestic. Secure control of an international boundary, in Japan as in any other country, is premised upon secure control of the surrounding area—the periphery—and vice versa. Although the area around Hakata itself was relatively safe in the Nara period, other parts of Kyushu were not necessarily so (nor was Hakata itself in other historical periods).

Control over Kyushu was also necessary in order to secure personnel and materiel for frontier administration. Admittedly, some manpower was imported from elsewhere; all the important posts at Dazaifu were filled by career bureaucrats from the capital, and, as described below, *sakimori* were conscripted in eastern Honshu. But minor officials, service personnel, construction workers, and ordinary soldiers were all, of necessity, recruited in Kyushu. And almost all of the material requirements of frontier administration—official salaries; provisions for government workers, guards, and foreign guests; military supplies and building materials—were met through taxes collected in Kyushu, principally from the six richest provinces: the two Chikus, the two Bus, and the two His.[92]

So while the Dazaifu officials were certainly involved in administering Kyushu, much of this work was secondary in the sense that it either served to maintain the Dazaifu organization itself, or more directly subsidized the needs of frontier administration.[93] And of course, we also know from copious historical sources that Dazaifu officials were directly involved in receiving diplomatic envoys and other visitors at the Tsukushi Lodge and in supervising defense-related activities (including the stationing of border guards) throughout northern Kyushu, Iki, and Tsushima. These frontier-related functions, and not local government, were the original business of Dazaifu. In simplest terms, the office was designed for the purpose of letting in people whom the state deemed desirable and keeping out those deemed undesirable. In the words of *Veritable Records of Japan's Emperor Montoku,* an official chronicle from the mid-ninth century, Dazaifu "is at the hub of foreign countries; it is a barrier-gate between inside and out."[94]

Nothing to Fear but Fear Itself?

Although the crisis of the 660s soon passed, the defense system established at that time functioned for well over a century. Maintaining vigilance in Kyushu was a very high priority with Japan's rulers, whose self-stated motto was "Always think of danger, even when at peace."[95] In their eyes, Kyushu's proximity to the continent was sufficient reason for maintaining constant alert: "The Tsukushi Dazai abuts the Western Sea. Various foreign countries come [there] to pay tribute, their ships and rudders face to face [with ours]. For this reason we drill men and horses and sharpen our weapons in order to display our might and prepare for emergencies."[96] This statement may seem incongruous, juxtaposing as it does the image of tribute-bearing foreigners with the need for defense. But to Japanese courtiers, the equation made perfect sense: as they knew from experience, foreigners, including diplomatic envoys, came to Japan for their own reasons, not all of which were benign.

Defense was the responsibility of Dazaifu, or more specifically of the *sakimori* under its command.[97] Altogether there were about three thousand *sakimori* deployed on Tsushima, Iki, and at strategic points near Hakata and elsewhere on the Kyushu mainland. Perhaps surprisingly, these troops were not recruited locally, in Kyushu. Rather, they came from all the way across the country from the Tōsandō and Tōkaidō regions of eastern Honshū. *Sakimori,* like other soldiers in eighth-century Japan, were originally peasant conscripts. (Military service, along with tax paying, was one of the obligations laid on adult men.) The guards were selected by local provincial officials and then escorted down the eastern seaboard of Honshu as far as the port of Naniwa (modern Osaka), where they boarded ship for Hakata.

Sakimori were allowed to bring "servants, slaves, cattle or horses"[98] with them to Kyushu, but not, apparently, family members. The *Man'yōshū* poetry anthology contains a group of verses written by frontier guards on their way to Dazaifu in 755. Most of them revolve around the theme of parting from loved ones. The pathos of the guards' situation evidently struck a chord in Ōtomo Yakamochi, the anthology's editor, who contributed the following:

Tsukushi, land of the white sun,
Is a distant outpost of the realm,
A secure fortress to protect us from our foe.
The lands that stretch in four directions
Under our lord's rule
Abound with people,
But the man from the cock-crowing East
Goes forth with never a look back
To serve as a soldier strong and brave.
He leaves his mother's watchful eye,
His mother of the drooping breasts;
No longer sleeps beside his wife,
His wife like the young grass,
And counts off the changing months and days.
A great ship is set with myriad true oars
In the royal bay of Naniwa
Where men cut reeds,
On the morning calm
They row out in cadence,
On the evening tide
Pull the oars till they bend.
"May you who set off rowing
To the boatman's chant,
Thread your way between the waves
And safely reach your port.
May you keep your spirit true
As ordered by our sovereign lord,
And when your time of sailing round
From cape to cape is done,
May you come safely home,"
Thus his wife must pray,
Setting a jar beside the bed,
Folding back her white hemp sleeves,
Spreading out her seed-black hair—
Long days she waits with yearning.[99]

The journey to Kyushu was difficult, as were the three years of required service on the coastal watches. As noted above, newly conscripted *sakimori* traveled by ship from Naniwa down the Inland Sea to Kyushu. Not all of them arrived safely; according to *Chronicles of*

Japan, a group of *sakimori* en route to Kyushu in 685 "drifted about at sea, and all of them lost their clothing."[100] (But why? Perhaps the text refers to the guards' luggage rather than the actual clothes on their backs.) After arriving in Kyushu, *sakimori* first went to Dazaifu to receive their assignments (which were changed every three months "so that hardship and ease are shared equally").[101] Following commencement of their duties, they were largely expected to fend for themselves. The government allotted guards "vacant land" in the vicinity of their posts: "Where the water and land are good, seeds should be planted as appropriate, and miscellaneous greens used to provide food for the *sakimori.* The necessary ox power shall be supplied by the government."[102] However, there cannot have been much time to tend the fields: *sakimori* received but one day of rest out of every ten.[103]

Why were *sakimori* conscripted so far from the border they defended? This is actually two questions: "Why not Kyushu?" and "If not Kyushu, why eastern Honshu?" With regard to the first question, men from Kyushu were not used because, at least initially, there were not enough of them to go around (Kyushu residents had borne the brunt of the 663 war). More fundamentally, however, local conscripts were considered unreliable, partly because they might have been distracted by family matters and partly because growing up so close to the frontier might have "contaminated" them with empathy for those on the other side. (Almost universally in world history, residents of frontier regions are mistrusted by central authorities. This is why the Roman Empire, for example, used legions from Rome, rather than local residents, to guard its frontiers.[104]) Second, guards were recruited in eastern Honshu in preference to other locations in that island or Shikoku because the Tōsandō/Tōkaidō area had long ties to Yamato and because its male residents were famed for their bravery and martial prowess—a result of their unique historical experience with the Emishi, the unruly aboriginal inhabitants of northeast Honshu. Perhaps another factor influencing the selection of *sakimori* from eastern Japan was the sheer distance involved: fully a thousand kilometers from home, *sakimori* had little recourse but to serve faithfully if they ever hoped to see their loved ones again. (Poignantly, not all of them did. The law codes of the time make provisions for *sakimori* who fell ill or died on the road to or from Kyushu. In the case of death, the deceased guard was to "be provided with a coffin and be cremated and buried as convenient"; his personal possessions were to be "sent to the Ministry of War for return to the family."[105])

As noted, the *sakimori* system survived one way or another for more than a century—a respectable period of time, especially given that there was objectively little need to "drill men and horses and sharpen our weapons in order to display our might and prepare for emergencies." Tang posed no danger to Japan after 668. Silla never threatened Japan, either—although the reverse was not necessarily true. (Korean records note a Japanese attack in 731, and a full-scale invasion was planned—although not carried out—by court leader Fujiwara Nakamaro in the late 750s and early 760s.[106]) And the only other state in the region—Parhae, to the north of Silla, in the region later known as Manchuria—was consistently friendly to Japan.[107]

So over time it was perhaps natural that the hyped-up defense arrangements of the postwar period were abandoned. The tendency to "let go" was reinforced by what has been called the "decline of the *ritsuryō* system."[108] The reasons for the court's gradual loss of direct control over the countryside and its residents are matters of scholarly debate, which I will not enter into in detail here.[109] In short, however, a Tang-style, authority-intensive state was probably necessary to overcome the crisis of the late seventh century but less necessary once the position of the central elite (and in particular, the emperor) had been firmly established and the threat of war subsided. In other words, once the purpose of the state had been fulfilled, there was no real need to maintain it as is. Also, and probably equally important, the creation of the state in and of itself engendered changes in local society (e.g., economic growth and consequent differentiation of the peasant class) that could not be adequately managed within the relatively rigid confines of the system.

Table 1 shows some of the institutional changes in frontier defense during the late eighth and early ninth centuries, corresponding to the last few decades of the Nara era and the first few decades of the Heian.[110] (The court moved to a new capital, Heian-kyō—modern Kyoto—in 794.) In general, three major trends can be identified. First, responsibility for providing guards was shifted from eastern Japan to the seven provinces of mainland Kyushu. Reasons cited for this shift include the cost of transporting *sakimori* long distances, the hardships faced by the guards themselves, and the need for additional manpower along the Emishi frontier. Next, the geographic scope of recruitment gradually narrowed from Kyushu as a whole to the immediate vicinity of each frontier watch. Here again this measure was ostensibly intended to alleviate suffering among guards and their families and to reduce costs. Concurrently with these changes, there was a tendency to replace peasant conscripts with other categories of guards, especially *senshi* (literally, "picked troops," i.e., professional warriors recruited from among "sons of the idle rich"[111]) and *fushū* (literally, "barbarian captives," i.e., naturalized Emishi). Peasant conscription in Kyushu was abandoned somewhat later than in the rest of the country, but for the same reason: abuse of the system by local officials, who were said to overwork ordinary soldiers, treating them as a source of private labor. The replacement of peasant conscripts with semiprofessional fighters, meanwhile, was an attempt to harness the energies of the increasingly militarized local elite. Taken as a whole, these various reforms represent a sustained, largely successful effort to maintain a workable defense system in the face of social change. As is clear from the many lamentations contained in the primary sources, however, they were seen at the time (especially by officials at Dazaifu) as a retreat from the "ideal" defense system of the late seventh and early eighth centuries.

Ironically, just after the *sakimori* system was dismantled, a security threat did emerge for the first time since the 660s. This was a plague of coastal piracy occasioned by the political decline of Silla. I explore the matter more thoroughly in chapter 3, but suffice it to say that pirate raids, while by no means inconsequential, were neither sustained enough nor damaging enough to substantially affect the course of Japanese history. During the ninth century, efforts were made to maintain and improve coastal defense by "picked troops," but after about 900, the court abandoned any attempt to maintain working defenses in Kyushu—partly because of its declining monopoly on power, but more fundamentally because such defenses were not really needed. The surrounding oceans did, for the most part, protect Japan from harm.

However, being an island country was a mixed blessing. Although isolation protected the country from casual invasion, it also allowed weak regimes to persist, regimes that in a rougher, continental environment would have fallen. In China, and in Korea, dynasties were born and died in the flames of revolution of invasion. In Japan, it seems, old warriors never died, they just faded away. The court got weaker, but it was never toppled or replaced. Military regimes—shogunates—came on to the scene during the Kamakura (1185–1333) and Muromachi (1336–1573) periods, but they lacked the authority (or perhaps the will?) to supplant the court and establish unitary states of their own. The country became increasingly decentralized and divided. Thus,

TABLE 1. Changes in military administration in Kyushu, 757–826

DATE	EVENT	SOURCE
757/int. 8/27	Eastern *sakimori* sent home (reasons: burden on provinces along route to Kyushu, difficulty for guards to make living, problems caused by Emishi uprisings); guards (total: 1,000 men) henceforth to be recruited from main seven Kyushu provinces	*Shoku Nihongi,* Tenpyō Hōji 1/int. 8/27 and 3/3/24; *Ruijū sandai kyaku* 18, Enryaku 14/11/22 *Daijōkanpu* (p. 548)
759/3/24	Dazaifu petitions for reinstatement of eastern *sakimori;* denied	*Shoku Nihongi,* Tenpyō Hōji 3/3/24
766/4/7	Dazaifu petitions for reinstatement of *sakimori* (reason: Kyushu guards "neither brave nor strong"); court allows redeployment of eastern guards still resident in Kyushu	*Shoku Nihongi,* Tenpyō Jingo 2/4/7
792/6/7	Peasant brigades disbanded except in "strategic frontier areas" *(hen'yō)* including Kyushu; guard duties given over to "stalwart youths" *(kondei)* (reason: abuse of conscripts by local officials)	*Shoku Nihongi,* Enryaku 11/6/7; *Ruijū sandai kyaku* 18, Enryaku 11/6/7 *Daijōkanpu* (pp. 558–559)
795/11/22	Court orders *sakimori* to be recruited locally, except on Iki and Tsushima, where guards will continue to be sent from six main Kyushu provinces (reasons: guards sent from Kyushu provinces are exhausted and abandon their family affairs; also require many expenses)	*Ruijū sandai kyaku* 18, Enryaku 14/11/22 *Daijōkanpu* (p. 548)
804/6/21	*Sakimori* on Iki also to be recruited locally (total: three hundred men)	*Nihon kōki,* Enryaku 23/6/21
806/10/3	640 *fushū* from Ōmi sent to Dazaifu as *sakimori*	*Ruijū kokushi* 190 (vol. 6, p. 336)
813/8/9	Number of peasant conscripts recruited and deployed in Kyushu reduced from 17,100 to 9,000	*Ruijū sandai kyaku* 18, Kōnin 4/8/9/ *Daijōkanpu* (pp. 550–551)
826/11/3	Peasant brigades disbanded in Kyushu; guard duties given over to "picked troops" (*senshi;* total: 1,720; 400 to be stationed at Dazaifu) (reason: abuse of conscripts by local officials)	*Ruijū sandai kyaku* 18, Tenchō 3/11/3 *Daijōkanpu* (pp. 553–555)

Japan's geographic isolation and its relative safety from attack encouraged political fragmentation within the archipelago: Japanese people squabbled with each other because there was no menacing foreign Other to bring them together.

In these circumstances, if an invasion did occur, it might find the inhabitants of the islands ill-prepared to deal with it. Such an event happened just twice in premodern Japanese history,[112] both times at the hands of the great Mongol empire in the late thirteenth century. The Mongol ruler Khubilai Khan wished to establish suzerainty over Japan, and when the Kamakura shogunate refused to have anything to do with this plan, Khubilai resolved to invade the island country.

The Mongol invasions of Japan (Bun'ei-no-eki, 1274; Kōan-no-eki, 1281) have been the subject of innumerable books and articles in Japanese as well as several important works in English.[113] I discuss the invasions again in chapter 3; here suffice it to say that both were unsuccessful (from the Mongol point of view). In 1274, the Mongol navy (which also included many Koreans, whose country had already been overrun) plowed through Tsushima and Iki and made serious inroads at Hakata before mysteriously disappearing from the bay in the middle of the night. In Japan, credit is usually given to a "divine wind" or *kamikaze,* although the historical evidence for this claim is slim.[114] There *is* strong evidence for a storm in 1281, when a typhoon sank many of the Mongol ships at Takashima—"Hawk Island"—at the mouth of Imari Bay in what is now Nagasaki Prefecture. These events—suitably embellished in legend—strengthened the belief that Japan was the "land of the gods" (an idea still held by ultrarightists and some politicians, including ex-prime minister Mori, who caused a furor with his public remarks to this effect in May 2000).

While premodern Japanese generally ascribed their country's survival to benevolent otherwordly forces, no serious modern historian takes this view. The consensus is that Japan was saved by a run of good luck, not only meteorological but also medical (the Mongol ruler, Khubilai, died before a third invasion could be undertaken). Thomas Conlan argues, to the contrary, that the Japanese "provided stiff resistance to the Mongols" and that "military skills and not the storms proved decisive in the encounter."[115] While it is clear from the sources Conlan cites that the samurai defenders indeed fought bravely and well, we should not conclude that Japan was any match for the Mongol empire. Luck and military prowess may both have played a role in thwarting the invasions, but what really saved Japan was geography. The country was close enough to Mongolia (and China, which Khubilai also ruled at this time) to attack, but it was too far away to attack successfully, much less rule (although it seems doubtful that the Mongols would have wanted to rule Japan directly; more likely they were simply after a pledge of submission and regular payments of tribute). Geopolitics worked against Mongol ambitions in Japan, just as they did in other remote regions such as Vietnam and Java.[116]

But Japan's rulers can be forgiven for having been worried. The Kamakura shogunate—like the court five centuries earlier—was quick to set up a system of coastal defenses in Kyushu. In this case the hardware consisted of a massive wall built around the entire circumference of Hakata Bay—a distance of approximately twenty kilometers. The software consisted, not surprisingly, of guards stationed along the bay and at other strategic points. Since as far as Japan's leaders knew, a third invasion might occur at any time, vigilance was maintained for half a century—until the shogunate itself collapsed in 1333. Responsibility for wall building and guard duty fell squarely on the shoulders of shogunal vassals *(gokenin)* in Kyushu and was a substantial burden, contributing to their dissatisfaction and the weakening of shogunal rule in Kyushu.[117]

The Mongol defense wall can still be seen along some stretches of Hakata Bay—not in the downtown area of Fukuoka, where it lies buried under landfill and rubble, but farther to the west in Nishijin, the Iki-no-matsubara pine grove, and the Itoshima Peninsula. Here the wall lies toward the back of the beach, largely covered by sand drifts and overgrown with pine trees. In a few portions, the city of Fukuoka has made an effort to dig out and repair the wall for public view. One such section, prepared in conjunction with the Group of Eight (major industrialized countries) Kyushu/Okinawa Summit of July 2000, is shown in figure 8.

One interesting and important question is why the invasion scare of the 660s prompted political centralization and state building whereas the actual invasions of the thirteenth century did not. Although to my knowledge this question has not been posed before, the answer seems fairly clear. The events of the 660s took place within a very different historical context from those of 1274 and 1281. In the first case, fear of invasion certainly pumped some extra adrenaline into Japanese veins, but these events occurred within a very broad historical and international context—a long cycle of geopolitical competition among the various states of East Asia, ultimately caused by the

FIGURE 8. Mongol defense wall at Iki-no-matsubara. Photograph by author.

expansion of the Sui and Tang empires. Japan's defeat at Paekchon River was just another link in the long chain of events leading to the emergence of a centralized, bureaucratic state. In the thirteenth century, by contrast, the Mongol invasions, while preceded by some diplomatic overtures, were akin to drive-by shootings, devoid of a larger historical context (on the Japanese side). They struck fear in the hearts of contemporary authorities, but offered no compelling reason for a fundamental reorganization of Japanese state or society, which this time seemed adequate to the task of dealing with the crisis. (The country was already on a wartime footing, this being the middle ages.) The Mongol invasions did allow the Hōjō family of shogunal regents to seize more power for themselves in Kyushu and elsewhere, but this was autocracy, not centralization, and it eventually backfired by contributing to the malcontent that found expression in the destruction of the Kamakura regime in 1333. The differing effects of the two foreign crises thus resulted from differences in context and timing.

CHAPTER 2

Diplomacy

Although war was an important form of interaction between Japan and its continental neighbors, it was also, fortunately, unusual: six centuries elapsed between the Korean unification wars and the Mongol invasions. In premodern times, even more than today, an overseas war was not undertaken lightly, and few regimes were up to the task. Also, many of the same goals could be achieved through other, less costly, forms of interaction. One such form—the most important foreign policy tool of all states in the region—was diplomacy.

SUMMIT MEETINGS AND SOUND BITES

To most of us, the word "diplomacy" probably calls to mind images and sound bites of meetings between heads of state or other high government officials. We think of the U.S. president flying across the Pacific on Air Force One to discuss nuclear containment or trade barriers with his Asian counterparts. We think of the secretary of state headed to Europe to ask for understanding and support of U.S. policy in the Middle East. We think of group photos of smiling G8 leaders taken between rounds of discussions on intellectual property rights. We think of the joint declarations issued after these summit meetings, often masterpieces of compromise and finesse—that is to say, of "diplomacy." We think of tension and high security, pressure and counterpressure, give and take, shadowboxing, pomp and circumstance, and media displays designed for public consumption.

High-profile meetings between heads of state are one aspect of diplomacy, but not the only one. Today, and indeed from the beginning of modern times, most countries maintain embassies and consulates abroad. These offices are staffed by professional diplomats from the home country, together with a variety of support personnel, mostly hired from the local labor market. I think, for example, of the U.S. embassy in Tokyo, a huge, well-guarded building situated on a hill in Akasaka. The U.S. ambassador lives next door in his magnificent official residence, while several hundred other American personnel, together with their families, reside in the embassy compound (actually, a walled apartment complex) a short distance away. These diplomats, and the Japanese staff who support them, provide services to U.S. citizens living in Japan, issue visas to would-be Japanese visitors to the U.S., and conduct mid- to low-level negotiations with counterpart organizations—ministries, trade associations, and the like—in Japan. Most of the actual work of diplomacy is carried out not at flashy summit meetings, but at embassies such as this.

Such is diplomacy today; how was it conducted in premodern times? With a few exceptions, diplomacy in early periods of history made use of neither summit meetings nor fixed, permanent embassies. Except in the case of closely neighboring countries, it was impractical for heads of state to visit their counterparts before the invention of the airplane. Permanent embassies were perhaps possible, but in most cases neither necessary nor welcome. Relations between countries, even neighboring ones, were far less intense (for better or worse) than they are today.

At least in Asia, diplomacy was a matter of intermittent comings and goings by embassies—not ferroconcrete structures like those today, but groups of diplomats sent by one state (or, more accurately, one sovereign) to another for a specific, one-time purpose or purposes. Those sending the mission might be interested in discussing military strategy, picking up information on the latest cultural trends, or importing exotic foreign goods. Sometimes they just wanted the prestige accruing from official recognition by a superior, imperial power; if already powerful, they perhaps wished to emphasize this fact by obtaining the submission of a weaker neighbor. Sometimes these desires were expressed directly, while at other times they were visible only through diplomatic smoke screens and mirrors.

More often than not, the perceptions of the sending party were far different from the perceptions of those on the receiving end. Then, as now, states needed each other. Yet their needs were often mutually contradictory; they could not be reconciled on the basis of open, jargon-free discussion. Diplomacy was a means of obfuscation, but obfuscation for a higher, positive goal: to allow each party to satisfy its needs in the least disruptive way. The smoke screens and mirrors were not secondary to the practice of diplomacy; they were its very heart and soul. And in that sense, perhaps there is no fundamental difference between diplomacy today and diplomacy in premodern times.

Japan and Silla: A Relationship Goes Sour

Nowhere were these contradictions and obfuscations more evident than in the relationship between Japan and its nearest neighbor, Silla. Many scholars, at least in the West, think of early Japanese foreign relations mostly in terms of *kenzuishi* and *kentōshi*—respectively, Japanese missions to Sui and Tang China.[1] But although China was certainly the center of the East Asian world, and although Japan was clearly influenced by it in many ways, Japan's relationships with the various Korean kingdoms were more intense.[2] This section provides a brief survey of the country's relations with one such kingdom, Silla.[3]

As described in the previous chapter, Silla and Japan fought a bloody war in 663—a war occasioned by Silla's desire to unify the Korean Peninsula and Japan's badly informed decision to aid Paekche, one of Silla's doomed rivals. Strangely enough, though, Silla and Japan were back on speaking terms within a matter of years: in 668, just five years after Japan's defeat, Silla sent its first postwar embassy to Japan, initiating a series of diplomatic exchanges that was to last a full century.

Silla's sudden about-face—from threatening enemy to placating diplomatic partner—reflected its changing geopolitical circumstances. Tang, Silla's partner in the war against Paekche, Koguryŏ, and Japan, turned out to have its own designs on the Korean Peninsula, bringing it into conflict with Silla. Silla managed to oust Tang, unifying the peninsula, in 676, but the shadow of the Chinese behemoth encouraged Silla to maintain good relations with Japan for several decades thereafter. Japan, for its part, was happy to be free of the threat of war and flattered by the constant stream of attention from Silla.

Traffic between the two countries was brisk throughout the remainder of the 600s. Silla sent a total of twenty-three embassies to Japan in the thirty-two years from 668 to the end of the century, while nine Japanese missions traveled to Silla during the same period. (The imbalance in numbers perhaps indicates that Silla was more interested in Japan than vice versa.) One unusual feature of this period is that Korean ambassadors visiting Japan generally spent their entire visit in

Kyushu without being invited to the court in Yamato and without meeting the Japanese sovereign. Instead, they took part in various diplomatic ceremonies (exchanges of messages and presents, banquets, et cetera) orchestrated by the head of Dazaifu or special agents of the court. In the immediate postwar years, one reason for this odd arrangement may have been security concerns; after all, Silla had until recently been an enemy state. Another reason was probably prestige; at this point, Japan had no real capital city, certainly nothing to compete with Silla's capital of Kyŏngju. Very likely Japanese sovereigns of this period—Tenji, Tenmu, and Jitō—did not want to reveal to Silla that in some respects Japan was still very much a "developing country."[4]

All of this changed following the construction of Japan's first Chinese-style capital, Fujiwara-kyō, in 694. When a Korean embassy led by Kim P'iltŭng arrived in Hakata in the tenth month of 697, the party was invited to Fujiwara-kyō, where they attended the New Year's audience held by Emperor Monmu in the Great Throne Hall or Daigokuden. This annual ceremony, which was attended by the entire central bureaucracy as well as representatives of "barbarian" tributary societies such as the Emishi of northeast Honshu, was meant to reaffirm the participation of all of these individuals, and those beneath them, in the ritual order presided over by the emperor, Japan's "living god."[5] Inviting guests from Silla to participate in these ceremonies can be seen as an attempt to incorporate them, and their king and country, within the Japanese "world order."

During the first three decades of the eighth century, relations between Japan and Silla remained polite, although interaction declined from previous levels. Silla sent nine embassies to Japan in the period, and Japan also sent nine missions to Silla. As in the case of Kim P'iltŭng, most of the Korean visitors to Japan were automatically invited to Fujiwara-kyō or Heijō-kyō, the new capital constructed in 710, for an audience with the emperor.

This period of stable diplomatic relations came to an end during the 720s and 730s as the result of changing international conditions. Silla grew closer to Tang, reducing its need for a diplomatic counterweight to the east. Japan, for its part, acquired another "tributary" in the form of Parhae, a Manchurian state hostile to both Silla and Tang. Parhae sent its first mission to Japan in 727, and as a result of this unexpected diplomatic windfall, Japanese rulers had less interest in maintaining good relations with Silla. Because Japan and Silla were no longer bound together by ties of mutual interest, relations began to deteriorate quickly. Silla began arming itself against Japan, and Korean records tell of a Japanese attack on Silla in 731. Later, following the 755 An Lushan Rebellion in China, Japanese leaders began planning a full-scale invasion of Silla (which they eventually abandoned for domestic political reasons).

Despite this context of mutual distrust and enmity, Japan and Silla continued to exchange diplomatic envoys through the 770s. In the fifty years from 730 to 779, Silla sent twelve missions to Japan and Japan sent seven to Silla. However, these exchanges were marked by constant bickering. Symbolic of the change in attitude on the Japanese side, visiting Korean envoys were no longer automatically invited to Heijō-kyō. When ships from Silla arrived in Hakata, commissioners were sent from the capital to question the envoys regarding their "reasons for coming" and, if the envoys bore a "state letter" *(kokusho)* from the Silla king, to open and read this as well.[6] The results of this screening were then used by the central government to determine whether or not the envoys should be allowed to proceed to Heijō-kyō. A few embassies, such as the one described in the following section, managed to obtain permission and fulfill their mission. In the majority of cases, however, the Japanese court found fault with either the envoys or their goals, and used this as an excuse to deport the Koreans directly from Hakata. On one such occasion in 760, the Japanese rubbed salt in the wounds of a departing ambassador, Kim Chŏnggwŏn, by telling him to inform his government that any future embassies must meet the following four conditions: "men with proper credentials; faithful adherence to protocol; tribute as of old; and clear, truthful speech."[7] Is it any wonder that Silla ceased to send diplomatic envoys to Japan after 779?

In sum, diplomatic relations between Japan and Silla started out friendly but gradually deteriorated to the point of "divorce." That having been said, the two countries did manage to maintain relations for a full century after 668. What was the content of this diplomacy? What forms did it take? What was at stake on both sides, and to what extent were diplomatic goals achieved? Let me attempt to answer these questions through a case study of a particular Korean embassy, one that arrived in Hakata in the spring of 752. This was the largest, and also one of the last, such missions to reach Japan before official relations between the two courts fell into abeyance. As such it is perhaps not entirely typical; but it is well-documented, and it provides much food for thought, regarding both the nature of Japan-Silla relations and the reasons for their eventual breakdown.

A Prince from Silla

Our knowledge of the embassy of 752 comes largely from *Chronicles of Japan, Continued,* the second of six "national histories" that survive from ancient times. The account begins as follows:

> *Fourth year of Tenpyō Shōhō [752], intercalary third month:*
>
> *Twenty-fifth day.* Dazaifu reported, "Silla's Prince Kim T'aeryŏm, of *hanach'an* [fifth] rank, Tribute Ambassador Kim Hwŏn, and the prince's escort Kim P'irŏn, together with more than 700 men, have arrived on board seven ships."
>
> *Twenty-eighth day.* Messengers were sent to the imperial mausoleums at Ōuchi, Yamashina, Ega, Naoyama, and elsewhere to convey news of the arrival of the Silla prince.[8]

By the conventions of the chronicles, the date of the first entry shows when news of Kim T'aeryŏm's arrival reached the court in Heijō-kyō. The news arrived by mounted courier from Hakata, where the Korean ships had weighed anchor. The couriers, low-ranking Dazaifu officials, would have first traveled up the northwest coast of Kyushu along the Saikaidō highway, stopping only for rest, food and water, and fresh mounts at the government post stations placed at convenient intervals along the broad, well-maintained highway (map 5).[9] After taking the ferry across the narrow (and dangerous) Kanmon Strait into Honshu, they would have continued up the San'yōdō highway along Honshu's Inland Sea coast, with a final brief jog inland from Naniwa, present-day Osaka, to Heijō-kyō. The total distance from Hakata to the capital was approximately six hundred kilometers, a journey of ten days to two weeks. Counting backward, this means that Kim T'aeryŏm and his companions probably arrived in Japan around the middle of the intercalary third month, not on the twenty-fifth as reported in *Chronicles of Japan, Continued.* During the intervening time, we presume, the prince and other members of the diplomatic corps stayed, under Dazaifu supervision, in the Tsukushi Lodge. They would have plenty of time to become familiar—and bored—with their lodgings before the next stage in the journey, to the capital itself, could commence.

As noted above, three days after the court learned of the diplomats' arrival in Kyushu, messengers were sent to several imperial mausoleums to convey the news to the ancestors of the current empress, Kōken (r. 749–758). Kōken, who had assumed the throne three years earlier

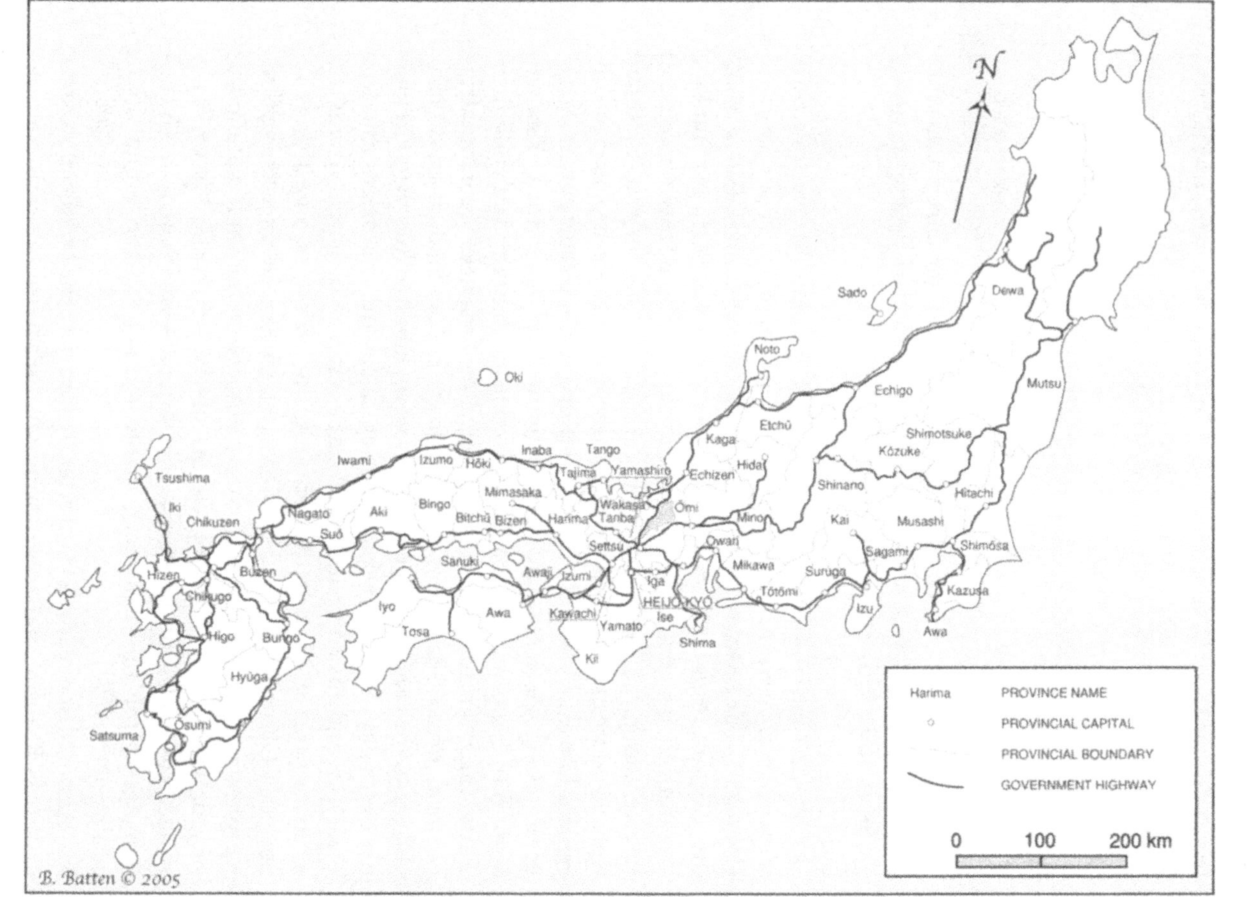

MAP 5. Japanese provinces and highways in the 8th c. *Source:* Adapted from map in Asao Naohiro et al., *Kadokawa shinpan Nihonshi jiten.*

upon the (semi-) retirement of her father, Emperor Shōmu (r. 724–749), was presumably overjoyed by the arrival of the embassy: Japan's sovereigns were always eager to receive "tribute" missions, which afforded proof positive of Silla's subsidiary status to Japan, and thus of their own legitimacy and prestige. Silla, not surprisingly, was loath to use the word "tribute" *(chōkō),* and the two countries had a long history of squabbling over this issue.

That being the case, why did Silla choose to send a "tribute" mission this time? One possibility, of course, is that it did *not*—that the Japanese blandly treated the envoys as tribute bearers regardless of their actual intentions. Although possible in theory, this hypothesis seems unlikely to me because it requires us to discount most of the remaining Japanese records of the visit, described below. At the very least, the Koreans were cognizant of and went along with (at least superficially) their hosts' interpretation of the visit. The decision to comply may have been made in the planning stages of the mission back in Silla; equally likely, it may have been made by the envoys themselves following their arrival in Japan. In either case, the decision would not have been publicized widely in Silla itself: it would have been a "plausibly deniable" expedient made known to as few people as possible. But why was such an expedient necessary? Why, in other words, was it necessary to adopt the pretense of a "tribute mission" in the first place? Probably because the mission had other objectives, which could be met only by at least a superficial acknowledgment of Japan's claims to suzerainty.

Those objectives will be discussed below; for now let us return to the description of the envoys' visit in *Chronicles of Japan, Continued:*

> *Fourth year of Tenpyō Shōhō, sixth month:*
>
> *Fourteenth day.* Silla's prince Kim T'aeryŏm appeared at court and presented tribute. Accordingly he stated, "The King of Silla addresses the court of the empress who rules gloriously over Japan. The country of Silla has from times long past continuously plied the waters with ships coming to serve your state. Now the king desires to come in person to your realm to present tribute. However, upon reflection, were the sovereign to be absent for even one day, the affairs of state would fall into disorder. Therefore, Prince T'aeryŏm, of *hanach'an* rank, has been sent in the king's stead to lead more than 370 other envoys to enter your realm and also to present diverse tribute. [So] I respectfully state."
>
> In reply, the empress proclaimed, "The country of Silla has since times long past continuously served the state. Now Prince T'aeryŏm has

> also been sent to enter our realm and to present tribute. We are pleased with the king's diligent faithfulness. May he long be given solace from afar."
>
> T'aeryŏm again stated, "There is nowhere under heaven that is not part of the royal domain, and no one on [even] the furthest shores of the realm who is not a royal subject. T'aeryŏm is overcome with happiness to have been blessed with the opportunity to come to serve you during your divine reign. I respectfully present some small items coming from my own land."
>
> The empress again proclaimed in reply, "Let it be as T'aeryŏm has said."

This entry is dated roughly three months after the court learned of T'aeryŏm's arrival. During that time, much had happened. Ordinarily in the mid-eighth century, the arrival of an embassy from Silla would have been followed by the dispatch of central inspectors to Dazaifu to question the envoys (either using written Chinese, which both Japanese and Koreans understood, or orally, through an interpreter) and make copies of their official papers. Then the commissioners would have returned to Heijō-kyō to report to the throne so that a decision could be made on whether or not to allow the Koreans to complete their mission. In 752, it is possible that these procedures were waived in view of the ambassador's princely status and self-acknowledged desire to present "tribute." Even so, however, inviting the prince to court could not be accomplished overnight. Possibly the task was delegated to the same Dazaifu functionaries who had informed the court of the embassy's arrival in the first place (and were now probably languishing in the capital). More likely, separate "escorts" were appointed and sent to Hakata with orders to bring the embassy (or rather, the diplomatic component of it, 370 members strong) back to Heijō-kyō. Whoever was sent, it would have taken another ten days to two weeks for the messengers to reach Hakata. By that time, the men from Silla had already been in Japan for a month, eating up provisions stored at the Tsukushi Lodge and, no doubt, fervently hoping for an end to their enforced state of boredom. Caring for so many visitors over such an extended period must have also taxed the resources of the Dazaifu officials, all the more so because Japanese supervision of the mission was absolute. In no case were embassy personnel allowed to roam freely or have contact with the local population (although even if they had, it is difficult to see how they could have communicated, since most Japanese in this period were illiterate). The Tsukushi Lodge, in any case, was guarded and relatively isolated—an early version of Deshima,[10] the artificial island in Nagasaki Harbor that was the sole permitted abode of Dutch visitors during the Edo period (1600–1867).

Finally, in any case, the long-awaited invitation arrived, and preparations began for the next stage of the mission. Japanese sources are ambiguous regarding travel arrangements for foreign embassies from Hakata to Heijō-kyō. The earliest clear record, involving a Chinese embassy in 608, describes the use of ships.[11] However, a tenth-century book, *Procedures of the Engi Era,* implies that embassies had a choice of coming by land or sea.[12] Regarding the land journey, which would have made use of the above-mentioned system of official highways, the text states:

> When envoys from vassal states are to enter the capital with presents from their country, they are to wait for the arrival of escorts [from the court]. The escorts are to let provinces and districts along the way arrange for the necessary horses and conscripts. Calculate the amount of tribute and clothing brought by the guests, and make provisions accordingly for meeting them and seeing them on their way. Then order one provincial official in each province to take charge of the conscripts and watch over the crossing of the border. On the way there must be no interaction with the guests. Also, the guests must not be allowed to converse with people. Nor should officials of the provinces and districts they pass through be allowed to look at the guests, or vice versa, unless there is a reason. Do not allow the guests to freely wander in and out of lodges where they stay. Other miscellaneous items not brought into the capital should be kept as convenient in local storehouses, and taken out when [the envoys] return. Horses and conscripts necessary for the round-trip should not be forced to undergo unreasonable hardship.[13]

Note again the emphasis on keeping foreign visitors away from contact with ordinary people: the movements of the envoys were under official control from start to finish.

Procedures of the Engi Era notwithstanding, in practice most—if not all—embassies from Silla seem to have made the journey from Kyushu by sea.[14] The use of ships was more convenient and less expensive, and it also solved the vexing problem of containment. No doubt the sea route was also chosen for the visit of Prince T'aeryŏm and company in 752. If so, they would have been escorted up the Inland Sea to

Naniwa Harbor, where they were greeted by a fleet of Japanese ships. Following a brief on-board welcome ceremony, the envoys would have disembarked and proceeded to the Naniwa Lodge, another official guesthouse for foreign visitors.[15] Several days later they would have traveled overland to the capital and been met on its outskirts by a mounted ceremonial guard.[16] Finally, once the delegation had entered the capital, it was led to yet another official guesthouse, which the Korean diplomats would call their home for the month or so they spent in Heijō-kyō.[17]

As noted earlier, on the fourteenth day of the sixth month, Prince T'aeryŏm visited the court for a formal audience with Empress Kōken, to whom he related greetings from the King of Silla and presented "small items coming from my own land" (i.e., tribute). *Chronicles of Japan, Continued* itself is silent on the nature of the gifts, but records of similar missions in the late seventh century mention, among other things, animals such as horses, donkeys, dogs, and birds; metals such as gold, silver, copper, and iron; fine silks and other textiles; tiger and leopard skins; Buddhist statues; and medicines and pigments.[18] Many of these same items appear among the "Silla goods" purchased by Japanese nobles after T'aeryŏm's presentation of tribute (see discussion below).

Three days after the exchange of official greetings and the presentation of tribute, Prince T'aeryŏm and the other guests from Silla attended an official banquet held in their honor, which offered Empress Kōken yet another opportunity to assert Japan's superiority to Silla:

> *Fourth year of Tenpyō Shōhō, sixth month:*
>
> *Seventeenth day* . . . On this day, the envoys from Silla were feasted in the Courtyard of the Halls of State *(chōdō)*. The empress proclaimed, "The country of Silla has served the court since Empress Jingū pacified that country until the present; [Silla] is our outer palisade. However, the previous king Sŭnggyŏng [Hyosŏng, r. 737–742] and the minister Ŭngong were lax in their words and deeds and always lacked propriety. We were therefore about to send a messenger to inquire into their crimes, but now, [the present] King Hŏnyŏng [Kyŏngdŏk, r. 742–765], ruing the earlier transgressions, desires to come to court himself. However, thinking of the affairs of state he has sent Prince T'aeryŏm in his stead to enter our realm and also present tribute. We are thus well pleased to advance him to [court] rank and bestow presents upon him." [The empress] again proclaimed, "From now on, the king should come to speak for himself. If

others are sent to enter the realm, they should in all cases bring a written memorial *(hyōbun).*"

This episode must have been galling in the extreme to Prince T'aeryŏm and his colleagues. The empress's speech, if accurately translated into words they could understand, cannot have pleased them with its derogatory references to their country and its former king. Nor can Prince T'aeryŏm have been very happy with his appointment to court rank, since by this device Empress Kōken was in effect treating him as a Japanese subject. Even the presents received—judging from other sources, pongee, silk thread, silk floss, and linen cloth[19]—could hardly compare with the exquisite gifts the prince had brought from Silla.

Finally, the "written memorial" mentioned at the end of the empress's speech was a continual sore point between the two countries. The Japanese wanted Silla to acknowledge its subordinate status in black and white, while the Koreans were understandably reluctant to do so. Oral communication, particularly when undertaken through interpreters, offered many opportunities for face-saving "creative misunderstandings." Each party was able to come away from the proceedings with its pride intact. Written documents, by contrast, were generally less flexible, constraining the two parties to a particular relationship—something only possible if they agreed in principle on the nature of the relationship or if power relations were so unequal that one party could unilaterally impose its will upon the other.

The Japanese, while eager to impress their will upon Silla, were aware of the problems inherent in written communication. The second Japanese embassy to Sui China, in 607, carried a written message from Queen Suiko to Emperor Yangdi. This document, which began, "The Child of Heaven in the land where the sun rises addresses a letter to the Child of Heaven in the land where the sun sets," enraged the Sui ruler with its implied assertion of equality.[20] The Japanese ambassador, Ono Imoko, conveniently "lost" Yangdi's reply edict on the way back to Japan, presumably because its contents would have been unacceptable to the Japanese court.[21] Until recently, it was believed that subsequent Japanese envoys to China avoided carrying diplomatic letters because of their explosive potential. Actually, this seems not to have been the case. They did carry letters from the Japanese sovereign to his Chinese counterpart, but made use of an interesting device that allowed each side to construe the relationship according to its own needs: the Japanese ruler referred to himself not with the Chinese characters for "emperor," which would again have given offense to his Tang counterpart, but with a string of characters spelling out *sumera mikoto,* a phrase that indeed meant "emperor" in Japanese, but could be (and apparently was) interpreted on the Chinese side as a personal (or family) name.[22] But needless to say, the possibilities for multiple interpretations were far greater in oral, as opposed to written communication, and that was why Silla, with very few exceptions, preferred to send its ambassadors to Japan without formal letters of state.

If the presentation of tribute was but a means to an end, what was the purpose of the mission of 752? Some scholars—the majority, in fact—have suggested that the real motivation was economic.[23] The evidence for this view comes from a collection of documents dating from the period immediately following T'aeryŏm's presentation of tribute to Empress Kōken. These documents, which were later recycled (paper was a scarce commodity) for use in the lining of a painted folding screen (now in the Shōsōin, the imperial repository at Tōdaiji), are "petitions to buy Silla goods" filed by Japanese aristocrats of the fifth court rank and above with the Treasury Ministry and the Palace Storehouse.[24] Each petition lists the items to be purchased, together with their quantity and price. The Silla goods mentioned include spices, fragrances, medicines, and dyes from tropical Asia, together with various items of Korean (or perhaps in some cases Chinese) manufacture including tableware, accessories (mirrors, combs, hairpins, and the like), and Buddhist accoutrements (table 2). In terms of quantity, the two most popular items seem to have been sappanwood, a product of South and Southeast Asia that was boiled to produce a dark red dye, and polished metal mirrors. Japanese nobles paid for their purchases not with cash, but with silk fabric, floss, and thread, which served as money substitutes in this period.[25]

Basing their arguments on these documents, most scholars conclude that the Korean envoys of 752 were little more than merchants in disguise—that Silla, in other words, caved in to Japanese demands for tribute because powerful interests at the Korean court, or their merchant backers, wanted access to the Japanese market. This argument seems questionable to me. Even assuming that we can impute modern economic motives—the desire for profit—to people living in the eighth century, it is hard to see why merchants would travel all the way from Silla to trade exotic spices and luxurious accoutrements and accessories for silk and linen. (Admittedly, of course, the envoys could have turned around and—with government permission—used these same textiles to purchase other, more desirable Japanese goods, at one of

TABLE 2. Goods from Silla purchased by Japanese nobles, 752*

CATEGORY	ITEMS
Spices and fragrances	Frankincense (or retinite), birthwort root, cloves, aloeswood (i.e., agalloch, garroo/gharu), agastache (or patchouli), fenugreek, Chinese spikenard, borneol (i.e., camphor), benzoin
Medicines	Musk, myrobalans, ginseng, cinnamon, rhubarb, bezoars (i.e., ox gallstones), long pepper, licorice, broomrape, milkwort, beeswax, Epsom salt
Cosmetics	Gamboge, cinnabar, white lead, orpiment
Pigments	Sappanwood, gromwell root
Metals	Gold, iron
Tableware and furnishings	Mirrors, incense-burners, metal bowls, platters, spoons, chopsticks, vases, priest's staffs, candle stands, saddles, reins, cruppers, combs, hairpins, felt products, folding screens
Other	Lipstick, soapberry rosary beads, pine nuts, honey, cloth, dried hides

Source: Tōno Haruyuki, *Shōsōin monjo to mokkan no kenkyū* (Hanawa shobō, 1977), pp. 312–316.

*This is a partial list; I have omitted several items that are either unidentifiable or untranslatable. I follow Tōno's classification of the items (see chap. 2, n. 24), although some had more than one use. (For example, pepper was used both as a medicine and a spice.) Translations of the terms for aromatics and medicines were made with the aid of Shiu-ying Hu, *An Enumeration of Chinese Materia Medica;* Friedrich Hirth and W. W. Rockhill, *Chau Ju-Kua;* and Shibata Shōji and Kunaichō Shōsōin jimusho, eds., *Zusetsu Shōsōin yakubutsu.* The last book also contains photographs and detailed descriptions (in both English and Japanese) of imported medicines from the eighth century preserved in the Shōsōin. Edward H. Schafer, *The Golden Peaches of Samarkand,* contains fascinating descriptions of most of the items listed in table 2. Also see Shafer, *The Vermilion Bird.*

Heijō-kyō's two official marketplaces.) Further, it is not even clear that the envoys were directly involved in these transactions. The fact that the petitions are all addressed to the Japanese government suggests to me that the latter may have been auctioning off part of the tribute presented by T'aeryŏm, after the best items had been appropriated by the empress and her household.[26]

This still leaves us with the question of the embassy's motives. Lee Sungsi, for his part, finds them in contemporary interstate relations.

Specifically, during these same years, Silla's relations with its northern neighbor, Parhae, were becoming increasingly strained. Silla, in Lee's interpretation, sought Japanese support (whether ideological or material or both) in its struggle against Parhae and for this reason agreed, if only temporarily, to play the role of a tributary.[27]

However, this is only part of the picture; a second and probably equally important factor was religious. Take a look at the next related entry in the *Chronicles of Japan, Continued,* which dates from five days after the above-described banquet:

> *Fourth year of Tenpyō Shōhō, sixth month:*
> *Twenty-second day.* T'aeryŏm and others worshiped the Buddha at Daianji and Tōdaiji.

Daianji and Tōdaiji were major temples in Heijō-kyō. Of the two, Tōdaiji was the more important, indeed the single most important religious institution in Nara-era Japan. Tōdaiji was patronized by Emperor Shōmu and his immediate heirs, who overtly subscribed to the doctrine of *chingo kokka* or "protection of the state," according to which the Buddhas, boddhisattvas, and guardians of the four heavenly directions would actively guard Japan from harm. Tōdaiji also housed the Great Buddha or *daibutsu,* a huge gilt-bronze effigy completed and unveiled in the fourth month of 752, after the envoys from Silla docked in Hakata but before their arrival in the capital. The gala opening ceremony, presided over by a priest from "Tenjiku" (India or vicinity), was attended by the empress, her entire court, and (probably an exaggeration) "ten thousand" monks.[28] It seems likely that the arrival of the Silla embassy was timed (not quite correctly, in retrospect) for the unveiling of the Great Buddha and that many of the participants had religious motivations. Perhaps they were even invited by the Japanese, who had a vested interest in the cosmopolitan nature of the ceremony, which was designed to show their country's central place in East Asia.[29]

It is easy for those of us living in the secular twenty-first century to play down such motives, to doubt that anyone would have made the long and arduous trip from Silla for the purpose of visiting a "mere" temple. Skeptical readers are urged to pay a visit to Tōdaiji and its Great Buddha, which despite the ravages of time have retained some of their original splendor, for an instant cure to such foolish notions. The temple is magnificent. In the far more religious climate of the eighth century, the mere rumor of it could have been—and was—sufficient to bring travelers from all over Asia.

A month after accomplishing their religious (and other) goals, the Silla envoys were on their way home. According to the *Chronicles of Japan, Continued:*

> *Fourth year of Tenpyō Shōhō, seventh month:*
> *Twenty-fourth day.* T'aeryŏm and others departed and were [staying] in the Naniwa Lodge. A messenger was dispatched by imperial edict to bestow them with pongee and cloth, as well as wine and delicacies.

Again, the Naniwa Lodge was in what is today Osaka at the eastern terminus of the Inland Sea. Presumably the prince and other members of his party spent a day or two there before heading down (probably again by sea) to Hakata. They would have been accompanied, of course, by official escorts charged with the envoys' protection and supervision, and we may assume that the party reached Hakata sometime in the early part of the seventh month. A brief reunion with the sailors and lower functionaries left behind in Hakata would have followed, and then perhaps an official banquet at the Tsukushi Lodge, or more likely the Dazaifu headquarters. Return to Silla would have followed not long afterward, possibly in the eighth month. All in all, the envoys of 752 would have spent about five months in Japan—just over a month in the capital, their ultimate destination, and the rest at Hakata or on the road. Roughly half the party, more than three hundred people, would have spent the entire period docked near the Tsukushi Lodge at Hakata.

At the Tsukushi Lodge

It is now time for a brief survey of what we know about this intriguing and important diplomatic facility. The goal of visiting embassies from Silla was always, of course, an audience with the Japanese sovereign and the exchange of messages and presents. However, as noted just now, even when diplomats achieved this goal, most of their time in Japan was spent not in the capital but on the road or in Hakata. And most support personnel and sailors never left Hakata in the first place: the Tsukushi Lodge and its immediate vicinity was the start and the end of their visit to Japan. Probably most of them were not happy campers. To have come all the way to Japan just to be kept confined to a single facility, no matter how well appointed, must have been extremely frustrating, especially considering the long duration of some of these visits.

Moreover, as noted earlier, many Korean embassies (except in the first three decades of the eighth century) were never invited to court at all. In such cases, not only the lower functionaries, but everyone up to the ambassador saw no more of Japan than Tsushima (possibly), the port facilities at Hakata, and the inside of the Tsukushi Lodge, with perhaps the odd, strictly supervised, visit to the Dazaifu headquarters. Although the Tsukushi Lodge certainly loomed large in the perceptions of all Korean envoys, for those not invited to the capital the lodge became the very symbol, the core, of their experience in Japan and, by extension, of Japan-Silla relations as a whole.

To reiterate, the Tsukushi Lodge was one of the many facilities constructed around Hakata Bay in the wake of Japan's defeat in 663. Several of these—the Mizuki, Ōno Fortress, and Ki Fortress—can be precisely dated, thanks to entries in *Chronicles of Japan,* the official record of the period. This text does not mention the building of the Tsukushi Lodge, but there is no reason to doubt that it dates from the same general period and was built to accommodate Chinese envoys in the immediate postwar years.[30] As described in the previous chapter, representatives of the Tang military visited Japan on five separate occasions between 664 and 671. Clearly these people needed a place to stay.

The physical location and appearance of the Tsukushi Lodge symbolized the ambivalence the Japanese government felt toward the Chinese envoys. On the one hand, the court would not have wanted to give offense to representatives of the great Tang empire. The guests had to be treated with dignity and in style—hence the need for a luxurious, well-appointed guest lodge. On the other, the last thing the Japanese hosts wanted was to give these unwanted visitors free rein of the country—hence the need for a guarded facility far away from centers of population. The Tsukushi Lodge was convenient to port facilities on Hakata Bay, but it was not convenient to Dazaifu or other population centers in Japan; that was the whole point.

The need for security is easy to understand in the case of the Tang embassies of the 660s: after all, they were representatives of a country that had recently defeated Japan in war. Security concerns probably also had something to do with the above-mentioned practice of isolating visitors from Silla throughout the seventh and eighth centuries. Like Tang, Silla was a past, and possibly future, enemy. But the same policy of isolation was applied to diplomats from friendly states such as Parhae and also to private individuals such as the Chinese merchants who began to visit Hakata in the ninth century. Indeed, with the possible exception of the Sengoku (Warring Provinces) period (ca. 1477–ca. 1568), close supervision of foreign visitors was the norm for all Japanese regimes until Japan's "opening" to the West in the nineteenth century.[31] (Cynics would argue that vestiges of this exclusivist attitude remain even today.)

Why such close supervision? Were Japanese people xenophobes? There is in fact some evidence of xenophobia, particularly among the social elite, during the Heian era. In the late ninth century, for example, bureaucrats in both Kyoto and Dazaifu responded to Korean piracy with strong negative feelings about Silla and its inhabitants. (Consider the following statement, from an official document of 870: "The puny [country of] Silla is venomous and corrupt."[32]) More generally, beginning in this same general period and continuing through medieval times, elites embraced a peculiar ideology centering on the pure, sacred body of the emperor. In this view of the world, society became increasingly degraded and defiled the further one traveled from the emperor's abode; foreign lands, by reason of their distant location, were the most polluted of all.[33] It is probably no coincidence that from the tenth century there was a strong taboo against bringing people of foreign birth into the emperor's physical presence.[34]

It is important, however, to put this "xenophobia" into perspective: It existed, but not in all periods. During the seventh and eighth centuries, as we have seen, many embassies from Silla visited Japan, and these visits culminated, at least ideally, in an audience with the emperor. Even after diplomatic ties with Silla fell into abeyance, envoys from Parhae continued to visit Japan, and meet with the emperor, until the early tenth century. It is also worth noting that negative attitudes toward foreigners, even when present among elite courtiers, were by no means typical of Japanese society as a whole. Even in Kyushu there were few opportunities to meet foreigners, and so the most common attitude was curiosity, sometimes tinged with mild racism born of ignorance. (An example from the Edo period is given in the Conclusion.) Those who did have an opportunity to interact with foreigners, however, seem generally to have been open-minded, except during outbreaks of piracy or the like. On occasion, in fact, those living and working in Kyushu were a bit too open-minded. In the ninth century, for example, there are several well-known cases of conspiracy or collusion between residents or local officials in northern Kyushu and their counterparts in Silla. In 866, for example, three district officials in coastal Hizen were accused of planning to go to Silla, teach the residents how to make weapons (as if they didn't already know!), and come back to capture Tsushima.[35] Or again, in 870, Dazaifu Junior Assistant Governor-General Fujiwara Motorimaro, together with one of his "retainers" and three "vagrants," was accused of "plotting with the king of Silla to harm the state."[36]

If xenophobia was not the reason for isolating foreign visitors, what was? Very broadly speaking, there are three answers to this question. The first is suggested by the fact of collusion, noted above: the government was afraid that unsupervised contacts between Japanese and foreigners could prove disruptive. Open social systems are unpredictable and thus difficult to control; governments thus had a vested interest in preventing unauthorized foreign contacts.[37]

Second, although foreigners themselves were not usually targets of discriminatory attitudes, they were seen as potential carriers of disease and thus as public health menaces. As an island country, Japan was to a large extent isolated from the disease pools of continental Eurasia.[38] This was both good and bad. Diseases such as smallpox, influenza, and measles were not ordinarily present in Japan, which was a good thing. On the other hand, precisely because these diseases were not endemic, people lacked natural immunities. As a result, when a disease was accidentally introduced from the continent, the results could be, and were, devastating. Smallpox introduced from Silla in 735, for example, set off an epidemic that eliminated as much as one-third of Japan's total population. This epidemic (and others) had no respect for social boundaries: among its victims were the so-called four Fujiwara brothers, who represented the up-and-coming generation of leadership in Heijō-kyō.[39] Japanese people were well aware that plagues could (and did) come from abroad: an outbreak of "coughing disease" in Kyoto in 872, for example, was attributed to "noxious vapors from foreign lands"—specifically, "noxious vapors" brought from Parhae by a visiting group of diplomats.[40] The chief weapon used to combat the spread of disease was prayer. For example, the court's initial response to the news of the arrival of disease in 735 was to offer prayers at Shinto shrines and to read sutras at Buddhist temples throughout Kyushu.[41] The idea that foreign visitors brought disease perhaps also accounts for the fact that purification rituals were performed on the borders of the central provinces and the four corners of the capital before foreign diplomats were allowed to enter.[42] However, the effort, both at the Tsukushi Lodge and on the road, to isolate foreign envoys from contact with Japanese people suggests that not everything was left to the gods: there was also some awareness of the effectiveness of quarantine.

A third reason for limiting foreign contacts had to do with political legitimacy. The government—or more precisely, the emperor and his court—derived some of its political authority from its ability to monopolize foreign contacts. As we have seen, the emperor's effective control over access to imported goods, cultural knowledge, and news of the world allowed him to redistribute these commodities to other members of the central aristocracy. This ability not only strengthened the emperor's authority over other elites but, by excluding nonelites from access to foreign goods, reinforced the prevailing status order of Japanese society as a whole. Strict supervision of foreign visitors was the linchpin of the entire system.

What sort of experiences would visiting Korean envoys have had in Kyushu? How would they have interacted with their Japanese hosts? How would their daily needs have been met? There are no certain answers to these questions, but for purposes of illustration let us go back to the case of Kim T'aeryŏm and company. As noted, a fleet of seven ships carrying a total of 700 men (and they probably *were* all men; women rarely seem to figure in East Asian diplomacy or, for that matter, trade or piracy, either) arrived in Hakata about the middle of the intercalary third month of 752. As discussed earlier, the entire party stayed in Kyushu for perhaps two months, and then a group of 370 departed for the capital, probably in the second half of the fifth month. The remaining 330 (presumably sailors and support personnel) remained in Kyushu until early in the seventh month, when their colleagues returned from the capital. Then all 700 got back in their ships and went home. In short, officials at Dazaifu were responsible for housing 700 men for two months, then a smaller party of 330 men for another two months, and then the entire contingent of 700 for perhaps a few more days prior to departure.

How was this accomplished? It would have been difficult for all of these people to stay in the Tsukushi Lodge. The lodge has not been fully excavated, but by present estimates it consisted of two rectangular compounds, each measuring 74 meters east–west and 56 meters north–south, aligned along a north–south axis atop a plateau by the sea (figure 9). These are large buildings, but were they large enough to house several hundred men? In the opinion of the chief investigator for

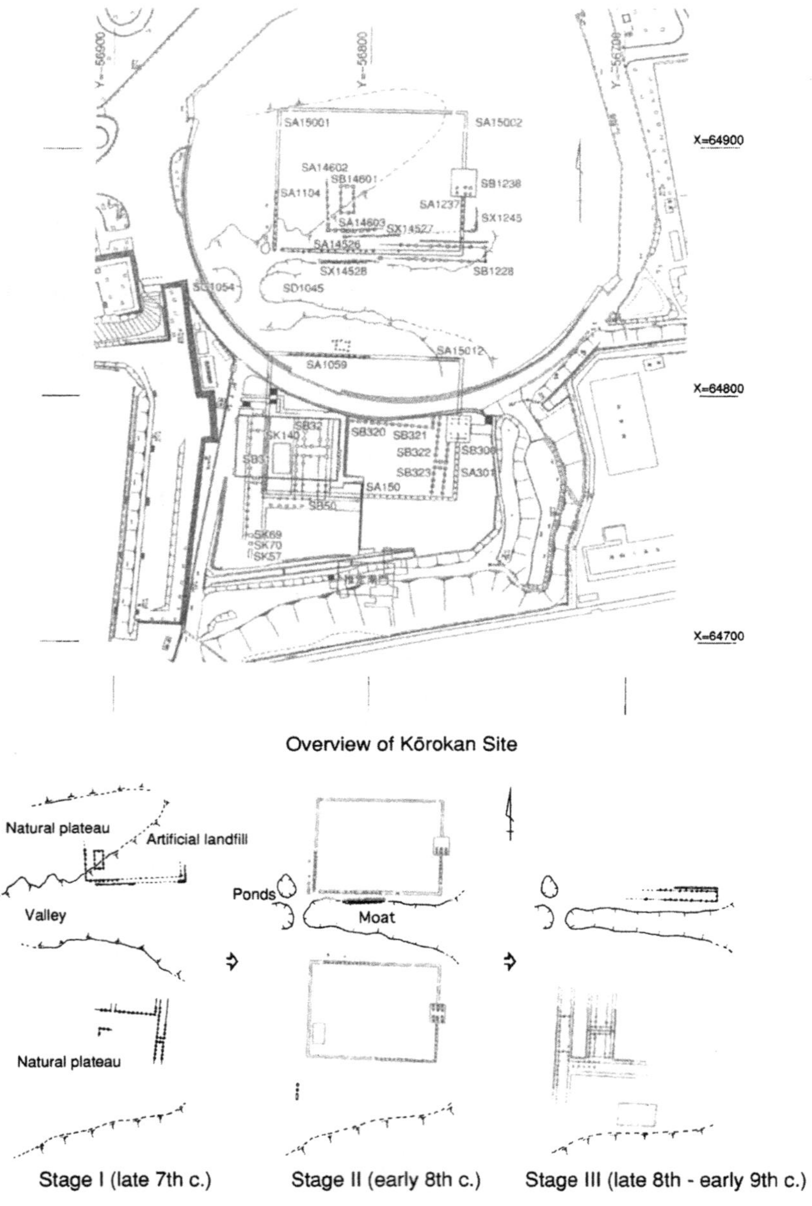

FIGURE 9. Kōrokan site map. As shown at the bottom of the figure, the original lodge facilities, dating from the late 7th c., were rebuilt on two occasions. *Source:* Fukuoka-shi kyōiku iinkai, ed., *Kōrokan 14: Heisei 11, 12 nendo hakkutsu chōsa hōkoku,* p. 5. Reproduced with permission.

the site, Ōba Kōji, yes, the buildings could have held everyone, but the experience would not have been pleasant: the diplomats would have been the human equivalents of sardines in a can.[43] Although there is no way of knowing, it seems to me more likely that to avoid overcrowding, berths at the lodge would have been reserved for the ambassador and perhaps several dozen other high-ranking diplomats, while support personnel and ordinary sailors would have had to camp outside the lodge or simply stay on board ship. (The Korean ships were probably docked just outside the lodge, which faced east toward a small harbor.[44]) Both the lodge area and the ships, of course, would have been under twenty-four-hour surveillance by border guards to make sure that none of the visitors took an unauthorized tour of Hakata.

What about food and water? Water would probably have been obtained from wells in the vicinity of the Tsukushi Lodge, although none has yet been archaeologically identified. As for food, diplomats certainly brought provisions for their journey, but these were intended for the sea voyage itself, not the duration of their stay in Japan. Given the emphasis on supervision, it is unlikely in the extreme that Japanese officials would have allowed foreign diplomats to forage for their own food in Japan—although conceivably those staying aboard ship could have done some fishing from the deck. So most of the visitors' food, like their other requirements, would have been provided by their Japanese hosts.

Table 3 shows foodstuffs known to have been available in Kyushu during the Nara and Heian eras. The list was compiled by Ishibashi Akira on the basis of references in traditional historical sources (e.g., *Chronicles of Japan, Continued; Procedures of the Engi Era,* etc.) as well as newly discovered *mokkan.* Because of the official nature of these sources, the result probably tells us more about the diet of Japanese bureaucrats than that of farmers or fishermen. Nonetheless, it is all we have. Many of the items on the list will be immediately familiar to anyone who has spent time in Japan today—or, for that matter, inside a Japanese restaurant overseas. Then, as now, the Japanese diet seems to have consisted largely of rice, vegetables, and seafood.

Although the foodstuffs in table 3 represent the diet of Japanese officials, foreign visitors apparently received much the same fare. Preparing their food was the responsibility of the Dazaifu kitchen officer (*shuchūshi,* perhaps more felicitously rendered as "chief chef"), who also cooked for the governor-general and other high officials. According to the chef's official job description, which appears in an eighth-

TABLE 3. Foodstuffs available in Kyushu during Nara and Heian eras

CATEGORY	ITEMS
Grains and legumes	Rice, wheat, soybeans, adzuki beans
Vegetables	Taro, Japanese radish, bamboo shoots, leeks, amaranthus *(hiyu),* lotus roots, ginger
Fruits and nuts	Sesame seeds, figs, chestnuts, water chestnuts, pine seeds, peaches
Seaweed	Thickhaired codium *(miru),* kelp
Other seafood and freshwater fish	Sweetfish, abalone, cuttlefish, oysters, bonito, whale, jellyfish, salmon, horned turbans *(sazae),* mackerel, shark, sea bream, octopus, murex snails *(tsubu),* sea cucumbers, croaker *(nibe),* pike conger *(hamo),* crucian carp *(funa)*
Fowl and game	Wild boar, venison, pheasant, chicken*
Condiments and alcoholic drinks	*Amazurasen* (sweetener made from ivy resin), salt, vinegar, soy, sake
Milk products and oils	Cheese,† sesame oil, perilla oil

Source: Ishibashi Akira, "Dazaifu seichō jidai Saikaidō no tabemono," *Tofurō* 11 (1991): 51–58.

*The original list also mentions cows and horses; while these were certainly raised in Kyushu, it is doubtful that their flesh was widely consumed because of Buddhist prohibitions against the eating of red meat. On consumption of beef, see Kaneko Hiromasa et al., *Nihonshi no naka no dōbutsu jiten,* pp. 13–14. Also note that during the "Toi Invasion" of 1019 (discussed in detail in chapter 3 herein), Japanese residents of Kyushu were shocked to see Jurchen raiders slaughtering horses and cows for consumption.

†"Cheese" is a tentative translation of *so.* This was a milk product of some kind, but its exact nature is unknown.

century legal compilation (the Yōrō Code), he was responsible for preparing "vinegar and pickled meats, seasoned vegetables, pickled vegetables, fermented bean paste, and dried fish."[45]

The chef and his staff ran a fishery-cum-supply depot on the sand spit connecting Shikanoshima to the mainland, but most of the ingredients they used came from tax goods sent to Dazaifu by the various Kyushu provinces.[46] In the 1990 field season, archaeologists working at the Kōrokan came upon three eighth-century latrines outside the southwest corner of the southern compound. One of them, referred to as SK-57, contained a number of inscribed wooden slips originally used as labels for foodstuffs shipped to the lodge. (After the goods were delivered, these *mokkan* were apparently scrapped and—incredible as it may seem—used as a substitute for toilet paper.) Figure 10 shows some of the tags recovered at the site. Judging from the inscriptions, they were used to label food products such as rice, fish, and venison from the Kyushu provinces of Chikuzen, Buzen, Hizen, and Higo. One tag (no. 11) mentions Miki district, Sanuki Province, in Shikoku—a surprising find inasmuch as Dazaifu, which coordinated the tax flows, had no jurisdiction on that island.

Interestingly, SK-57 and the other two latrines have also provided more direct evidence of eighth-century dietary habits.[47] When the sediments therein were sent out for lab analysis, they were found to include numerous seeds of melons, eggplants, and *Actinidia rufa,* a relative of the kiwi fruit known in Japanese by the evocative name *shimasarunashi* or "striped monkey-pear." Also recovered in quantity were eggs of human parasites, including intestinal worms and liver flukes. Most of these have specific natural hosts. Armed with knowledge of the parasites' life cycles, the investigators (Kanehara Masaaki and Masako) concluded that the users of SK-57 had a diet consisting primarily of vegetables and fish, while those of the other two latrines, SK-69 and SK-70, were eaters of meat, specifically pork or wild boar. On this basis it was further suggested that the users of SK-57 were Japanese, while those of SK-69 and SK-70 were foreign.[48] If true, this is interesting because it supports my idea that foreign guests were segregated to the extent possible from their Japanese hosts. However, one has to wonder to what extent this conclusion is "scientific" and to what extent it is simply based on cultural stereotyping. Japanese people tend to think that their ancestors ate no red meat, which is untrue; as can be seen from table 3, venison and boar were part of the premodern Japanese diet. There is also a strong tendency, perhaps even among archaeologists and parasitologists, to equate Korean cuisine, now and then, with barbecued meat.

As if one dubious claim about the toilets were not enough, we have another regarding the sex of those using the facilities: Nakano Masuo of Obihiro University of Agriculture and Veterinary Medicine has hypothesized, on the basis of coprostanol/cholesterol ratios from the latrine residue, that SK-57 was used by men while SK-69 and SK-70 were used by women. This claim, which seems never to have been

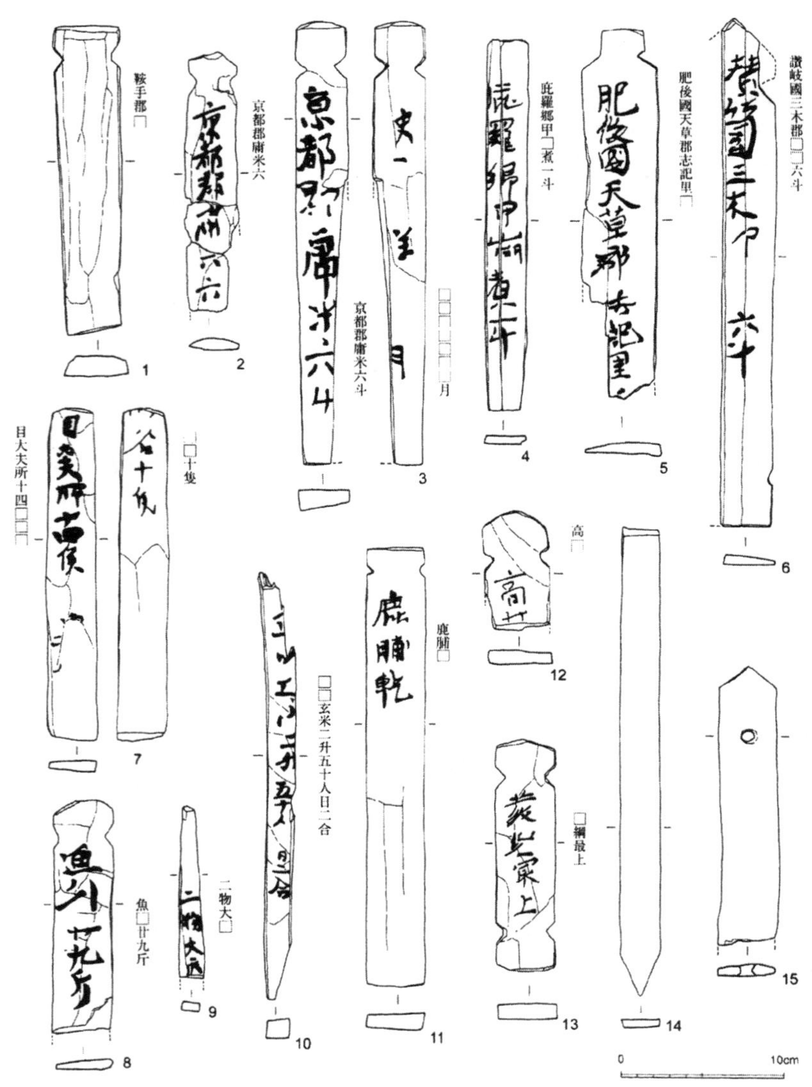

FIGURE 10. Inscribed wooden slips from Kōrokan site. Food products mentioned include polished rice (2, 3); unpolished rice (10); fish (8); and venison jerky (11). Places mentioned are Kurate district, Chikuzen Province (modern Fukuoka Prefecture, 1); Miyako district, Buzen (Fukuoka, 2, 3); Hira township, Hizen (Nagasaki, 4); Shiki township, Amakusa district, Higo (Kumamoto, 5); and Miki district, Sanuki (Kagawa, 6). *Source:* Fukuoka-shi kyōiku iinkai, ed., *Kōrokan 14: Heisei 11, 12 nendo hakkutsu chōsa hōkoku,* p. 35. Reproduced with permission.

FIGURE 11. Eighth-century latrine at Tsukushi Lodge (Kōrokan). This picture was taken in late March 2004, days before the pit was refilled for safety reasons. Photograph by author.

published formally (but was nonetheless cited in a general-audience book called *The Archaeology of Toilets*[49]), is also intriguing because there is no other evidence, either historical or archaeological, for the presence of women at the Tsukushi Lodge. However, it should be noted that Nakano's argument and that of the Kaneharas cannot both be correct. If they were, we would have Japanese men using SJ-57 and foreign women using SK-69 and SK-70—an impossibility, given that all foreign emissaries were male. If women were indeed present, they must have been Japanese—in which case the Kaneharas' arguments regarding ethnicity are wrong.

All of which is to say that further work is required before we can draw any firm conclusions about the sex or ethnicity of those using the Tsukushi Lodge toilets. Actually, the opportunity seemed to present itself during the 2003 field season, when investigators discovered two more eighth-century latrines, this time on the west side of the northern compound (figure 11). Unfortunately, however, neither of the new finds contained residue suitable for analysis.

Finally, what about entertainment and other activities? Did visiting envoys spend all their time cooped up in the Tsukushi Lodge? The answer to this, fortunately, seems to be "no." As part of his official duties the Dazaifu governor-general was held responsible for "guests from vassal states, immigrants, and banquets."[50] During the late seventh century, for reasons noted earlier, diplomatic ceremonies that would normally have been carried out at court were held instead in Kyushu. Instead of submitting tribute directly to the Japanese sovereign, visiting diplomats in this period surrendered their gifts to Dazaifu, which later forwarded them to court. The Dazaifu governor-general, usually acting in concert with special representatives of the central government, also sponsored official banquets for foreign guests. All of these activities were probably held at the Dazaifu compound itself, not at the Tsukushi Lodge. If so, the foreign guests would have had the opportunity to stretch their legs and enjoy the round trip to Dazaifu. And although some of the formal ceremonies were probably stiff and tiresome, the banquets that followed would have offered welcome opportunities to interact with Dazaifu officials, and perhaps even their families. Toasts would have been given, and poems would have been composed and recited to an appreciative audience.[51]

Dazaifu lost some of its importance as a site for diplomatic ceremony in the early eighth century, when it became routine to invite Korean ambassadors to Heijō-kyō. However, official banquets were still held in Kyushu (again, probably at Dazaifu), usually on the occasion of the envoys' departure for home following their return from the capital. Banquets for departing envoys continued to be held upon occasion even after relations with Silla took a turn for the worse in the 730s. As late as 770, Dazaifu is seen holding a banquet for visiting ambassador Kim Ch'ojŏng, despite the fact that he never received an invitation to Heijō-kyō.[52]

But ceremonies and banquets, by their very nature, were exceptional events: whether in the seventh century or the eighth, Korean diplomats in Kyushu could probably have expected only a few days of excitement amid many months of boredom at the Tsukushi Lodge. One recalls the words of *Procedures of the Engi Era:* "There must be no interaction with the guests. Also, the guests must not be allowed to converse with people. Nor should officials . . . be allowed to look at the guests, or vice versa, unless there is a reason. Do not allow the guests to freely wander in and out of lodges where they stay." Of course, there would have been some limited interaction with Japanese officials at mealtime, as well as discussions regarding provisions for the return journey (also the responsibility of Dazaifu) and, if necessary, repairs to the envoys' ships, which were sometimes damaged in the initial crossing to Japan. But that would have been about all.[53] And then, one day, the guests would be gone, with the wind in their sails and the broad expanse of Hakata Bay at their backs. Given the envoys' experiences, the beautiful setting probably looked less attractive on the way out than it had coming in so many months before. No doubt most of the diplomats were happy to be on their way home.

The Rest of the Story

With the departure of the last embassy from Silla in early 780, Japan was left with but two diplomatic partners, Tang and Parhae. Missions to Tang, or *kentōshi,* were dispatched in 779, 804, and 838, and the hundreds of Japanese diplomats, lesser functionaries, and sailors who took part in these gala events all went through Hakata both on their way out and, if they managed to avoid shipwreck (an all too common professional hazard), on their way back home from China. At Hakata, of course, they stayed at the Tsukushi Lodge. But the mission of 838 was the last ever sent to Tang; another embassy planned for 894 was scrapped at the recommendation of the ambassador-elect, Sugawara Michizane. Michizane cited the dangers of the journey and the tumultuous political conditions then prevalent in China.[54] Michizane's reading of the situation was correct: the Tang dynasty collapsed as the result of internal rebellions in 907. This left Japan with but one diplomatic partner, Parhae.

Parhae, like Silla, had been treated as a vassal state by Japan ever since the first Parhae embassy showed up on the Sea of Japan coast in 727.[55] But relations with Parhae were generally smoother than those with Silla. As understood by Japanese historians, Parhae leaders (who traced their ancestry to the ruling class of Koguryŏ) had a strategic interest in maintaining good relations with Japan in the eighth century, when Parhae was generally at odds with Silla and Tang. Later, in the ninth century, the strategic imperative declined, but Parhae continued to put up with Japanese demands, this time for largely economic reasons: the country's rulers, it is said, were willing to suffer the possible loss of prestige associated with tributary status because they placed a high value on trade with Japan. (The actual content of the trade was much the same as in the case of Silla.) Parhae embassies to Japan were technically required to enter Japan through Hakata,[56] but this requirement made little geographic sense, given Parhae's location just across the Sea of Japan from Honshu. After a while the court in Heijō-kyō gave tacit permission for Parhae envoys to disembark in Honshu. Provincial governors along the Sea of Japan coast were given powers similar to those of the Dazaifu governor-general, and a reception facility modeled on the Tsukushi Lodge, the Matsubara (Pine Grove) Guesthouse, was built on the shores of Tsuruga Bay in Echizen Province (modern Fukui Prefecture).[57] However, Parhae came to an unpleasant end at the hands of Khitan tribesmen in 926, very nearly on the two-hundredth anniversary of its first embassy to Japan. This event left Japan with no formal diplomatic partners.

Did it matter? Apparently not. One of the striking features of tenth-century Japanese history is the court's near-total withdrawal from international politics. This was not for want of opportunities. Liao (916–1125) sent an ambassador in 929, while Wu Yue (907–978), one of the "ten kingdoms" to appear in southern China following the collapse of Tang, attempted to establish diplomatic relations on at least four separate occasions. After a hiatus of more than a century, ambassadors even began to arrive from the Korean Peninsula. The kingdom of Later Paekche (900–935), a short-lived rival to Silla, sent envoys in 922 and 929, while Koryŏ (935–1392), which absorbed Silla and went on to conquer Later Paekche, sent official representatives in 937, 939, and 940. Without exception, these diplomatic initiatives were rebuffed by the Japanese court, which in most cases refused to recognize the legitimacy of the new states. The king of Later Paekche, for example, was treated as a subject of Silla, not the head of an autonomous state. Lacking sovereignty, it was argued, he was unqualified to initiate diplomatic contacts.[58]

Thus began a remarkable period of diplomatic isolation for Japan, one that was to last for nearly half a millennium. Domestically, this period was characterized by political decentralization, violence and social disorder, and the emergence of semiautonomous warrior regimes, based first in eastern Japan (the Kamakura shogunate) and then in Kyoto (the Muromachi shogunate). Internationally, Japan remained in contact with continental Asia, but through vehicles other than formal diplomacy.[59] Among peaceful forms of communication, the most important was maritime trade, the subject of chapter 4. Also important, although not treated in detail in this book, were religious contacts; Japanese pilgrims, often riding on merchant ships, went to China to study, and Chinese missionaries, making use of the same form of transportation, went to proselytize and found temples in Japan. Some of these religious endeavors were aided and abetted—or even sponsored—by political authorities. But they did not constitute formal diplomacy in the sense of direct, government-to-government (or, more precisely, sovereign-to-sovereign) contacts. (Quite possibly, they provided a needed avenue for the content of diplomacy in an age when the forms, for whatever reason, could not be adequately observed.) In the late twelfth century, the Mongolian ruler Khubilai Khan, following his conquest of China, attempted to establish diplomatic relations with Japan (which, naturally, was expected to play the role of a Mongol tributary). However, Khubilai's approaches were repeatedly rebuffed by the Kamakura shogunate. As we have seen, Khubilai rewarded this impudence by arranging two separate invasions of Japan, one in 1274 and the other in 1281. In the end, it was not until 1401 that a Japanese regime (the Muromachi shogunate) reestablished formal diplomatic relations with its counterpart in China (the Ming dynasty).

What is to account for the long-standing hiatus in Japanese diplomacy after 900, which contrasts so sharply with the relatively intense diplomatic engagements of the preceding three centuries? To answer this question, all we need to do is recall what benefits earlier Japanese rulers got out of diplomatic relations with Tang, Silla, and Parhae: cultural capital and information, on the one hand, and political legitimacy, on the other. But by the tenth century, foreign luxuries and news of the world were available through other channels, specifically via Chinese merchants operating out of Mingzhou (Ningbo), Quanzhou, and other ports. And as for political legitimacy, by 900 the position of the emperor was unquestioned. Perhaps the court would have been willing to enter into diplomatic relations with a foreign state openly calling itself a Japanese tributary, but such states were in noticeably short supply following the demise of Parhae. (Notably, when diplomatic relations with China were restored in the fifteenth century, the instigator was not the imperial court but the Muromachi shogunate, which indeed was in need of legitimacy to secure its position against domestic rivals.)

Throughout premodern history, Japanese leaders looked upon foreign relations as means to domestic ends. They wanted luxury products, information, and most of all political leverage against domestic rivals or underlings. If these could be obtained through diplomatic channels, and if the perceived benefits of state-to-state relations outweighed the perceived costs, then diplomacy was the order of the day. If the costs were too high, or if the same results could be obtained more easily through other channels, then diplomacy was no longer a priority. Japanese rulers had a choice, and they had a choice because they lived in an island country whose relative isolation gave them the luxury of engaging in, or withdrawing from, diplomatic relations with other states at their own convenience.

But even if Japan's leaders chose to withdraw, foreigners might still come to Japan for their own purposes, whether they were to raid or to trade. So while Japanese authorities could abdicate from active participation in the East Asian world, they could not back away from basic boundary functions such as defense and immigration control. In the next two chapters we examine, respectively, the imperial court's attempt to deal with visitations by foreign pirates and foreign merchants during the Heian period.

CHAPTER 3

Piracy

The word "pirate" calls to mind images of Blackbeard and Captain Kidd—or, to the less historically minded, Captain Hook in *Peter Pan* or Johnny Depp as Captain Jack Sparrow in *Pirates of the Caribbean.* Pirates are the stuff of legend—romantic, larger-than-life figures who are incurably evil and yet undeniably fascinating. Pirates seize other people's ships and hoard other people's gold. Pirates bury treasure—"X marks the spot"—and sometimes die before returning to claim it.

Blackbeard (Edward Teach) and Captain (William) Kidd were English pirates active in the Caribbean around 1700, but pirates have existed in many other times and places. Some of them conformed to the swashbuckling stereotype; others, probably the majority, did not. In this chapter I will look at some of the others: brigands from Korea, Manchuria, and Japan itself who were active in the seas off northern Kyushu in ancient times, hundreds of years and half a world away from their better-known counterparts in the Caribbean and the Atlantic.

There is a perfectly good word for "pirate" in Japanese: *kaizoku,* a two-character compound meaning literally "sea brigand" or "sea rebel." Early historical sources, however, generally use just the second character, *zoku,* a more general term for troublemakers and enemies of the state. *Zoku* might be either foreign or Japanese, might consist of anything from a few men to an entire army, and might be active either on land or at sea. When more specificity was called for, the authors of these sources might add a geographic modifier, as in *Shiragi zoku,* "brigands from Silla." Even terms such as this, however, could conceal tremendous diversity. Some "brigands from Silla" were indeed pirates in the narrow sense of the term—seafaring plunderers operating outside the law, independent of political authorities. But some were in fact acting on government orders; others were independent but only involved in piracy on a part-time basis, out of necessity; and still others were not raiding at all but merely falsely accused of such crimes. Similar ambiguities, of course, applied to "brigands" from other countries and from Japan itself.

This chapter aims to provide a brief account of piracy and raiding on the Kyushu coast in ancient times. I start out by examining a few attacks by Korean pirates in the ninth century, go on to consider the even greater damage caused by native marauders in the tenth, and end with an account of the little-known but fascinating "Toi Invasion" of 1019. One of the principal, if perhaps obvious, conclusions to emerge is that, all other things being equal, pirates thrive in the absence of government authority. Pirate activity waxed and waned in inverse proportion to the success of Japanese and Korean officials in maintaining control over their respective populations and coastlines.

Korean Pirates of the Ninth Century

As I described in the previous chapter, Silla and Japan allowed diplomatic relations to lapse in the late eighth century—not just because their worldviews clashed, which had always been the case, but because neither party any longer required the services provided by the other. Japan had a new, better-behaved vassal state, Parhae, that could satisfy its need for prestige and foreign goods. Silla, for its part, had grown closer to Tang China and no longer needed Japan as a counterweight to Tang or Parhae.

The end of official relations meant that very few Japanese now had the opportunity to travel to Silla. The Japanese government, in its desire to monopolize foreign contacts, maintained a ban on private travel abroad.[1] Although exceptions were sometimes granted, for example to clerics seeking to visit the continent for the purpose of study, the ban was otherwise comprehensive and remained adequately well-enforced throughout most of the Nara and Heian eras. As late as 1082, for example, we find three Japanese monks trying to make an unauthorized journey to the continent cringing in the hold of a Chinese junk in Hakata to escape detection by Dazaifu inspectors. In the words of one of the monks, Kaikaku, "We lay like big sacks in the bottom of the ship, unable to go out [on deck]. There was no way to urinate or defecate, so we refrained from eating and drinking."[2]

Whereas Japanese visits to Silla decreased, those in the other direction increased, so that cross-border traffic became virtually a one-way street. Official visits by Korean diplomats were at first supplemented, and then wholly replaced, by the arrival of private individuals and groups from Silla. Instead of Korean diplomats, Japanese officials on Tsushima and at Dazaifu now found themselves confronted with Korean immigrants, castaways, traders, and—pirates.

Beginning in the 780s, Silla was beset by frequent succession disputes and palace coups. During the early ninth century, portions of the country—notably the southwest coast—more or less seceded from central control. Finally, in the 880s, Silla entered a terminal phase characterized by rebellions of rural gentry known as "castle-holders" or "generals."[3] From the 780s until Silla's final collapse in 935, the country's borders were increasingly porous to coastal residents looking for greener pastures abroad.

But while Silla's borders were porous, Japan's were not. Over the century and a half of Silla's decline, policy makers in Heijō-kyō and Heian-kyō, working with local officials at Dazaifu, retained strong control over their country's borders; foreigners might come to Kyushu, but they could not do so unobserved. (Remote areas such as the Gotō Islands, to be discussed in the next chapter, were perhaps an exception.) During the late eighth century and the early years of the ninth century, most arriving Koreans identified themselves (or were identified) as immigrants or castaways. Later, during the 830s and 840s, Korean merchants also made a brief appearance in Kyushu. But during the second half of the ninth century, peaceful visitors were gradually supplanted by pirates. By the year 900, Korean brigands were responsible for the vast majority of all interactions between Japan and Silla—a very sorry state of affairs, to say the least. In the remainder of this section I will describe the nature of the threat and how the Japanese government attempted to deal with it.

The first historical reference to Korean "pirates" is from the twelfth month of 811, when officials on Tsushima sent the following report to Dazaifu:

> On the sixth day of this month, three Silla ships [were seen] sailing in the ocean to the west. Suddenly one of the ships arrived at Sasanoura, Shimoagata district. Aboard the ship were ten men. They spoke a language we did not understand, so it was impossible to comprehend their tidings. The other two ships drifted away in the dark of night. We do not know where they went.
>
> On the seventh day, there were at least twenty ships at sea to the west of the island, contacting each other with signal flares, from which

> we at last realized that they were pirate vessels. Accordingly, we killed five of the men who had arrived earlier, but the other five escaped. Later, four of them were captured. A guard was then put on the weapons storehouse, and troops were mobilized. Furthermore, gazing toward Silla in the distance, we could see flames in several places every night. Therefore, our fears have not abated. This report is sent accordingly.[4]

This document is interesting chiefly for what it suggests about the nature of the "pirates." Although the residents of Tsushima seem to have assumed that the visitors had evil intentions, the only thing that seems clear is that their arrival had something to do with an internal disturbance in Silla. Perhaps the men in ships were seeking to take advantage of the disorder; but perhaps they were merely fleeing for their lives or looking for help. Just because people are referred to as "pirates" in Japanese sources does not mean that they really were.

Much the same point could be made about another incident that occurred a year and a half later, in 813. This time, five ships from Silla arrived at Ojika Island in the Gotō Archipelago. Fighting resulted, apparently because the Japanese residents of the island could not understand Korean or the Koreans couldn't understand Japanese.[5] Nine of the Koreans were killed and 110 were captured. As it later turned out, the people from Silla were not pirates but would-be immigrants. The Japanese government gave them the choice of going home or following standard procedures for immigration (which were handled by Dazaifu).[6] Possibly as a direct result of this tragic instance of miscommunication, a government interpreter was stationed on Tsushima later in the year.[7]

During the 820s and 830s we find no recorded attacks; among other things, the energies of any would-be pirates were being channeled into commercial activity under the charismatic leadership of Chang Pogo. Chang was an individual of uncertain background who spent his youth as a soldier of fortune in the Huai River area of China. After returning to Korea in the late 820s, he received a commission from the king of Silla and was placed in charge of maritime defense at the Ch'ŏnghae garrison on Wan Island. From this base Chang also created a commercial empire extending from northern China to Japan.[8]

Chang's followers went to Hakata on several occasions. At the end of 840, he sent a representative to present tribute (consisting of a saddle), which was roundly rejected by the Japanese court: "This Pogo, although the subject of another land, has dared to offer tribute directly.

According to the old writings, this is not the correct way of doing things." In short, diplomacy was the prerogative of the king of Silla, not a private individual such as Chang Pogo. Pogo's messenger was told to sell his goods and return to Korea. In its magnanimity, the court ruled that the messenger should be "treated with kindness and given provisions for his return, in accordance with precedent."[9] The precedent in question was the system for repatriating castaways, who were customarily supplied with provisions (and even ships, if necessary) for their journey home.[10]

Approximately one year later, toward the end of 841, a party of merchants led by Chang's follower Yi Chŭng arrived at Hakata.[11] After completing their business, the Koreans returned home, only to find that Chang Pogo had been assassinated in the meantime and that Silla was in turmoil. Having nowhere to go, Yi and company turned around and returned to Hakata, apparently intending to immigrate. When they arrived, their cargo was seized by the local provincial governor, Fun'ya Miyatamaro, who was seeking compensation for a shipment of pongee that he had previously consigned to Chang Pogo. Yi Chŭng appealed Miyatamaro's action to the court in Heian-kyō. Meanwhile, yet another party of men from Silla, this one dispatched by Chang's assassin, Yŏm Chang, arrived in Hakata. The leader of this group informed Japanese officials that "rebels" associated with the late Chang Pogo had been properly subdued and that "there is no longer anything to fear." He went on to state:

> However, it is possible that some rebels may escape the net and flee directly to your country, stirring up the common people. Should any ships arrive without going through official channels, I beg that [the local officials of] the place in question be promptly ordered to arrange their capture. Also, the freight brought last year by the trade envoys Yi Chŭng and Yang Wŏn was sent by subordinates and relatives of the late Chang Pogo. I beg that it [and they?] be swiftly returned.

Faced with these confusing stories and conflicting claims, the *kugyō* (the ruling council of nobles at the Japanese court) decided in favor of Yi Chŭng, both with respect to Governor Miyatamaro and with respect to the new visitors from Silla. Regarding Miyatamaro, Dazaifu was ordered to make an inventory of the cargo he had seized and then return it to Yi Chŭng. Regarding the new visitors, to surrender Yi Chŭng and company to Chang Pogo's killers would be "like casting a lost beast to a starving tiger." The men were to be questioned regarding their preferences and allowed to leave "earlier or later, according to their wishes."

The events of 840–842 are of interest because they show that—notwithstanding the organization of this book—foreign visitors to Japan did not always fall cleanly into one category or another. Chang Pogo was on the one hand a subject of the Korean king but on the other a potential rival; his tribute mission to Japan might be seen as a bid (albeit an unsuccessful one) for independent sovereignty. His followers, such as Yi Chŭng, were merchants but also potentially immigrants, depending on circumstances in Korea. And Yŏm Chang's followers were either diplomats speaking on behalf of the Korean government (their point of view) or dangerous troublemakers, perhaps even pirates.

This series of events also shows that unregulated traffic across the Silla frontier did indeed pose a security threat to Japan—a fact that was widely recognized at the time. For example, half a year after the arrival of Yŏm Chang's lackeys, Fujiwara Mamoru, junior assistant governor-general of Dazaifu, petitioned the central government as follows: "[Men from] Silla have been presenting tribute for a long time. However, from the time of Emperor Shōmu [r. 724–749] until the present reign, they have failed to observe the old precedents and always have evil intentions. They offer no gifts as tribute and spy on the affairs of state under the guise of commerce. I beg that they be completely prohibited from entering our borders."[12] Although policy makers in Heian-kyō were not prepared to go this far, they did agree to place a ban on immigration from Silla: "The Imperial Benevolence spreads far and wide, and foreigners seek to immigrate. To completely prohibit their entry seems unkind. Let them be given provisions and sent home, as in the case of castaways."[13] This was an important change of policy, as it signified that government leaders were so worried about security that they were willing to forgo the prestige accruing from immigration.[14]

And they were indeed justified in these concerns: the death of Chang Pogo signifies a turning point, not just in Japanese attitudes toward Silla, but in the nature of visitors making the journey from Korea to Japan. After 842, there was no longer much diversity or ambiguity: Koreans making an appearance on Japanese shores were nearly all pirates or desperadoes. In the remainder of this section I will briefly examine two important episodes for what they tell us about the nature of these unwanted visitors and about Japanese defense capabilities. The first episode was a spectacular pirate raid on Hakata in 869; the second was an extended series of attacks on Tsushima, Iki, and mainland Kyushu during the period 893–895.

The first raid occurred without warning and was over almost as soon as it had begun. In the fifth month of 869, according to a report later filed by Dazaifu, "pirates from Silla came to Hakata Bay aboard two warships, plundered Buzen Province's annual tribute of silk fabric and floss, and fled immediately." The report continues, "Troops were raised to give chase, but failed to capture the enemy."[15] The silk in question was on its way to the capital. Every year a great convoy of ships left Hakata carrying tax goods from the Kyushu provinces to Kyoto, and on this particular occasion, the ship carrying Buzen's dues had "walked into the maw of a starving tiger" by weighing anchor before the rest of the fleet.[16] (The "starving tiger" metaphor was evidently a popular one. Perhaps significantly, tigers were native to Korea but not Japan.)

The attack caused great consternation at court. "Not only have tax goods been lost," government leaders bewailed, "but state prestige *(kokui)* has been injured as well. On searching the past for examples, none has ever been heard of. We shall surely lose face in the eyes of posterity."[17] To prevent a recurrence, the court appointed Sakanoue Takimori, a courtier renowned for his love of the martial arts and his skill as an archer, to the post of Dazaifu provisional junior assistant governor-general and sent him to Kyushu to supervise defense. Over the course of the next year and a half, a great number of military reforms were implemented, mostly following specific suggestions by Takimori. These and other related events are summarized in table 4.

The raid of 869 was followed by several decades of relative peace, but Korean pirates renewed and intensified their attacks in the early 890s. The main events are summarized in table 5. Raids occurred on Tsushima, Iki, and Hizen; the largest, on Tsushima in 994, reportedly involved twenty-five hundred pirates, several hundred of whom were slain by provincial authorities and island residents. Every time a raid occurred, details were reported to Dazaifu by local officials and then relayed to the court by "flying post" *(hieki),* that is, by mounted courier. The journey from Dazaifu to Heian-kyō normally took about a week to ten days. Invariably, the couriers were sent back to Kyushu in possession of an edict *(chokufu)* ordering Dazaifu to "subjugate" the raiders. The events of the 890s, like the raid of 869, were followed by various military reforms proposed by Dazaifu officials; a good example

TABLE 4. The raid of 869 and its aftermath

DATE	EVENT	SOURCE
869/6/15	Dazaifu reports that two pirate ships from Silla entered Hakata Bay and made off with tax goods from Buzen (5/22); Dazaifu dispatched troops to give chase but was unsuccessful	*Nihon sandai jitsuroku,* Jōgan 11/6/15
869/7/2	Dazaifu censured for laxity; ordered to release men from Silla placed under custody following attack	*Nihon sandai jitsuroku,* Jōgan 11/7/2
869/12/5	Dazaifu petitions court to station *fushū* (naturalized Emishi) in strategic areas; granted	*Nihon sandai jitsuroku,* Jōgan 11/12/5; *Ruijū sandai kyaku* 18, Jōgan 11/12/5 *Daijōkanpu* (pp. 568–569)
869/12/13	Sakanoue Takimori appointed provisional junior assistant governor-general	*Nihon sandai jitsuroku,* Jōgan 11/12/13
869/12/14	Offerings made at Ise Shrine	*Nihon sandai jitsuroku,* Jōgan 11/12/14
869/12/28	Dazaifu petitions court to transfer troops and suits of armor to Kōrokan; granted	*Nihon sandai jitsuroku,* Jōgan 11/12/28; *Ruijū sandai kyaku* 18, Jōgan 11/12/28 *Daijōkanpu* (p. 555)
869/12/28	Dazaifu petitions court to double number of *senshi* on watch; granted	*Nihon sandai jitsuroku,* Jōgan 11/12/28; *Ruijū sandai kyaku* 18, Jōgan 11/12/28 *Daijōkanpu* (p. 555)
869/12/29	Offerings made at Iwashimizu Hachiman Shrine	*Nihon sandai jitsuroku,* Jōgan 11/12/29
870/1/15	Dazaifu relays petition from Iki for allotment of helmets and gauntlets; granted	*Nihon sandai jitsuroku,* Jōgan 12/1/15; *Ruijū sandai kyaku* 18, Jōgan 12/1/15 *Daijōkanpu* (p. 562)
870/1/15	Court orders transfer of suits of armor, greaves, and gauntlets to Kōrokan	*Nihon sandai jitsuroku,* Jōgan 12/1/15; *Ruijū sandai kyaku* 18, Jōgan 12/1/15 *Daijōkanpu* (p. 562)

DATE	EVENTS	SOURCES
870/2/12	Dazaifu relays report of militarization in Silla; coastal provinces and districts put on alert	*Nihon sandai jitsuroku,* Jōgan 12/2/12
870/2/15	Offerings made at Hachiman Usa and other Kyushu shrines	*Nihon sandai jitsuroku,* Jōgan 12/2/15
870/2/20	Dazaifu petitions that all residents from Silla be sent to live in Mutsu; granted	*Nihon sandai jitsuroku,* Jōgan 12/2/20
870/2/23	Dazaifu petitions court to reinstate watch fires, prohibit export of horses from Kyushu, etc.; granted	*Nihon sandai jitsuroku,* Jōgan 12/2/23; *Ruijū sandai kyaku* 18, Jōgan 12/2/23 *Daijōkanpu* (p. 566)
870/3/16	Dazaifu relays petition from Tsushima for flax to make banners and provision bags; granted	*Nihon sandai jitsuroku,* Jōgan 12/3/16
870/5/2	Dazaifu petitions to inspect weapons in storehouse; granted	*Ruijū sandai kyaku* 18, Jōgan 12/5/2, *Daijōkanpu* (pp. 562–563)
870/6/7	Court orders fifty *senshi* to be stationed on Tsushima	*Nihon sandai jitsuroku,* Jōgan 12/6/7
870/6/13	Dazaifu reports mysterious events at Hizen weapons storehouse plus escape of seven men from Silla; divination at court reveals needs for vigilance; coastal areas put on alert	*Nihon sandai jitsuroku,* Jōgan 12/6/13
870/9/15	Men from Silla relocated to Musashi, Kazusa, and Mutsu in eastern Honshu	*Nihon sandai jitsuroku,* Jōgan 12/9/15
870/11/13	Chikugo provincial clerk accuses Dazaifu Junior Assistant Governor-General Fujiwara Motorimaro of plotting with Silla to harm state	*Nihon sandai jitsuroku,* Jōgan 12/11/13

TABLE 5. The events of the 890s

DATE	EVENT	SOURCE
893/5/22	Dazaifu dispatches couriers to report arrival of pirates in Hizen (5/11); court authorizes Dazaifu to subjugate them	*Nihon kiryaku*, Kanpyō 5/5/22
893/int. 5/3	Dazaifu dispatches couriers to report burning of dwellings by pirates; court grants Dazaifu edict of subjugation	*Nihon kiryaku*, Kanpyō 5/int. 5/3
893/int. 5/7	Dazaifu dispatches couriers	*Nihon kiryaku*, Kanpyō 5/int. 5/7
893/6/6	Dazaifu dispatches couriers; court grants edict	*Nihon kiryaku*, Kanpyō 5/6/6
893/6/20	Dazaifu dispatches couriers; court grants edict	*Nihon kiryaku*, Kanpyō 5/6/20
894/2/22	Dazaifu dispatches couriers; court grants edict of subjugation	*Nihon kiryaku*, Kanpyō 6/2/22
894/3/13	Dazaifu dispatches couriers to report invasion of "outlying islands" by pirates from Silla; court grants edict of subjugation	*Nihon kiryaku*, Kanpyō 6/3/13
894/4/10	Dazaifu dispatches couriers; court orders offerings to Kyushu deities	*Nihon kiryaku*, Kanpyō 6/4/10
894/4/14	Dazaifu dispatches couriers to report arrival at Tsushima of pirates from Silla; court grants edict	*Nihon kiryaku*, Kanpyō 6/4/14
894/4/16	Dazaifu dispatches couriers to petition court for appointment of commander; court appoints Fujiwara no Kunitsune as provisional governor-general	*Nihon kiryaku*, Kanpyō 6/4/16
894/4/17	Court grants Dazaifu edict of pacification; Hokuriku, San'yō and San'in provinces ordered to ready weapons and troops and make defense preparations	*Nihon kiryaku*, Kanpyō 6/4/17
894/4/18	Tōsan and Tōkai provinces ordered to recruit soldiers	*Nihon kiryaku*, Kanpyō 6/4/18
894/4/19	Offerings made at Ise Shrine	*Nihon kiryaku*, Kanpyō 6/4/19
894/4/20	Mutsu and Dewa placed on alert; offerings made to various shrines	*Nihon kiryaku*, Kanpyō 6/4/20

DATE	EVENT	SOURCE
894/5/7	Dazaifu dispatches couriers to report fleeing of pirates; court orders persistence	*Nihon kiryaku*, Kanpyō 6/5/7
894/8/9	Dazaifu petitions court to reinstate border guards on Tsushima; granted	*Ruijū sandai kyaku* 18, Kanpyō 6/8/9 *Daijōkanpu* (pp. 556–557)
894/9/9	Dazaifu relays report from Tsushima of arrival of forty-five pirate vessels (9/5)	*Fusō ryakki*, Kanpyō 6/9/5
894/9/13	Dazaifu petitions court to assign master crossbowman to Tsushima; granted	*Ruijū sandai kyaku* 5, Kanpyō 6/9/13 *Daijōkanpu* (p. 216)
894/9/17	Dazaifu reports slaying of 302 pirates by Tsushima governor; captured pirate tells of crop failure and starvation in Silla, says purpose of raid was to obtain rice and silk	*Fusō ryakki*, Kanpyō 6/9/5
894/9/18	Dazaifu dispatches couriers	*Hokuzanshō* 4, *Zasshō hieki no koto* (vol. 27, p. 57)
894/9/19	Dazaifu dispatches couriers to report slaying of more than two hundred pirates (same events as reported on 9/17?); court reinstates signal flares in various coastal provinces	*Nihon kiryaku,* Kanpyō 6/9/19; *Fusō ryakki,* Kanpyō 6/9/19; *Hokuzanshō* 4, *Zasshō hieki no koto* (vol. 27, p. 57); *Ruijū sandai kyaku* 18, Kanpyō 6/9/19 *Daijōkanpu* (pp. 566–567)
894/9/30	Dazaifu dispatches couriers to report slaying of more than twenty pirates; court orders Dazaifu to take defense measures	*Nihon kiryaku,* Kanpyō 6/9/30
894/10/6	Dazaifu dispatches couriers to report repelling of pirates; court grants edict	*Nihon kiryaku,* Kanpyō 6/10/6
895/3/13	Dazaifu petitions court to station fifty additional *fushū* at watch station; granted	*Ruijū sandai kyaku* 18, Kanpyō 7/3/13 *Daijōkanpu* (p. 569)
895/9/27	Dazaifu reports burning of Iki government offices by pirates	*Nihon kiryaku,* Kanpyō 7/9/27

is the redeployment of *sakimori* from the Kyushu mainland to Iki in the eighth month of 894.

I have presented detailed information on these various episodes of pirate activity not just because they are important in and of themselves, but because they permit some general observations about frontier administration in the late ninth century. First, authority over coastal defense remained highly centralized. Details of each pirate raid were reported immediately to the central government, which authorized, often ex post facto, counter actions by Dazaifu as well as institutional reforms to improve the quality of defense. Second, in spite of, or perhaps because of, the centralized nature of the system, defense preparations were not very effective. Pirates carried out raids at will and were only rarely captured or punished. Third, institutional reforms were frequent, but compared to earlier efforts such as reforms of the *sakimori* system in the eighth century, they were trivial and reactive in nature—probably because the government no longer had a firm hold on local society and because officials were unable to conceive, much less implement, any fundamental reform of the system.

Finally, a note on the causes of these various raids. As noted earlier, just because Japanese bureaucrats attributed raids to "pirates" does not mean that the perpetrators were always professional marauders. In some cases, such as in the early 800s, Koreans who simply wanted to immigrate to Japan were treated as pirates by Japanese authorities. In the case of the raid of 869 and the numerous attacks during the 890s, of course, it is difficult to ascribe honest intentions to the Korean perpetrators. But we have to recognize that their actions were dictated largely by internal conditions in Silla. Specifically, the state was in decline and civil unrest was on the rise. The 890s, in particular, were characterized by near-continuous peasant revolts and local secessions.

Noteworthy in this context is the description in *Fusō ryakki* of the attack on Tsushima in the ninth month of 894.[18] During a battle in which "arrows [fell] like rain," the local governor, Fun'ya Yoshitomo, and other defenders managed to kill 302 of the attackers, including three "great generals" and eleven "vice generals." Japanese forces also seized eleven ships, 50 swords, 1,000 halberts, 110 bows, 110 quivers of arrows, and 312 shields. There was only one survivor, who told his captors (in what language, it is not recorded) that in Silla, "the annual grain harvest has failed, the people are starving, the storehouses are all empty, and the capital city is in a state of unrest." The man went on to claim that the raid had been authorized by no less than the king of

Silla.[19] This statement seems implausible, but the link between internal unrest in Silla and piracy seems undeniable.

Interlude: Japanese Pirates and the Torching of Dazaifu

So far the discussion has focused solely on foreign pirates in Japan, whose comings and goings were dependent upon conditions overseas: bad times encouraged people to turn to piracy, and weak governments were powerless to prevent them from doing so. But were there no Japanese pirates? Were there no bad times and weak governments in Japan itself? Indeed there were. In this section I shall take a brief look at piracy in the Inland Sea, culminating in the rebellion of Fujiwara Sumitomo and the (temporary) destruction of Dazaifu in 941.

In Japan as well as in Korea there is often little to distinguish merchants from pirates; the one could turn into the other at the blink of an eye. Merchants—perhaps shippers would be a better word—first emerged in the Inland Sea region in the Nara era, where they contracted with the government to transport tax shipments. By the end of the eighth century, Dazaifu was complaining that "villains" were making "habitual illegal crossings" from Honshu to Kyushu without obtaining the proper "check-station passes."[20] One wonders whether some of the raids ascribed to Korean pirates in the early Heian period were not conducted with the assistance of some homebred villains. Certainly by the year 900, the situation in the Inland Sea was nearly out of control.

Enter Fujiwara Sumitomo, one of the most famous pirates in Japanese history. Sumitomo came from a moderately high-ranking lineage in the Fujiwara clan. His grandfather Nagara had been a provisional middle counselor in the Great Council of State (Daijōkan), and his father Yoshinori was, among other things, a junior assistant governor-general at Dazaifu. Sumitomo himself served in the early 930s as a provincial secretary in Iyo on the southwest coast of Shikoku. When his term was up, however, he decided not to return to the capital, opting for a new career as the leader of a local federation of pirates.

Sumitomo is said to have commanded more than a thousand ships from his base at Hiburishima, conducting raids throughout the Inland Sea. After suffering a military setback in early 940 at the hands of Bizen Assistant Governor Fujiwara Kunikaze, Sumitomo embarked on a prolonged rampage, among other things looting and burning the Awa provincial headquarters. The court responded by dispatching

FIGURE 12. Ruins of Dazaifu headquarters. The foundation stones are from the third and final phase of construction, which took place after the rebellion of Fujiwara Sumitomo. Photograph by author.

Lieutenant of the Right Palace Guards Ono Yoshifuru to capture Sumitomo, who promptly fled to Kyushu.

There followed one of the more dramatic episodes in the history of that island. In the fifth month of 941, according to the *Record of the Pursuit and Capture of Sumitomo,* "the pirates arrived at Dazaifu." The text continues: "The troops stationed there put up resistance at the wall [i.e., the Mizuki?] but were defeated by the pirates, who then plundered Dazaifu of its accumulated valuables and set fire to the headquarters"[21] (figure 12). Ono's forces, belatedly arriving on the scene, forced a confrontation at Hakata Bay, where they boarded and torched the pirates' vessels, putting an end to the rebellion. "Eight hundred ships were taken; several hundred people were killed or injured by arrows; and countless men and women threw themselves into the sea for fear of the government army. The pirate commanders and their followers all dispersed, some to die and others to surrender, breaking up like clouds."[22] Sumitomo himself fled back to Iyo, where he was apprehended by Defense Commissioner Tachibana Tōyasu. Soon afterward, he died (perhaps not entirely of natural causes?) in prison.[23]

As noted, Sumitomo burned the Dazaifu headquarters. Although Kyushu was the scene of many tumultuous events in the Nara and Heian eras, 941 was the only time when Dazaifu, the greatest bastion of imperial power in western Japan, was actually attacked and destroyed. This event is known not just from *Record of the Pursuit and Capture of Sumitomo* but also from the archaeological record. Excavations at and near the site of the headquarters, mostly conducted by the Kyushu Historical Museum, have been ongoing since 1968. As a result, we know that the Dazaifu office complex was first constructed in the late seventh century and then rebuilt twice, once in the early eighth century and then again in the tenth. The first time, the original post-and-lintel buildings were replaced by a more grandiose structure resting atop large foundation stones. (These not only gave the headquarters a more imposing appearance, but also made the structure more durable, since posts driven directly into the ground are subject to rot.) The second time, in the tenth century, the headquarters buildings were rebuilt after a fire, represented by a layer of scorched earth—evidently the work of Sumitomo and company.[24] So the damage recorded by *Record of the Pursuit and Capture of Sumitomo* was real. Nonetheless, reconstruction seems to have been accomplished fairly quickly. The events of 941, in other words, had only a temporary dampening effect on the functioning of Dazaifu—a good thing, as it turns out, because by the end of the century the office was once again needed to defend Japan from external enemies.

The Toi Invasion

Luckily for Japan, Korean piracy was at an all-time low when Sumitomo was doing his mischief; had there been a simultaneous threat on both sides of the border, the result could have been a lot worse than the burning of Dazaifu. There were few Korean pirates in the tenth century because Silla was replaced by a more stable regime, Koryŏ, in 936. But there were other fish in the sea, so to speak, and throughout its history Japan remained vulnerable to the odd attack by foreign marauders.

Two such episodes are known from the mid-Heian period. First, just a century after the last attacks by "Silla pirates," Kyushu was subjected to a series of raids in the years 996–999. Most of these are ascribed to "southern barbarians" from Amami Island in the Ryukyu Archipelago, although men from Koryŏ are also implicated in a few cases. Although the background of these incursions is obscure, some

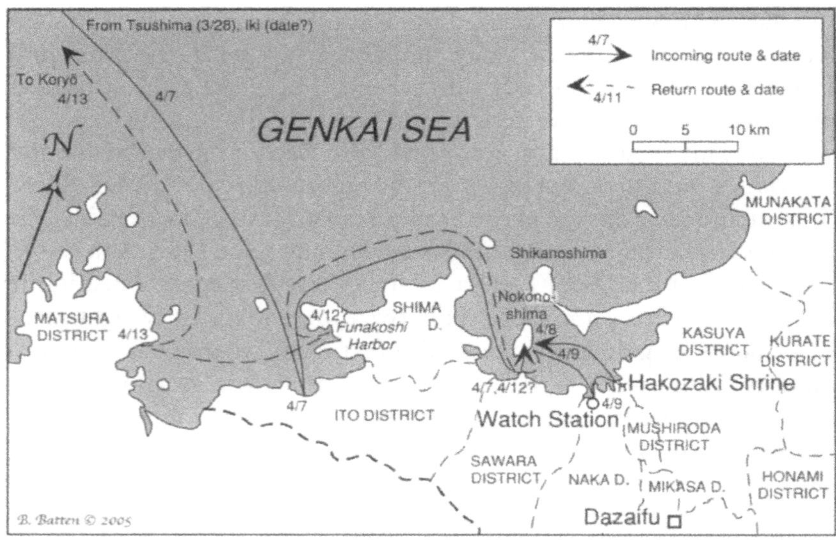

MAP 6. Route of Toi Invasion. *Source:* Based in part on map in Kawazoe Shōji et al., eds., *Fukuoka ken no rekishi,* p. 60.

of them were impressive in scale, with four hundred residents of Kyushu abducted in 996 and three hundred taken away the following year.[25] However, even these attacks pale in comparison to the second incident—the "Toi Invasion" of 1019 (map 6).

The Toi Invasion was as unexpected as it was violent. At Hakata, the first hint of trouble came on the seventh day of the fourth month, 1019, with the arrival of ships from Tsushima and Iki islands, each carrying news of harrowing events.[26] Tsushima, it seems, had been "plundered" by fifty pirate vessels. Iki had suffered even worse devastation: according to Jōgaku, the teacher-priest who brought the news, he was the only survivor of a massive attack on the island. (A later report gives the number of survivors as thirty-five, including nine provincial officials, seven district officials, and nineteen commoners.[27]) The Dazaifu officials who received these reports must have quaked in their boots, for marauding pirates who had attacked Tsushima and Iki would almost certainly next turn their attention to Hakata.

The officials did not have long to wait. On the same day that these reports arrived, the enemy fleet suddenly materialized off the Itoshima coast west of Hakata. According to the official report later filed by Dazaifu Provisional Governor-General Fujiwara Takaie, the invaders

> attacked Ito district, Chikuzen Province, and passed through the districts of Shima and Sawara, capturing people and burning their dwellings. The enemy's ships were in some cases twelve armspans in length, and in some cases eight or nine. There were about thirty or forty oars on each ship and fifty or sixty men on board. [Once on land,] twenty or thirty men danced around with their swords glistening. After them followed about seventy or eighty men carrying bows and arrows and bearing shields. Ten or twenty such units climbed the hills and cut across the meadows, killing horses and cattle to eat. Dogs were also slaughtered, and all the old men and women and children were slain. Four or five hundred frightened men and women were captured and put aboard the ships. An untold amount of grain is also said to have been carried away.

Resistance on this first day of the invasion was slight because the Japanese were taken almost completely by surprise—much as was the case two and a half centuries later during the first of the Mongol invasions. Provisional Governor-General Takaie dispatched some troops, who with the help of local residents managed to kill several dozen of the invaders, dispatching some with arrows on the battlefield and chopping off the heads of others as they sought refuge in their ships. The Dazaifu forces also suffered ten or more casualities during this initial day of fighting.

On the following day, the eighth, the attackers retreated to Nokonoshima Island, strategically situated in the center of Hakata Bay. This was to serve as their base of operations for the next few days. Meanwhile, Provisional Governor-General Takaie dispatched a number of local warriors, most of them holding official posts at Dazaifu, to the Hakata Watch Station (Keigosho), near the Kōrokan, "to defend it and repel the enemy."

The defenders' chance came on the morning of the very next day, when the enemy ships left their base on Nokonoshima and "attacked, attempting to burn down the Watch Station." Once again the invaders came "fifty or sixty men to a ship. On the field of battle each man carried a shield. The first formation carried spears; the next formation carried long-swords; and the next formation carried bows and arrows. The arrows were about one *shaku* [roughly a foot] in length and were shot with great force." The defending troops, who fought on horseback, suffered no losses, although some of the servants *(genin)* who accompanied them into battle were apparently killed.[28]

The marauders then returned to their ships and staged another

FIGURE 13. Nokonoshima. This was the island seized and used as a base by the Toi marauders in 1019. The view is from Iki-no-matsubara on Hakata Bay. Photograph by author.

attack near Hakozaki, where they tried to burn down Hakozaki Shrine (ironically, dedicated to Empress Jingū, a mythical figure renowned for her supposed foreign conquests). Once again unsuccessful, the enemy retreated to Nokonoshima, which they were unable to leave for the next two days because of "fierce wind and high waves" (figure 13). Takaie took advantage of this respite to make further defense preparations, among other things stationing "picked troops" along the coast from Sawara district to Funakoshi Harbor on the Itoshima Peninsula.

The next attack came late in the afternoon of the twelfth day. The enemy lost forty men in battle with Dazaifu forces and then fled, with thirty Japanese ships in pursuit. Provisional Governor-General Takaie gave the troops orders to "go first to the islands of Iki and Tsushima; attack [the enemy] only within Japan's borders, without entering the borders of Silla." (Note here the presence of something akin to the modern concept of territorial waters; Takaie seems to have envisioned a line in the sea between Japan and what he called "Silla"—an anachronistic reference to Koryŏ, the current regime on the peninsula.)

The final act in the invasion of 1019 came on the thirteenth day of the fourth month—six days after the invaders had arrived in Hakata and fifteen days after they had decimated Tsushima. On this day, the invaders—apparently using plundered Japanese ships—appeared on the coast of Matsura district, Hizen. They attacked a village but were repelled—again after suffering casualties—by troops under the command of Minamoto Shiru. Shiru was the former assistant governor of the province and also, most ironically, the progenitor of the infamous Matsura League, a clan of Japanese pirates that came to dominate the seas in this region during medieval times.

With Japanese ships in hot pursuit, the invaders now turned to the high seas, never to return. They had left a wake of death and destruction leading from Koryŏ to Tsushima, Iki, and the Kyushu mainland. Based on the final accounting later submitted by Takaie to the central government, nearly four hundred Japanese were killed in the attacks, and more than twelve hundred were abducted. Nearly four hundred cows and horses were butchered for food, and many houses were also torched (table 6). The repeated references to livestock, incidentally, show that rural Japan in the eleventh century was a far cry from rural Japan today, where the sight of even a single horse or cow is cause for excitement.

What was Japan's central government doing while all of this was going on? Absolutely nothing, and for a good reason: the court did not even learn of the attack until it was over. Takaie, good bureaucrat that he was, was diligent to a fault about sending reports up the pipeline: he (or more likely a scribe following his instructions) wrote the first one, probably by candlelight, on the night of the initial attack on Hakata. This, together with a follow-up report, was dispatched on the very next day, the eighth of the fourth month. The couriers entrusted with the devastating news made every effort to get it to court quickly; we can imagine them galloping up the San'yōdō, changing mounts at every station house and probably chronically deprived of sleep. Nevertheless, it took nine full days for them to reach Heian-kyō. When the couriers arrived in the capital on the seventeenth, the invaders were no longer even in Japan, having fled four days earlier from Matsura. Of course, the bureaucrats reading Takaie's reports did not know this. Working on the false assumption that there was actually something they could do, the highest lords of state gathered for an emergency meeting, the results of which were summarized in an edict issued the next day. This document authorized the "defense of strategic points," the "pursuit and capture" of the enemy, and

TABLE 6. Damage from Toi Invasion, 1019

PROVINCE	DISTRICT / LOCATION	RESIDENTS		LIVESTOCK BUTCHERED	STRUCTURES BURNED
		SLAIN	ABDUCTED		
Chikuzen	Shima	112	435	74	—
	Sawara	19	44	6	—
	Ito	49	216	33	—
	Nokonoshima	9	—	68	—
Iki	(all)	149	239	—	—
Tsushima	Silver mine	18	116	—	mine shaft
	Kamiagata	9	132	—	—
	Shimoagata	9	98	—	—
—	(unspecified)	—	—	199	45 houses
Total casualties		374	1,280	380	

Source: Shōyūki, Kannin 3/6/29.

the granting of rewards to deserving individuals. (At the same time, prayers were offered to the "Buddhas and Gods" to "protect the border"; in the religious atmosphere of the day, courtiers put as much or more stock in otherworldly protection as they did in the works of men.)[29] Assuming that top priority was given to conveying the court's edict to Dazaifu, Takaie probably received it a week or ten days later, near the very end of the month and more than two weeks after the invaders had forever disappeared from Japan. At this point, the only real significance of the scrap of paper rushed down from Heian-kyō was to provide Takaie with retrospective authorization for the defensive actions he had taken and to give local warriors concrete reason to hope that they might be rewarded for their heroic efforts. (Most of them eventually were.[30])

Put in other terms, Dazaifu was on its own when it came to defending Japan against pirate attacks. Hakata was too far away from Heian-kyō for frontier defense to be micromanaged by the central government. This in itself was nothing new: during the ninth century, as well, pirate attacks occurred without warning and were generally over before the government even learned of them. In both periods, sheer distance prevented courtiers in Kyoto from influencing the course of events on the frontier. By default, responsibility for defending Japan from attack lay squarely on the shoulders of officials at Dazaifu.

What was new was that by the time of the Toi Invasion, central officials no longer seemed to care about the details of coastal defense. Recall that in the ninth century, pirate attacks were routinely followed by scores of centrally authorized military reforms, many concerned with the most minute aspects of frontier administration. This was no longer true: now, everything was left to the ranking official at Dazaifu, in this case Fujiwara Takaie. This was perhaps not such a bad thing; Takaie and his cohorts put in a credible performance, probably just as good as could have been mustered by Nara-era border guards in the same circumstances. The central government was weaker than in the Nara period, but this weakness did not lead immediately to anarchy or administrative breakdown. What it did lead to was militarization of local society (as people armed themselves for protection) and the emergence of warrior chiefs who in their desire for legitimacy were as eager to obtain titles and official positions as the court was to disburse them. It was a symbiosis born of mutual need, and, as shown by the events of 1019, it provided a relatively good defense against pirates even in the absence of direct central controls over the border.

Who were the invaders of 1019? Where did they come from and why did they perpetrate these attacks against Tsushima, Iki, and the Kyushu mainland? First, regarding the invaders' identity, a number of prisoners were taken by the Japanese on the last day of fighting at Matsura, and all of them turned out to be Korean. When questioned through an interpreter, they claimed to have been been forcefully conscripted by "Toi" (K. *doe,* "barbarians") from across the "border," presumably meaning Koryŏ's land border to the northeast. That would place the Toi in the former territory of Parhae, which was now inhabited by a people known as the Jurchen. The Jurchen were seminomadic tribesemen who eventually went on to conquer part of northern China and found the Jin dynasty in the twelfth century. (They were also ancestral to the Manchus, who founded another conquest dynasty, the Qing, in the seventeenth century.) Taking the account of the Korean prisoners at face value, then, we have a Jurchen expedition sweeping down Koryŏ's eastern seaboard, impressing local residents into service, and then moving on to Japan.

Regarding the motivation of the attackers, there are no clear answers. One background factor was certainly the state of military tension along Koryŏ's continental frontiers.[31] To the northwest, just across the Yalu River, lay the Khitan state of Liao. Koryŏ and Liao were constantly squabbling, and as recently as 1018 Liao had launched a major (but ultimately unsuccessful) invasion of Korea. Koryŏ's relations with the Jurchen were also strained, so it is perhaps not surprising that Jurchen raiders would have been active along the eastern Korean coast in 1019. But this does not explain why the perpetrators came all the way to Japan. Perhaps the Toi Invasion represents nothing more than sheer opportunism. (Perhaps even the very idea came from the Korean conscripts; at the very least, without their cooperation the invaders' apparent familiarity with the sea routes to Tsushima, Iki, and Hakata is difficult to explain.) In this context, it is worth noting that for the Jurchen, as for other tribal peoples of Northeast Asia, the ability to lead men in battle was the mark of a leader, and would-be leaders were frequently testing their mettle against rivals and neighboring peoples. Personal ambition on the part of the fleet's leaders, then, might explain the decision to push on to Japan.

Another goal of the raid was clearly plunder. It is interesting to note that one of the structures burned during the course of the raid was a "mine shaft" on Tsushima. This mine, which was run by provincial officials, produced most of Japan's silver at the time, and we may speculate that the Toi helped themselves to whatever stock of that precious metal was at hand. More generally, wherever the marauders struck, they seized livestock and local residents. Most of the former were butchered for food on the spot; most of the latter, one presumes, were either impressed into service (like the Koreans before them), or, more likely, later sold into slavery or prostitution. The vast majority of the abductees, one notes, were women and children. Fortunately, many of these eventually made their way back to Japan. On the twenty-ninth day of the fourth month, two weeks after the invaders had left Japan and probably just about the time when the court's belated initial response reached Dazaifu, Koryŏ seized eight pirate ships containing 259 Japanese captives, who were escorted back to their homeland.[32] They, or perhaps another group of captives (this time said to number about 270) reached Tsushima during the ninth month, at which time their Korean escorts were rewarded with presents and an official letter of thanks from Dazaifu. (The letter was issued by order of the court in Heian-kyō, which evidently wanted to call all the shots behind the scenes while retaining its official policy of diplomatic seclusion.)[33] Meanwhile, in the seventh month, a minor functionary on Tsushima had gone to Koryŏ (illegally, since leaving Japan without government permission was a crime) to search for tidings of family members. He eventually returned with ten women from

Sawara district, Chikuzen, who had been rescued from the Toi by the Koryŏ army.[34]

The events of 1019 bear comparison not just with the pirate raids of the ninth century, but also with the Mongol invasions of the thirteenth. On the surface, the differences between the Toi episode and the Mongol invasions are striking. First, the intentions of the attackers were completely different: the Toi were "merely" raiding whereas the Mongols hoped to conquer Japan for political or ideological reasons. Second (and for the same reason), the scale of the invasions also differed: the Mongol forces numbered in the tens of thousands, while in 1019 enemy ships contained but two or three thousand men.[35] Finally, on the Japanese side, by the time of the Mongol invasions coastal defense was no longer in the hands of the imperial court and the Dazaifu, but in those of the Kamakura shogunate and its Kyushu vassals.[36]

These points aside, however, there are some uncanny similarities between the two series of events. Specifically,

- In both cases the invading forces were seminomadic peoples from Northeast Asia.
- Identical invasion routes were used: the Korean Peninsula through Tsushima and Iki and then to Hakata. (In the second Mongol invasion, of course, a second and larger navy came directly from the southern Chinese coast.)
- In both cases the invading forces contained numerous Korean conscripts.
- In both the eleventh century and the thirteenth, the invaders fought on foot using swords and bows (and in the case of the thirteenth, gunpowder as well).
- In both cases the Japanese defenders were led by mounted warriors, early samurai, who fought bravely and effectively under the command of local officials, there being no time for central authorities to dispatch commanders or otherwise control the flow of events.
- Inclement weather played a role in thwarting the enemy's advance. In 1019, the Toi were unable to leave Nokonoshima for two days because of high winds and seas. The two Mongol invasions are said to have been ended by *kamikaze.*
- In both 1019 and 1281, the invaders' return route took them through Hizen, to the west of Hakata. (In 1274, the enemy departed immediately from Hakata.)

- In the aftermath of the attacks, central authorities (the court in 1019 and the Kamakura shogunate in the case of the Mongol invasions) were besieged with (and most often acceded to) requests from the defending warriors for rewards.
- At the same time, authorities were also careful to acknowledge the role of the deities in protecting Japan. As is well known, the Mongol defeats were widely ascribed to otherworldly forces.[37] A great deal of praying also followed the events of 1019.

At first glance these similarities are so striking as to create the impression that the Toi attack was virtually a dress rehearsal for the Mongol invasions—albeit a dress rehearsal held two and a half centuries before the performance. A closer look, however, shows that many of the similarities stem from geography or geopolitics. That identical routes were used for the invasions simply resulted from the fact that Tsushima, Iki, and Hakata formed a natural corridor from the Korean Peninsula to Japan. The hit-and-run nature of the attacks can be explained as a consequence of distance: Japan was close enough to the Asian mainland to be a tempting target, but too far to successfully conquer, even in part. (Of course, the Toi were not interested in conquest, just plunder.) Finally, distance also had important consequences on the Japanese side. Much as central authorities were aware of Hakata's vulnerability, much as they wished to protect it, in the end they had no choice but to entrust its defense to those actually on the scene: by the time news of an invasion came from Kyushu, it was too late to do anything about it. Praying to the gods for protection may have been a natural—if fatalistic—consequence of this knowledge.

In short, northern Kyushu was indeed a natural crossroads. Because of this fact, the area was a target for all men of ambition: to control Hakata was to control access to all other points on the regional political map. And yet, precisely because of Hakata's in-between geographical status, it was too far away to control easily by any interested power. In the end, the area remained "Japanese" partly because it was relatively closer to Heian-kyō than to, say, China, and partly because Japanese leaders were more eager to keep Hakata than foreign aggressors were to conquer it.

CHAPTER 4

Trade

As we have seen, human traffic across the maritime frontier could take many forms. On the public side of the spectrum, states in Japan or on the Asian continent could resort to war to achieve their aims, dispatching armadas across the sea. But foreign wars required a huge commitment of resources and were thus relatively rare. Far more common were diplomatic interactions—attempts by government leaders to achieve their goals through peaceful means. Meanwhile, on the private side of the spectrum, independent individuals or groups also occasionally braved the international waters separating Japan from the continent. The pirates and raiders of the previous chapter are one such example; the merchants of this chapter are another. I will start with a case study of a Chinese junk that arrived in Kyushu in 945—a visit that was entirely typical, but is better documented than most.

A CHINESE JUNK IN HIZEN

It was midsummer when the ship left Wu Yue for Japan. Wu Yue was one of the "ten kingdoms" to emerge in southern China after the demise of the Tang empire in 907. Like all of these ephemeral states, Wu Yue was eager to find support where it could, and its rulers attempted on at least four occasions to establish diplomatic ties with Japan.[1] All of these initiatives, however, were rebuffed; Japan's leaders were no longer interested in diplomacy, for reasons described earlier. They were still interested in foreign goods, but these could be obtained quite easily, without the muss and fuss of diplomatic entanglements, from foreign merchants—many of them also from Wu Yue, whose territory included several major ports on the southeast Chinese coast.

It was with an eye to this market that Jiang Gun, Yu Renxiu, and Zhang Wenyu departed from their hometown—probably Mingzhou (Ningbo), just south of the Yangtze River mouth[2]—on the third day of the fifth month (equivalent to mid-July by today's calendar).[3] The three "captains" (of whom Jiang Gun seems to have been first among equals[4]) were in command of a seagoing junk—a large two- or three-masted ship with bamboo sails, a pointed bow, square stern, flat deck, multiple holds, and a knife-edged underside[5]—that had a capacity of 1,000 *koku,* about 250 tons. On board were a hundred men, perhaps half of them sailors and most of the rest petty merchants who had scraped together enough capital to buy a berth for themselves and storage for their wares on what promised to be a lucrative journey. The vessel was owned either by the captains themselves or perhaps by richer merchants back home who could afford the tremendous up-front expenses required to finance such an expedition.[6] Their decision to leave in early summer was standard; given the prevalent monsoon winds, this was one of the best times to head east across the East China Sea.[7]

We know virtually nothing about the actual voyage except that it was successful and made first landfall in Japan in the Gotō Archipelago of Hizen Province (modern Nagasaki Prefecture). This archipelago, which consists of five main islands (Gotō literally means "five islands") and perhaps two hundred smaller ones, is in the East China Sea to the west of mainland Kyushu (map 7). Historically, it was the last piece of Japanese territory to be seen by Japanese departing for China (*kentōshi,* for example, routinely stopped there on their way to Tang) and the first to be seen by people coming the other way—people such as Jiang Gun and company. Jiang Gun later stated to Japanese authorities that his party had spent "much time on the deep blue waters," but this phrase was just a time-tested formula devoid of real meaning: the voyage from China would normally have taken a week or two at most.

The ship dropped anchor at Kashiwa (Oak) Island, a microscopic piece of real estate (total area 0.12 km^2) within Aokata Bay on the west coast of Nakadōri, the northernmost of the five main islands. The setting must have been phenomenally beautiful at the time, as much of the Gotō Archipelago still is. The islands—green, forested gems, set against sparkling blue waters—were created when a mountain chain (technically, a "horst" or fault block) began to subside, resulting in a peculiar combination of drowned valleys, narrow straits, and an incredibly complex (that is to say, scenic) coastline. (Ironically, the specific location chosen by the Chinese captains to weigh anchor is now the site of

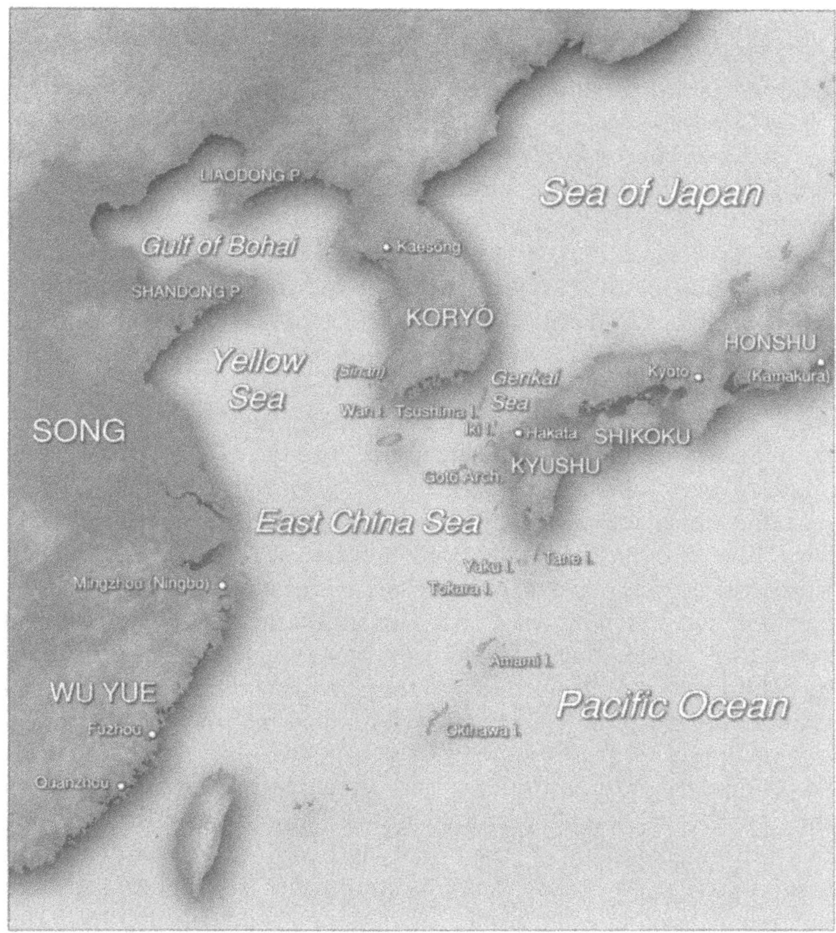

MAP 7. Japan in East Asia, 10th c.

a huge floating storage facility for petroleum—a perfect symbol of how many of Japan's scenic wonders have been sacrificed for economic growth.)

Oddly—or perhaps not so oddly, given the remoteness and inaccessibility of the region—the Chinese visitors seem to have escaped official notice during their brief stay on Kashiwa Island. At any rate, no news proceeded them as they left the Gotō Archipelago and headed for mainland Kyushu in the direction of Nagasaki Peninsula. Japanese guards at the government watch station at Himosaki,[8] on the tip of the peninsula, were therefore taken by surprise on the fourth day of the sixth month, when the junk, "flying its sails, suddenly ran in from the southern ocean . . . during the third watch." Following the sighting, "watch station soldiers in twelve pursuit ships had [the junk] anchor at the island in Himosaki Harbor, and during the hour of the tiger [3–5 a.m.] of the fifth day, [we] officials sent a messenger to conduct questioning." This initial questioning of the Chinese captains, in combination with a more comprehensive inspection later conducted at the watch station, established the nationality and tonnage of the vessel, together with the names of the captains and crew. (Probably all communications with the visitors were in writing; all Japanese bureaucrats were trained to read and write literary Chinese, but few if any could speak the language. Chinese-speaking interpreters would have been available at Hakata, but probably not in Hizen.)

Like petty officials everywhere, the watch station officials now passed the buck upward—in this case to the Hizen provincial office, in Saga district near the head of the Ariake Sea. Provincial officials learned of the ship's arrival in Himosaki on the tenth, six days after the fact. On the following day, they appended their own petition and passed the growing body of documents on to officials at Dazaifu, about forty kilometers to the northeast of the provincial office. The Hizen petition contained a recommendation—originating with the messenger originally sent to question the Chinese captains—that "men and ships be promptly sent, in accordance with precedent, to tow [the junk] to the Kōrosho" (that is, the Hakata Kōrokan).[9] Some time after receiving this recommendation, on the twenty-fifth day of the sixth month, officials at Dazaifu passed the buck still further by sending their own petition (including, again, copies of all previous documents) for a ruling from the Great Council of State in Heian-kyō. Should the visitors, Dazaifu asked, be permitted to stay and carry out trade?

The answer, as it turns out, was "yes." However, it was not immediately forthcoming. Dazaifu's petition probably reached the capital in a couple of weeks, but it was not acted on until the twenty-ninth day of the seventh month, when we find Regent *(kanpaku)* Fujiwara Tadahira perusing copies of directives issued by the Great Council of State upon similar occasions in the past. At issue was a rule instituted in 911 requiring Chinese merchants to observe a two-year interval *(nenki)* between successive visits to Japan. Jiang Gun and company, however, were in the clear on this point, and so Tadahira recommended to Emperor Suzaku (r. 930–946) that the merchants be "accommodated" (*anchi,* a code word for "permitted to stay and trade") at Hakata.[10] The directive carrying this order was issued a week later, on the fifth day of the eighth month,[11] and presumably reached Dazaifu sometime around the middle of the same month.

It is not clear where Jiang Gun and company were staying at this time; perhaps they were still in Hizen, or perhaps their ship had already been towed to Hakata to await the government's answer. In any case, the Chinese were probably growing frustrated with the slowness of Japan's bureaucracy; they had already been in the country for more than three months, and ideally would have wished to depart in the eighth month, when the seasonal winds were favorable for the return to China.[12]

However, this was not to be. Although the merchants were allowed to move from their ship to the Kōrokan when the government order arrived, the actual sale of their cargo could not begin until yet more officials had arrived from court—in this case, foreign trade commissioners *(karamono-kōekishi),* who were apparently not even appointed until the tenth month.[13] At this pace, trade could not have begun much before the end of the year. The trade commissioners were authorized to go through the cargo and select the best items on behalf of the government (meaning, in practice, the emperor and major officeholders at court).[14] The goods themselves consisted mostly of Chinese silk and porcelain, together with spices, drugs, and precious woods from tropical Asia (figure 14). Payment was in gold, but unfortunately (for the merchants) this was not always immediately forthcoming (figure 15). Typically, goods were transferred on faith to the trade commissioners, and merchants had to wait to be reimbursed by yet another set of central representatives.[15] (One of the more interesting discoveries during the 2003 field season at the Kōrokan site was a small nugget of gold, perhaps dropped by a careless trade commissioner.) While waiting for payment from the government, merchants sold off their remaining goods to officials stationed in Kyushu, representatives of the central nobility, and members of the local gentry. They also made efforts to obtain Japanese goods for sale back home, including objets d'art, sulfur, and perhaps even agricultural products. All of this trade took place at the Kōrokan under the strict supervision of Dazaifu officials.

It would seem that Jiang Gun and company finished their business in Japan around the end of 945 or the beginning of the next year. Regent Tadahira noted in his diary toward the end of the second month of 946 that he had selected a few foreign goods—presumably from

FIGURE 14. Trade ceramics recovered from Kōrokan site. *Source:* Fukuoka City Board of Education. Reproduced with permission.

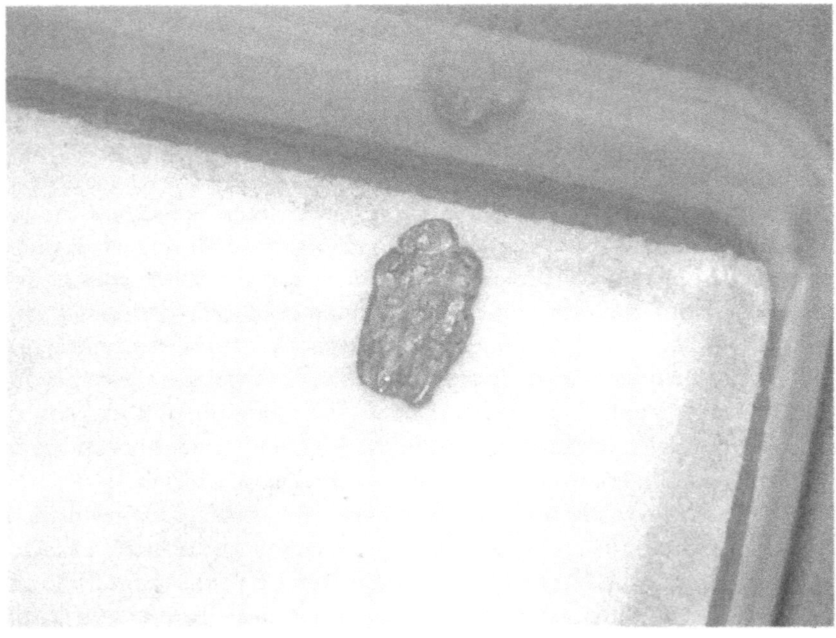

FIGURE 15. Gold nugget from Kōrokan site. Photograph by author.

Jiang Gun's cargo—and returned the rest to Emperor Suzaku.[16] If Jiang Gun and company were lucky and received their payment without delay, they might possibly have been able to leave that same month, when the winds were changing from northwest to southeast. If, however, the payment was slow to arrive, the Chinese would have been forced to wait another six months for the winds to change again in early fall. In the first case, their total stay in Japan would have been about nine months; in the latter, it would have been fifteen. Once back in Mingzhou, the merchants would have begun selling their Japanese goods, counting their profits, and perhaps making plans for another commercial venture several years down the line. Time moved slowly in the tenth century.

From Diplomacy to Trade

By the time Jiang Gun and his comrades made their journey, Chinese merchants were no rarity in Kyushu, and local officials all up and down the coastline were well acquainted with the procedures for dealing with them. However, it had not always been thus. In a sense, foreign trade had a long history in Japan, but until the ninth century C.E., almost all of it was conducted within the context of diplomacy. As we have seen, diplomatic embassies served as a vehicle for state-level exchanges of prestige goods—and also, on many or most occasions, for small-scale commercial transactions by the envoys themselves. But this is a rather different thing from trade conducted by professional merchants, motivated by profit, and operating their own vessels. Foreign trade in this sense of the term begins in Japan around 830, barely a century before Jiang Gun's visit.[17]

Maritime trade in East Asia began to flourish in the seventh and eighth centuries C.E. It was jump-started by Persian and Arab merchants, who traveled to and settled in ports as far from home as Guangzhou (Canton) in southern China.[18] Later, commerce spread eastward and northward along the coast to Quanzhou, Fuzhou, Mingzhou (Ninbo), and finally Hangzhou, where merchants could gain access to the Chinese interior via the Grand Canal. Foreign trade thus became integrated to a certain extent with China's domestic economy. Although pioneered by Arabs and Persians, this route soon fell under the domination of ethnic Chinese. Meanwhile, Korean merchants established their own trade networks connecting the west coast of Silla with Laizhou, Haizhou, and other ports in north China and entering the canal system through the mouth of the Huai River. In the early ninth century, semiautonomous communities of Korean traders were scattered along much of the north China littoral.[19]

These northern routes were further extended to Japan under the direction of the Korean tycoon Chang Pogo.[20] Chang himself is said to have visited Kyushu in 824 and met with the governor of Chikuzen, although the validity of this account has been questioned.[21] In any case Chang, acting by authorization of the king of Silla, was in charge of maritime defenses at the Ch'ŏnghae garrison on Wan Island by the late 820s or early 830s. It is probably no coincidence that the first Japanese record of "Silla merchants" in Hakata dates from 831.[22]

However, Korean domination of the Hakata trade was short-lived, to say the least. Merchants from Tang make their first known appearance in Hakata in 842,[23] and soon thereafter they completely replace their counterparts from Silla. Chinese merchants bypassed the Korean coastal route entirely, traveling directly across the East China Sea from locations such as Fuzhou and Mingzhou. These same ports continued to supply the bulk of foreign merchants visiting Japan after the demise of Tang (in 907), when they fell under the control, respectively, of the Wu Yue kingdom and then (after 978) the Song empire.

As noted above, the arrival of commercial junks was a new phenomenon in Japan, and we can readily surmise that the first such visits were occasions for much hand-wringing by local officials in Kyushu and their superiors in Heian-kyō. The visitors fit into none of the old categories used to classify foreign visitors. They were not immigrants, since they had no intention of staying in Japan. They were not diplomats, since they represented private rather than state interests. And they were not castaways or drifters, since their arrival was deliberate and their vessels generally undamaged.

But while the merchants posed problems of classification, their presence in Kyushu could scarcely be ignored. As early as 831, officials at court were complaining that visits by merchants were causing "foolish people" in Kyushu to "bid for goods at inflated prices" and "squander family fortunes" because of their "obsession" with things foreign.[24] As their choice of words reveals, courtiers embodied the typically Confucian sentiments of disdain for commerce and patronizing concern for the welfare of the people. Reading between the lines, however, one suspects that the real issue here was potential loss of control; the bureaucrats were worried that the merchants' activities might have a disruptive influence on local society.

At the same time, there were at least two good reasons—one ideological, the other practical—for permitting merchants to enter Japan. First, like diplomats and immigrants, merchants were coming of their own free will, a fact that reflected well on Japan and its emperor. Merchant visits thus validated and legitimated the worldview of contemporary courtiers. As late as 1070, government officials would nod their heads sagely when Pan Huaiqing, a Chinese captain seeking permission to trade, claimed (possibly with tongue in cheek?) to have "come from far across the deep blue sea out of yearning for the Imperial Virtue."[25] Second, on a more practical level, courtiers themselves, and not just "foolish people" in Kyushu, were obsessed with the outside world. Merchants brought the exotic goods they craved, goods that were no longer readily available through diplomatic channels (at least from Silla and Tang; diplomatic exchanges with Parhae continued until that country was destroyed by a Khitan invasion in 926).

Taken together, these various pros and cons led inescapably to the following conclusion: foreign merchants should be allowed to come and sell their wares, but only under strict supervision, with right of first refusal going to the government. As the Great Council of State decreed in 831, "When merchants arrive, all of the items on board are to be examined for items required [by the court], which shall be sent up by post [i.e., mounted courier]. Items that are not required may be sold under the supervision of headquarters [i.e., Dazaifu] officials. The amount [paid] shall in all cases follow the schedule of prices. Any offenders shall be punished severely. There shall be no leniency."[26] Again, the purpose of these arrangements was to prevent undue contact between foreign visitors and ordinary Japanese, while at the same time ensuring the court's access to desired foreign goods. Aristocrats could (and did) send representatives to purchase goods at the Kōrokan after the official trade was over. Also, as in the case of foreign "tribute," some of the items purchased by the state probably found their way into private hands after the emperor had taken his pick. Since it was the emperor's government that set the rules, oversaw the trade, and redistributed some of the spoils, the system also served—intentionally, no doubt—to highlight the authority of the ruler and his monopoly over foreign contacts.

Over the course of the next century and a half, a number of minor adjustments were made to this system, while leaving the basic principles intact.[27] These changes can be briefly described as follows: First, when Korean piracy became an issue following the death of Chang Pogo, merchants from Silla (but not those from China) were barred from using the Kōrokan. This step was taken in 842.[28] Second, at some unspecified point in the ninth century, responsibility for the official trade was shifted from Dazaifu to trade commissioners sent from Heian-kyō.[29] Third, beginning in 911, foreign captains were required to observe a two-year moratorium between consecutive visits to Japan, apparently as part of a program to limit private, illegal trading between foreigners and Japanese buyers. The introduction of the two-year rule essentially completed the system that we have already seen in operation during the visit of Jiang Gun and his colleagues in 945–946. Their experiences would have been typical for visiting Chinese merchants until the late eleventh century, when trade shifted from the Kōrokan to an emerging "Chinatown" in Hakata.

Supervised Trade at the Kōrokan

Discussion of foreign trade in Heian Japan inevitably raises three sets of questions: (1) What kind of goods were actually traded? What came in and what went out? (2) How well was the government able to supervise the trade? Could it actually enforce the rules described above? (3) Finally, what was the volume of trade? How many merchant vessels came to Japan each year, or each decade?

Imports and exports have already been described in passing, but the topic is of sufficient interest to merit another look. In essence, trade at Hakata was a continuation of earlier patterns of exchange conducted under the guise of diplomacy. Imports as well as exports were almost all luxury products, not bulk items of daily consumption. Imports consisted of raw materials and manufactures, not just from the merchants' home country of China but from all over Asia. Exports were almost exclusively products of Japan with, at least initially, a definite emphasis on raw materials and semifinished products. In terms of the circulation of goods, Japan thus played the role of a "developing country" in its relations with continental Asia.

Regarding imports, the best source is *Shinsarugakuki,* a work of fiction composed about 1052 that contains a long list of "Chinese goods" *(karamono)* known to its author, Fujiwara Akihira (table 7). It is highly instructive to compare these items with those sold three centuries earlier by Korean envoys in Heijō-kyō (see table 2). On the one hand, there are some obvious differences. Products of Korea and Manchuria, such as metal utensils, gold and iron, ginseng, pine nuts, and honey, are prominent in 752 but almost completely absent in 1052. In

TABLE 7. "Chinese goods" listed in *Shinsarugakuki,* ca. 1052*

CATEGORY	ITEMS
Spices and fragrances	Aloeswood (i.e., agalloch, garroo/gharu), musk, cloves, Chinese spikenard, frankincense (or retinite), birthwort root, borneol (i.e., camphor), sandalwood oil
Precious woods	Sandalwood, sanderswood, *Bischofia,* sappanwood
Medicines	Alum, elixir of gold, elixir of silver, croton oil, orpiment, myrobalans, betel *(Areca)* nuts
Pigments	Gamboge, indigo, lac,† verdigris, azurite, minium, cinnabar, ceruse
Textiles	Twill, brocade, scarlet raiments, "elephant eye" damask, "cloud-patterned" brocade, soft Koryŏ brocade, Tonkin brocade, "floating-line" twill, silk gauze and crape
Other	Leopard and tiger skins, rattan,‡ teacups, wicker baskets, rhinoceros horns, water-buffalo [horn] scepters, agate belts, glass urns, Chinese bamboo, sweet bamboo, hollow glass balls

Source: Fujiwara Akihira, *Shinsarugakuki, Hachirō no mahito jō,* pp. 280–281.

*As in table 2, I have omitted several items that are either unidentifiable or untranslatable.

†Mistranslated as "cochineal" in Batten, *To the Ends of Japan,* p. 193. Cochineal is a red dye made from the pulverized bodies of female scale insects native to tropical America—an item not very likely to have been in the hands of Chinese merchants during the eleventh century. Lac, however, is almost the same thing—a resinous substance secreted by similar insects from South and Southeast Asia, used to produce shellac and red dye.

‡Mistranslated as "wisteria stems" in Batten, *To the Ends of Japan,* p. 193.

1052, by contrast, we see many Chinese manufactures, especially fine textiles and porcelain. Clearly, the composition of imports was in part a function of the nationality of the bearers: visitors to Japan, whether from Korea or China, tended to bring products of their own countries.[30]

At the same time, there are also some remarkable similarities between the two lists. We have virtually the same spices and aromatic compounds for use in perfumes and incense. And we have many of the same medicines, dyes, and pigments. As noted before, the majority of these items (excluding mineral products, which generally originated in Central Asia) came from the forests of South and Southeast Asia and had made their way to East Asia by ship. Their presence in Japan in both 752 and 1052 is evidence of strong continuities in supply and demand. Japan was the eastern terminus of a surprisingly stable pan-Eurasian network of exchange. In the eleventh century, Japanese elites satisfied their wants by commercial instead of diplomatic means, but their shopping list remained much the same as before—and would until a new commodity, Chinese coins, piqued their interest in the twelfth century.[31]

Moving on to exports, we again find a mixture of continuity and change. As described in chapter 2, during the eighth century, foreign imports were generally purchased with Japanese silk (including silk thread and floss). In the ninth century, silk was largely abandoned in favor of alluvial gold from northeast Honshu. But an important point to keep in mind is that although merchants were paid with these items, they did not necessarily just turn around and carry them home. In many cases they probably used the silk or gold to purchase Japanese goods for resale in their home markets. One major item purchased for export was sulfur from Iōgashima (Sulfur Island), south of Kyushu. Sulfur found its way by domestic trade routes to Hakata. There it was purchased by visiting Chinese merchants on consignment for the Song government, which used the mineral to produce gunpowder for frontier defenses. Sulfur was also important because it provided ballast needed to stabilize the ships on the return voyage.[32] Merchants also purchased Japanese manufactures that commanded high prices back in China, including objets d'art and (especially during the medieval era) Japanese swords and armor.[33]

A good record of Japanese exports at the beginning of the eleventh century is provided by *Midō kanpakuki,* the diary of Fujiwara Michinaga. In one passage, Michinaga provides a list of gifts he sent to a Chinese temple in 1015.[34] Although this particular transaction was noncommercial, the items sent are typical of those exported via merchants at Hakata. They consisted of

- six soapberry rosaries (four decorated with amber, two with quartz)
- a split-level miniature shrine with mother-of-pearl and gold inlay
- two lacquer boxes with gold inlay
- a lacquer garment box decorated with a gold-inlay ocean scene
- six folding screen-shaped partitions
- three marten robes from Mutsu
- a seven-foot-long hairpiece
- one hundred taels of placer gold in a round lacquer box with gold inlay

- five large pearls
- ten bolts of cloth

Note the prominent position occupied by goods from the frontier region of northeast Honshu, including not just gold but also furs. Although one does not ordinarily associate furs with traditional Japanese (or Chinese) forms of dress, in fact they were highly prized, and the Heian court spared no expense in obtaining them from the proto-Ainu tribes that inhabited the northern reaches of the archipelago.

Regarding the government's ability to supervise trade, I would argue that they did very well indeed. Admittedly, there are some scattered records of Chinese merchants in ports other than Hakata, the only one officially open to trade. We know, for example, of perhaps a dozen junks that came to Tsuruga Harbor in Echizen (modern Fukui), on Honshu's Sea of Japan coast, during the late eleventh century. But it is abundantly clear that the vast majority of ships went to Hakata, either directly, or (as in the case of Jiang Gun's ship in 945) upon the instructions of local officials following initial landfall elsewhere.[35] Partly this was because it was in the merchants' own best interest to go to Hakata, with its well-developed infrastructure and dependable markets. But it was also because of the tight supervision exerted by the Japanese government. As we saw during Jiang Gun's visit to Japan in 945, foreign ships arriving in mainland Kyushu were inevitably detected by local officials, who reported the matter up the bureaucratic hierarchy while rerouting the visitors to Hakata.

Once in Hakata, certainly, merchants were subject to an extraordinary degree of control. A glance at the written evidence can hardly fail to leave one impressed with both the thoroughness of the supervision provided by Dazaifu and the degree of micromanagement attempted, and indeed achieved, by central officials, up to and including the emperor. Some examples follow.

The performance of Dazaifu is highlighted by a fascinating set of documents from 1105, which are contained in *Collected Official and Unofficial Writings* (Chōya gunsai), a compendium of prose and poetry intended for the edification of aspiring young bureaucrats (e.g., "How to draft a state council order in seven easy steps").[36] The first document in the set is a report by the Hakata Watch Station informing Dazaifu of the arrival of a Chinese ship in the waters off Shikanoshima. The second is a transcript of an interrogation of the captain by officials at Dazaifu, conducted with the aid of an interpreter (also a member of the

Dazaifu staff). The captain, Li Chong, is asked, among other things, to state his reasons for coming and to declare his freight, official sailing papers, the names of his crew members, and the tonnage of his vessel. The report is signed not only by the Dazaifu interrogators but also by Li Chong, indicating that the captain was given an opportunity to review its content for accuracy. The third item in the set is a copy of the sailing papers submitted by Li Chong, which were originally issued by port authorities in Mingzhou. Among other things, these list the names of the captain, his two mates, and the other sixty-six men on the ship. There is also a breakdown of Li's cargo, which consisted principally of Chinese textiles and porcelain. All of the above documents were forwarded by Dazaifu to Kyoto, where they were presumably used as a basis for deciding whether to give Li Chong permission to trade.

The end result in this case is unfortunately not clear, but the procedures involved are known from other sources. These reveal an extraordinary level of involvement by central officials in the details of trade regulation. Consider the following document, which is a verbatim transcript of a cabinet meeting *(jin no sadame)* held in 1070:[37]

> Concerning whether or not to accommodate *(anchi)* the merchant Pan Huaiqing of Fuzhou, Great Country of Song, whose arrival was reported by Dazaifu:
>
> Palace Minister and Master of the Crown Prince's Household Fujiwara *no ason* [and four others] stated: "The matter is much as Major Controller of the Right Minamoto *no ason* states [i.e., Huaiqing has violated the minimum two-year term between visits]. However, the freight declaration mentions presents of Buddhist icons and writings. If he is deported, it may be thought that such Buddhist icons and writings are not used here, and merchants arriving in the future may no longer bring them as presents. So what harm would there be in accommodating him and receiving the gifts?"
>
> Provisional Middle Counselor Minamoto *no ason* and Major Controller of the Right Minamoto *no ason* stated: "This Huaiqing came during the Jiryaku era [1065–1069], but because he was in violation of the term [between visits], he received an order of deportation, returning home last year. Nonetheless, he has come again this year. It is as if he has forgotten the laws of the land. Also, he has presented a copy of his sailing papers, but is it not customary to present the original? It was most inappropriate of Dazaifu not to ask him the reason for this. However, according to the interrogation record, despite his [earlier] deportation, he

has come again from far across the deep blue sea out of yearning for the Imperial Virtue. Regarding this, while we feel that he has truly erred in violating the term, one can certainly sympathize with his distant yearning for the Great Virtue. Moreover, it is the last month of the year, and the cold is at its most fearsome. Therefore, what special harm would there be in issuing an order to [this] effect and accommodating him? Since a term was [first] established for merchants, there have been cases where they have been accommodated without strictly following the stipulated term. This is because they serve the court and cause no special problems. At any rate, regarding the goods that have been sent up—if [Huaiqing] is to be accommodated, let them be inspected and received."

Second year of Enkyū [1070], twelfth month, seventh day

Admittedly, in this case the lords decided to waive their own rule that merchants observe a two-year interval between visits. But can anyone reading the document doubt that the central government was both well-informed about events in Hakata and actively involved in the nitty-gritty details of foreign trade in the late eleventh century? I trust not.[38]

This conclusion has important implications for the third question, regarding the actual volume of foreign trade in the tenth and eleventh centuries.[39] The question can be addressed both archaeologically and historically, but since the two approaches lead to the same conclusion, I will focus here on the written record, leaving an account of archaeological excavations for the next chapter. Thanks to the efforts of Japanese scholars, comprehensive chronologies are now available of all known foreign contacts in Heian times.[40] As a result, one can actually sit down and count surviving records of arrivals by merchants. Of course, possibly not all such arrivals were recorded by contemporary scribes, and of the records that were made, not all may have survived until the present day. Nonetheless, I would contend that extant sources present a surprisingly complete and accurate picture of the actual situation.

Most of our information on this period comes from courtier diaries. Heian-era nobles were inveterate record keepers, and their diaries survive in such numbers that for some periods it is possible to reconstruct events at court on a day-by-day basis. Among these events was the arrival of news from the provinces—specifically, in this case, news concerning the appearance of foreign vessels in the waters off Kyushu. Significantly, many merchant arrivals—particularly in the early tenth century, the first two decades of the eleventh, and the two decades surrounding 1100, from which the greatest number of diaries survive—are known from multiple, mutually reinforcing sources. This redundancy argues strongly, I think, that at least for these short periods, the documentary record contains a fairly complete inventory of merchant arrivals known to the courtiers writing these diaries. Of course it is possible to argue that the courtiers did not have access to full information about such events—that some traders, or more accurately smugglers, came and went without anyone's reporting the matter to the court. I would not go so far as to deny this possibility altogether, especially for remote locations such as the Gotō Archipelago. However, as I have argued above, the general level of central control was high. For the most part, high government officials were aware of the arrival of foreign ships: they noted them down in their diaries, and we have (at least for the subperiods mentioned above) those records in front of us today. In sum, it is possible to estimate the frequency of merchant visits.

Following that lengthy justification, my conclusion may now be stated briefly: the average number of merchant vessels visiting Japan each year was surprisingly low—perhaps as low as *one*. Basing conclusions on the same data set, we can say that each of these junks carried approximately fifty-five individuals. Note that Japan's population at this time was about six and a half million people.[41] By way of comparison, today it is 127 million, and the annual number of foreign visitors is five million.[42] What this means is that, per given unit of population, Japan—even now a relatively closed society in many ways—is nearly four thousand times more open to foreign contact today than it was during the Heian era. Of course, the numbers I have cited for the Heian period are probably a bit low, but even if they underestimate the total by a full order of magnitude—a virtual impossibility—Heian Japan was extraordinarily isolated by almost any standard.

The Dawn of a New Era

However, times were changing, both in Hakata and in Japan as a whole. The first harbinger of change was the abandonment of the Kōrokan sometime in the late eleventh century, roughly coincident with the emergence of a Chinese settlement several kilometers to the east along Hakata Bay. Trade itself, which now took place along the beaches and streets of this diaspora community, remained under Dazaifu supervision for a while. But in the twelfth century, the old imperial system of government began to totter. After 1185, the court was forced to share power with a warrior regime based in the eastern city of Kamakura. From that time on, no single authority in Japan had the wherewithal to monopolize transfrontier contacts. As a result, foreign trade, once limited to Hakata, spread to other ports in Japan and began to increase dramatically in volume.

The demise of the Kōrokan is apparent from both historical sources and the archaeological record. The last clear written reference to the facility is from the visit of Jiang Gun in 945.[43] However, it is plausible that another record from 1047, regarding the burning by arson of "lodgings for merchant guests from the Great Song," also refers to the Kōrokan.[44] By the early twelfth century, at any rate, the facility was clearly no longer in use; for example, the copious historical documentation of Li Chong's visit in 1105, summarized in the previous section, contains not a single reference to the Kōrokan. The archaeological record also supports this general chronology: in over fifteen years of investigation, not one artifact dating from later than the eleventh century has ever been found.[45] One is tempted to conclude that, indeed, the facility was burnt in 1047 and never rebuilt.

The reason is that trade had shifted to a new location: the newly emerging town of Hakata. "Wait a minute!" cries the reader. "Doesn't Hakata refer to the entire bay and vicinity?" Well, yes, it does. But in the narrow sense, Hakata is also the name of a more specific location. Recall the physical configuration of Hakata Bay: a semicircle open to the north, with numerous rivers and streams arrayed around the shore like spokes on a wheel. From east to west, the most important of these waterways are the Tatara, Umi, Mikasa (otherwise known as Ishidō), Naka, Hii, and Muromi rivers. The Kōrokan was on a promontory between the Naka and the Hii; Hakata, in the narrow sense of the term, was about three kilometers farther east, sandwiched between the Mikasa and Naka rivers.

Unlike the site of the Kōrokan, Hakata had no headlands or outcroppings of rock. In fact, it was nothing but a large sandbar, roughly a kilometer in length, that had formed between the mouths of the two rivers. The beach was formed by sedimentation and wave action no later than the eighth century, as attested by the Nara-era artifacts and structures that have been uncovered here. These indicate to archaeologists the presence of some kind of government office, perhaps an extension of the Tsukushi Lodge. Details are unclear, but in any case, this beach—and a second, parallel, sand spit that later emerged to the north as the Naka and Ishidō rivers continued to carry sediment into the bay—formed the nucleus of the medieval city of Hakata.[46]

To get back to my point, the city started as a diaspora community of Chinese merchants in the late eleventh century. Evidently, some of the Ningbo-based merchants visiting the Kōrokan decided to settle down in Japan, building houses—and eventually, docking facilities, temples, and roads—at Hakata.[47] As a result, by the twelfth century, a good portion of Japan's international trade was being run from "inside"—although admittedly, most or all of the principal actors were still ethnically Chinese (and remained so until they were assimilated within the surrounding Japanese community in the late Kamakura period). This situation represented a major change in the nature of Japan's foreign contacts because it was the first time that transfrontier contacts originating in the islands began to outnumber those originating elsewhere. An excess of outflows over inflows was one hallmark of Japan's medieval centuries.[48]

Another characteristic of medieval times was the emergence of a "borderless" Japan. Transfrontier contacts were no longer closely supervised and thus took place at more and more locations and in greater numbers than before. It is clear that Dazaifu retained control over trade for some time after the emergence of the Hakata "Chinatown." Certainly it was still actively in charge in 1105, when Li Chong's ship cast anchor at Shikanoshima. But after this there are relatively few records of Dazaifu involvement in foreign trade. The "last gasp" perhaps came during the so-called Taira regime of the late twelfth century. Both the Taira leader Kiyomori and his half-brother Yorimori served as Dazaifu senior assistant governor-general, and Yorimori actually made the arduous journey to Kyushu to conduct his duties in person. (This was unusual for the period; after about 1120, courtiers assigned jobs in the provinces generally stayed home in Heian-kyō, entrusting the details of local administration to personal deputies known as *mokudai*). Most historians assume that Kiymori and Yorimori sought positions at Dazaifu as part of a larger plan to seize control of, and milk profits from, the Song trade.[49]

But even if Hakata was still of immense importance, it no longer enjoyed the unique status it had in earlier centuries. The Taira clan, in addition to infiltrating the Dazaifu organization, also built port facilities at Ōwada (modern Kobe), apparently for use by Chinese merchants.[50] This would have been the first time in many centuries—and perhaps the first time ever—that ships of foreign nationality were allowed past Hakata into the Japanese interior. But it was not the last time. Following the eclipse of the Taira and the establishment of Japan's first warrior government in 1185, vessels of foreign registration not only sailed the Inland Sea but also traveled up the Pacific seaboard of Honshu as far as the new capital of Kamakura. And in Kyushu—far from Heian-kyō, even farther from Kamakura, and under the complete control of neither—the foreign trade spread from Hakata to other choice ports, notably Bōnotsu at the southern tip of the island in what is now Kagoshima Prefecture. And as more and more ports opened their doors to foreign trade, the number of transfrontier contacts increased dramatically—a point to which I will return in the next chapter.

CHAPTER 5

Medieval Hakata

A Forward-Looking Conclusion

This book began with a visit to the Kōrokan. It will end with a tour of the medieval city of Hakata, followed by a brief summing up.

A Tour of Medieval Hakata

During Japan's medieval era—the four hundred years from the establishment of the Kamakura shogunate in the late twelfth century until the rebirth of a unitary state in the late sixteenth—Hakata Bay was no longer the sole gateway to Japan. However, it remained one important gateway, and was also the location of one of Japan's largest commercial cities. Hakata was a city of, by, and for merchants, although—partly because of the wealth that flowed through it and partly for its strategic importance—it was also hotly contested by political authorities. Authority over Hakata was asserted by branch offices of the Kamakura and Muromachi shogunates, by the feuding barons of the Sengoku period, and finally, at the end of the sixteenth century, by the "great unifier" Toyotomi Hideyoshi (1536–1598).[1]

As we have seen, Hakata originated as a Chinese diaspora settlement on the shores of the bay between the mouths of the Naka and Ishidō rivers. Physically, the area took the form of an hourglass whose axis ran southeast-northwest along what is presently Taihaku Boulevard in Hakata ward, Fukuoka (map 8). The base of the hourglass was an oblong area known as Hakata-hama, "Hakata Beach," which extended roughly from what is today Japan Railways' Hakata Station in the southeast to Meiji Boulevard (Gofuku-machi intersection) in the northwest. (Meiji Boulevard runs southwest-northeast, perpendicular to Taihaku Boulevard and the Naka and Ishidō rivers that flank it.)

MAP 8. Area of medieval Hakata. *Source:* Kobayashi Shigeru et al., eds., *Fukuoka heiya no kokankyō to iseki ritchi,* p. 109 (fig. 4-14). Reproduced by permission of Kobayashi Shigeru and Kyushu University Press.

Hakata-hama was formed by sedimentation and wave action no later than the eighth century. It was joined in the eleventh or twelfth centuries by Oki-no-hama, "Beach in the Offing," which formed the top half of the hourglass. Oki-no-hama was a second, somewhat smaller sand spit to the northwest of Hakata-hama on the other side of present-day Meiji Boulevard. The neck of the hourglass was at Gofuku-machi crossing, where Meiji Boulevard intersects with Taihaku Boulevard. Here the two sand spits were connected by a narrow constriction that in medieval times generally remained above water even at high tide.

Rather than give a dry, chronological history of medieval Hakata, let me now take you on a virtual tour of the area, explaining the most important sites as we walk past them.[2] We will head northwest from Hakata Station and meander through the area of Hakata-hama. After visiting the important historical sites in this oldest portion of the city, we will walk across the old land bridge at Gofukumachi and take a tour of the newer portion of the city, Oki-no-hama. Keep in mind that today this area is heavily urbanized: everywhere the eye looks are tall buildings, busy streets, and many, many people. But it is still possible to discover traces of medieval Hakata in the lay of the land, in the many surviving temples and shrines, and in the occasional inscribed stele or other relic poking its head through the concrete veneer. To these remains may be added the countless artifacts and structures uncovered by archaeologists since 1977, when construction began on Fukuoka's (then) new subway system. In the intervening decades, the Fukuoka City Board of Education has conducted well over a hundred excavations in the subway tunnels and other construction sites in the area. Some of the most impressive finds from these ruins, known collectively as *Hakata iseki-gun* (Hakata group of ruins), are now on display at the Fukuoka City Museum and the Buried Cultural Properties Center.

We begin our tour a few blocks west of Hakata Station, where one encounters the remains of the moat, known as Bōshū-bori, that marked the southern boundary of Hakata in late-medieval times. It seems to have been constructed sometime during the late sixteenth century, probably for administrative as well as defensive purposes. Today all that remains of Bōshū-bori is a slight drop-off in the lay of the land, most visible in a vertical wall marking the south side of the temple Mangōji (also dating from the sixteenth century).

Immediately north of the moat, now on the southwest corner of what used to be Hakata-hama, stands Kushida Shrine (figure 16). The shrine is best known for Hakata Gion Yamagasa, an extended festival held each summer during the first two weeks of July. Yamagasa culminates during the wee hours of July 15, when seven large decorated floats, each representing a separate neighborhood in Hakata, are carried around the town on the shoulders of *yukata*-clad men in a race to Kushida Shrine. Wildly cheering crowds, who incite the float bearers to almost superhuman efforts, line the streets. The Yamagasa festival race draws up to a million spectators each year, many of whom drink themselves silly during the final night of celebration.

On most days of the year, as when I visited, Kushida Shrine presents a much more sober appearance. The precincts, marked by the traditional *torii* gateway (in fact, two gateways, one to the south and the other to the east), contain the main hall of the shrine, several secondary buildings (including a museum), and—as is the case at many religious establishments in Kyushu—several large camphor trees. Native to Southeast Asia, this species was reportedly introduced in medieval times to reduce Japan's dependence on imported camphor (borneol), an important ingredient in perfumes. (Recall that camphor

FIGURE 16. Kushida Shrine. Photograph by author.

was one of the items brought by diplomatic envoys in the Nara period and private traders in the Heian period.)

Also contained in one corner of the shrine precincts are two long (roughly 2 m) granite shafts (figure 17). These are proclaimed by the adjacent signboard to be anchors from the Mongol fleet. The sign is in error: actually these are the anchors of Chinese merchant vessels such as the junk described at the beginning of chapter 4. A number of similar examples have been discovered in recent years, not just in Hakata but also in other parts of northern Kyushu, on Okinawa, in Yamaguchi Prefecture in westernmost Honshu, and even in Ibaraki Prefecture on the Pacific coast of the same island. The discovery of a Chinese anchor in Ibaraki is proof that by medieval times foreign merchant vessels were no longer conducting trade just in Kyushu, but were actually taking their ships through the Inland Sea and up the eastern coast of Honshu to, and beyond, the warrior capital of Kamakura. So far, no anchors have turned up on the Sea of Japan coast of Honshu, where merchant activity is historically attested from the eleventh century, but their discovery is probably just a matter of time. Overseas, anchors of this type have been uncovered in China, of course, and also in

FIGURE 17. Granite anchor from seafaring junk. Photograph by author.

Vladivostok, Russia.[3] Surprisingly, none have been found in Southeast Asia—either as a result of bad archaeological luck or perhaps because maritime trade in the southern seas was dominated by Arabs rather than Chinese.

Heading northwest from Kushida Shrine we next arrive at Reisen Park, a refreshing area of open space in an otherwise congested urban environment. This general area, on the northwest corner of the old Hakata-hama, seems to have been the site of the original port facilities. Facing the park on the east side is the Fukuoka International House, which provides support to foreign students. Just up the street to the north is the headquarters of Kōwa New Pharmaceuticals Corporation. When these buildings were under construction, excavators discovered large quantities of porcelain dishes and bowls, most of them broken. Apparently these represent goods damaged in transit across the East China Sea that were summarily trashed upon discovery at the pier. This site, at least according to one theory, was the core of the original Hakata "Chinatown." Many of the ceramic vessels recovered here (and elsewhere along Hakata Bay, including the Kōrokan) bear ink inscriptions on the base composed of a Chinese family name (e.g., Zhou,

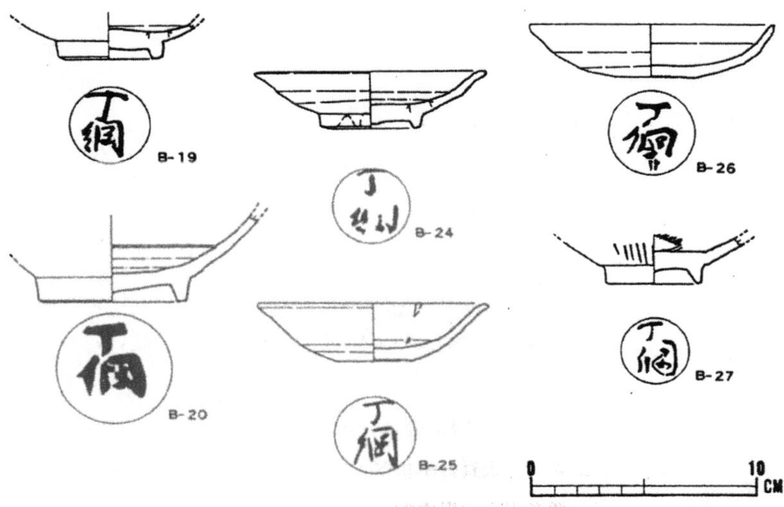

FIGURE 18. Inscribed ceramic vessels from Hakata group of ruins. The inscriptions refer to the "Ding Association," Ding being the surname of a Chinese merchant house. *Source:* Hakata kenkyūkai, ed. *Hakata isekigun shutsudo bokusho shiryō shūsei,* p. 5 (fig. 3). Reproduced with permission.

Ding) plus the character for "rope" or "tether" (J. *gō* or *kō;* C. *gang*), here apparently meaning something like "group" or "association" (figure 18).[4] These inscriptions were apparently used to label shipments as belonging to this or that commercial group. The wealthy shipowners in charge of these operations—pillars of the nascent community at Hakata—proudly bore titles such as *gōshu* (association head) and *sentō* (captain).[5]

Probably the most famous of these Hakata captains is Xie Guoming, who lived in the thirteenth century.[6] Hailing from southern China, Xie settled in Hakata in the vicinity of Kushida Shrine. He owned an entire island (Oroshima) in Chikuzen and donated part of his wealth to build Jōtenji, a Zen temple at the southwest corner of Hakata-hama. And it is to Jōtenji that we now turn, walking northeast past Taihaku Boulevard and then southeast to the temple precincts (figure 19). Jōtenji was founded in 1242; its first abbot was Enni, a Japanese priest born in eastern Honshu who traveled to Song China and studied Rinzai Zen with the master Wu Zhuo. Jōtenji itself is still a thriving center of Zen Buddhism, but unlike similar temples in Kyoto and Kamakura, it is not open to tourists, and there is little for the casual

FIGURE 19. Jōtenji. Photograph by author.

visitor to see. Just to the southeast of the temple grounds, near the Hakata post office, under a huge, but very dead, camphor tree, lies the grave of Xie Guoming.

At this point we turn around and head back to the northwest, past Jōtenji and another important Zen temple, Shōfukuji (figure 20). Shōfukuji was founded in either 1195 or 1204, depending on which source you believe. Its first abbot was Eisai, another Japanese priest to have studied Rinzai Zen in China. Shōfukuji was in fact Japan's first Zen temple, as a plaque hung in the rafters of its main hall proclaims. (The original of the plaque was supposedly a gift to the temple from Emperor Go-Daigo, who reigned in the early fourteenth century.) Shōfukuji, like Jōtenji, was built under the patronage of the Chinese merchant community. Both temples were originally equally magnificent, but Shōfukuji is by far the larger now. After World War II, when the city of Fukuoka began to rebuild from the ashes, Jōtenji cooperated with city planners and gave up about half of its land; Shōfukuji, meanwhile, refused to give in and as a result retains the scale and appearance of a medieval temple.

Visitors to Shōfukuji may notice that the orientation of the temple and surrounding precincts is skewed a few degrees counterclockwise

FIGURE 20. Shōfukuji. Photograph by author.

from that of the surrounding streets. A number of early medieval roads—mostly dating from the beginning of the fourteenth century—have also been uncovered in the area of Hakata-hama, and these agree in orientation with the temple, not the modern overlay of streets, which for the most part hew to a plan drafted by Toyotomi Hideyoshi in 1587. During the late sixteenth century, Hakata was a war zone and was burned down repeatedly, with major fires occurring in 1559, 1563, 1580, and 1586. Hideyoshi, well on his way to reestablishing a unified central government, rebuilt the city both to encourage trade (for his own profit) and as a commissariat, or supply depot, for the impending invasion of Korea.[7] Hideyoshi, revered as a hero in Japan for his role in reunifying the country, was also a warmonger who attacked the peninsula not just once but twice (in 1592 and 1597), simply because it lay on the route to his ultimate goal, Ming China. Fortunately, Hideyoshi died in 1598, and his troops in the peninsula all scurried home—but not before extensive damage had been done to Korea and, even more lastingly, to Korean-Japanese relations. As Hideyoshi's overseas "adventures" remind us all too starkly, all too often premodern foreign relations were ruled by the law of the jungle, and the Japanese, like some of their neighbors (e.g., the Mongols in the thirteenth century), were only too eager to play the role of top predator if given the chance.

Continuing to the northwest past Shōfukuji, we try to suppress these unpleasant thoughts. The attempt proves momentarily futile, because just past the temple there is a small granite marker commemorating Japan's role in the "Great East Asian War" and dated December 8, 1941—Pearl Harbor Day in Japan, where the calendar runs almost a day ahead of that in the United States because of the international date line. Wondering why the monument was not removed after the war, we continue walking northwest through some back alleys, finally emerging on a street that affords a fine view of the lay of the land. Ahead of us, the street drops off into what used to be the inlet between Hakata-hama and Oki-no-hama. The difference in elevation is not great—perhaps two meters at most—but it is visible if you know what to look for.

Next we take a 90-degree turn to the southwest, heading up the old inlet to Gofukumachi crossing at Taihaku Boulevard, where the two sandbars were originally connected. After another right turn at the intersection, we head uphill again into what was Oki-no-hama. During the Sengoku era, before the coming of Hideyoshi, Oki-no-hama was under the control of the Ōtomo family, military barons hailing from what is now Ōita Prefecture in northeastern Kyushu. Hakata-hama to the southeast was nominally ruled (until 1551, anyhow) by the Ōuchi, another family of warlords based in westernmost Honshu (Yamaguchi Prefecture). Most history books describe late-medieval Hakata, along with Sakai, as a "free city"—a commercial paradise ruled by merchants, a virtual beacon of light amidst the darkness of the surrounding samurai hordes. This picture is far from the truth. Merchants had little protection against warriors and depended upon their patronage and protection. Warlords, meanwhile, were highly desirous of Hakata for the wealth it offered. Medieval Hakata was contested ground, as its physical division between the Ōtomo and Ōuchi clans symbolizes.

We now continue up Taihaku Boulevard, eventually reaching Kuramoto crossing, one traffic signal to the northwest of Gofukumachi. We are now in the center of what used to be Oki-no-hama. On the north corner of the crossing is a stone bench, which upon closer inspection turns out to be yet another granite anchor—actually, a reproduction of an anchor found by archaeologists at this site. Excavations across the street on the west corner of the intersection—now the site of Hakata Elementary School—have revealed part of the Mongol defense wall, showing that this area was definitely dry land in the thirteenth century. At the same location the remains of a sixteenth-century merchant house were also discovered; these remains yielded, among many other artifacts, a Christian medallion depicting Jesus and Mary. Across the street on the south corner of the intersection the remains of another sixteenth-century merchant house were discovered, this one containing artifacts of Korean, Thai, and Vietnamese manufacture. Despite the ravages visited upon it by competing military houses, Oki-no-hama was evidently a cosmopolitan town in the sixteenth century.

On the other hand, most of its inhabitants were ethnically Japanese, as were those living at this time in Hakata-hama to the south. Although Hakata was originally a Chinese settlement, over the centuries its residents had assimilated with the surrounding Japanese population. By the sixteenth century, the merchant community along the bay shore was as thoroughly Japanese as that at Sakai or any other important commercial hub. Instead of passively waiting for foreign merchants to arrive, the city's residents now took their own ships overseas—to Korea, to China, and even to Southeast Asia. Indeed, some of them eventually settled abroad, forming diaspora communities—Japantowns—of their own.[8]

The sixteenth century was the most "open" period in premodern Japanese history, precisely because no single individual or group had the power to control Japan as a whole or (what is the same thing) to establish monopolistic control over its borders. This, of course, is the period when Westerners first came to Japan, as witness the Christian medallion noted above.[9] The house where the medallion was found probably belonged to a Japanese merchant; Westerners themselves were but transient visitors in Japan. Most scholars seem to assume that the owner of the house was a Christian convert. This is certainly possible. However, the medallion might also represent a trinket valued for its "foreignness" rather than its religious meaning. One thinks of the crosses seen so frequently on the jewelry worn by young Japanese women today. Appearances to the contrary, the crosses are merely a fad resulting from shifting consumer tastes and the whims of jewelry designers, and have little if any religious significance to those who wear them.

The area around Kuramoto intersection, and indeed all of Oki-no-hama, is today much more open than the Hakata-hama area around the station, which is cluttered and has many narrow streets. The reason has very little to do with premodern history. In 1945, toward the end of WWII, the bayside had a larger population than the area around Hakata Station, with the result that it was targeted by U.S. B-29 bombers and almost totally destroyed. Thus postwar city planners were able to give full rein to their imaginations in Oki-no-hama, whereas in Hakata-hama they had to live with the existing street plan, much of it again dating back to Hideyoshi. But even there, as we have seen, it takes a trained eye to see Hakata as it existed still earlier, in medieval times.

Here then at the end of our tour, looking south down Taihaku Boulevard in the general direction of Hakata Station, let us envision the city as it was. We are aided in this quest by the words of John Saris, an Englishman who visited Japan on business for the East India Company in 1613. Saris wrote:

> We were rowed through, amongst divers Ilands, all which, or the most part of them, were well inhabited, and divers proper Townes built upon them; whereof one called Hakata, hath a very strong Castle, built of free stone, but no Ordnance nor Souldiers therein. It hath a ditch about five fathome deep, and twice as broad round about it, with a draw bridge, kept all in very good repaire. I did land & dine there in the Towne, the tyde and wind so strong against us, as that we could not passe. The Towne seemed to be as great as London is within the wals, very wel built, and even, so as you may see from the one end of the streete to the other. The place exceedingly peopled, very Civill and curteous, onely that at our landing, and being here in Hakata, and so through the whole Countrey, whithersoever we came, the boyes, children, and worser sort of idle people, would gather about and follow after us, crying Coré, Coré, Cocoré, Waré, that is to say, You Coreans with false hearts: wondering, hoping, hallowing, and making such a noise around us, that we could scarcely heare one an other speake, sometime throwing stones at us (but that not in many Townes) yet the clamour and crying after us was every where alike, none reprooving them for it. The best advice that I can give those who hereafter shall arrive there, is that they passe on without regarding those idle rablements, and in so doing, they shall find their eares onely troubled with the noise.[10]

It is not completely clear what "castle" Saris is referring to. The only bona fide castle in this area in the early seventeenth century was Fukuoka Castle, built by Kuroda Nagamasa over the ruins of the Kōrokan—and thus not in Hakata, stricto senso, at all. During the Edo period, Fukuoka and Hakata were twin cities—the one, inhabited by samurai, on the west bank of the Naka; the other, inhabited by merchants and craftsmen, on the east bank. (Between them, on a sandbar in the middle of the river, was Nakasu, "Central Isle," one of Japan's most famous red-light districts, then as well as now.) So it seems strange that Saris refers to a "castle" in Hakata; perhaps he simply means that the city was fortified, as it undoubtedly was. As we have already seen, Hakata was bounded on the south by a moat, Bōshū-bori; perhaps this is the moat (complete with drawbridge) referred to by Saris.

The rest of the account, which clearly applies to Hakata proper, makes two important points. First, Hakata was relatively large (for the times) and densely populated. Admittedly, when looking at the area of the old city on a map it appears to be relatively compact, hardly more than a square kilometer in area. But as I can attest, it takes a surprisingly long time to circumnavigate on foot, even without tarrying to inspect historical monuments and temples. Regarding population, one record from the middle of the twelfth century mentions "1,600 households,"[11] and by 1471 Hakata's population is said to have numbered 10,000.[12] Figures of 19,500 and 13,500 are handed down, respectively, from 1690 and 1737.[13] These are not huge numbers (Edo already had a million residents by the 1720s), but they are not to be sniffed at, either.

Second, the residents of Hakata had ambivalent attitudes toward foreigners. On the one hand, the people were "very Civill and curteous." This civility was also noted by other foreign visitors; the travelogue of a Korean envoy who visited in 1420, for example, makes much of the lavish entertainment he received at the hands of local clerics and merchants (the latter no doubt hoping for new business opportunities).[14] On the other hand, the same Korean visitor also notes that the residents of Hakata, "from men and women, old and young, to monks and nuns,"[15] were wont to stare at him in curiosity—presumably the same sentiment that caused "boyes, children, and worser sort of idle people" to follow Saris around in 1613. The taunts Saris notes indicate that Hakata's residents, at least the "worser sort," were not above a bit of racial slander—even if they could not always tell the difference between an Englishman and someone from "Coré." In short, Japanese attitudes toward foreign visitors ran the gamut from warm hospitality to simple curiosity to outright racism. They were, in other words, human, with normal human reactions to outsiders in their midst.

Japan and the Outside World

Although he may not have enjoyed the attentions of the local populace, John Saris was fortunate to have been able to visit Hakata at all. Westerners were no longer as welcome in Japan as before. As early as 1587

Hideyoshi had proscribed Catholic missionaries in Nagasaki. During the subsequent Edo period, things went from bad to worse; just two decades after Saris's visit, the third Tokugawa shogun, Iemitsu (r. 1623–1651), began promulgating a series of laws that barred Japanese from traveling overseas and also effectively shut off the flow of Western visitors to Japan after 1639. The one exception was the Dutch, who were allowed to maintain a (completely secular) trading outpost on the artificial island of Deshima in Nagasaki Harbor, a hundred kilometers southwest of Hakata.[16]

Popular stereotypes to the contrary, Edo-period Japan was not a closed country. Not just the Dutch, but also Chinese traders were welcome at Nagasaki, and contacts with Korea, the Ryukyu kingdom, and the Ainu were maintained via other designated portals—respectively, the domains of Tsushima, Satsuma (in southernmost Kyushu), and Matsumae (in southernmost Hokkaido).[17] But the absolute level of traffic did fall off significantly, and for Hakata it was truly the end of the road. The city completely lost its international character, not to regain it until the reopening of Japan to the West in the nineteenth century.

The Edo period thus represents an anomaly in Hakata's long history—the one period when it was no longer the gateway to Japan (as during centuries covered by this book), nor even one portal among many (as in the medieval centuries), but just another castle town filled with soldiers, merchants, and craftsmen. When residents of Fukuoka look back on their past, they do not ignore the Edo centuries. Everyone is familiar with the Kuroda family's Fukuoka Castle and with Nakasu, the entertainment district that traces its ancestry to the pleasure quarters of the Edo period. Many of the festivals of the Hakata district also have their roots in the early-modern centuries. And yet, to most people, the primary fact about Fukuoka's history is its role as an international city, the crossroads of Asia. To the citizens of Fukuoka, the Kōrokan is the very heart and soul of that history—as it has been the very heart and soul of this book. What then does the story of the Kōrokan, and of Hakata's role as a port, tell us about Japan and the Japanese?

First and most obviously, Japan has always been an island country, and that fact has played an important role in the country's historical development. Japan developed in relative, although by no means total, isolation. As a result, Japanese society was, and is, homogeneous by world standards. These characteristics—isolation and homogeneity—were perhaps overemphasized by an earlier generation of scholars.[18] Partly in reaction to these stereotypes—but also in response to current trends and concerns such as globalization and multiculturalism—historians today are doing their best to paint a picture of a borderless, socially diverse Japan.[19] But this is going too far. The "borderless" label, in particular, holds only for the late-medieval period—and even then, the level of cross-border traffic was not that high, perhaps a few dozen ships per year according to the calculations of Charlotte von Verschuer.[20] The reason? Surrounded on four sides by ocean, and situated far from the population centers and principal trades routes of Eurasia, Japan was about as isolated as a country could be. Even when there was no one guarding the borders, Japan's place on the map consistently discouraged casual outside contacts.

This having been said, foreign relations nonetheless played an essential role in Japanese history. Although few people think about it, Japan is itself a nation of immigrants: everyone's ancestors ultimately came from overseas. So did rice agriculture, which—despite assertions to the contrary by revisionist historians[21]—indeed formed the basis of Japan's economy through premodern history. Other important imports from abroad include the writing system, Buddhism, Confucianism, Chinese legal and administrative institutions, and, later, guns and other aspects of Western culture and technology.[22] All of these were essential to the unfolding of Japanese history as we know it.

Precisely because foreign relations were so important, those in power tried to monopolize them whenever possible. They did so, characteristically, by bringing their political or military power or both to bear on natural crossroads or corridors connecting Japan to the outside world. Ancient Hakata is a case in point. So are the four mouths used by the Edo shogunate to regulate its external interactions. The use of gateways or portals to regulate cross-border traffic was characteristic of periods when Japan was ruled by a relatively strong, unitary state. In periods of weaker government, no single power was able to monopolize cross-border flows. This was all the more so because the frontier regions mediating such interactions were (almost by definition) far from the center, making them especially difficult to control. (As we have seen, just the journey from Kyoto to Hakata could take days or even weeks in premodern times.) In periods of weak government, the existence of multiple, competing power centers meant that foreign relations could no longer be channeled through designated gateways. Everyone wanted his own piece of the action.

All of this had several important consequences. For one thing, the prevailing mode of foreign relations changed systematically over time.

In periods of strong government—when control was a reality, not just a dream—foreign relations tended to be more assertive and public in character, taking the form of diplomacy or, when diplomacy failed (or leaders took leave of their senses), war. This was true during the heyday of the ancient imperial state and again under Hideyoshi and the Tokugawa shoguns. In periods of weak government, foreign policy became more reactive in nature, and private interactions began to flourish. During the Heian period, as we have seen, the court abandoned public diplomacy in favor of simple boundary maintenance: defense against incursion, coupled with controls over peaceful entry and exit. Later, as central controls over even these functions diminished, private forms of cross-border traffic came to the fore. The merchants of Hakata and elsewhere conducted trade under a minimum of supervision, while the pirates known as *wakō* (many of them, at least originally, Japanese from the Gotō Archipelago) began to haunt the sea lanes between Japan and the continent.[23]

Next, and even more important, there was a clear inverse relationship between the degree of political centralization in Japan and the volume of cross-border traffic. When there was a well-functioning central government, as in the Nara and Heian eras and the Edo period, relatively few people moved across the frontiers in either direction. In periods of weak government, such as the middle ages (particularly the Muromachi and Sengoku periods), the flow of people, goods, and information went relatively unimpeded. In addition to the historical arguments presented in earlier chapters, this point can be illustrated with archaeological data.

Consider figure 21, which shows the total number of archaeological sites in Japan that have yielded imported porcelain, arranged by century from the seventh through the nineteenth and also by prefecture of discovery. Note that this is a count of sites, not individual vessels or porcelain fragments recovered; the Kōrokan, where thousands of discoveries have been made, thus gets the same weight as another site that has produced just one broken bowl. Nonetheless, the general chronological trends are clear and can be interpreted as follows: Very small quantities of imported porcelain were brought to Japan, probably all through diplomatic channels, in the seventh and eighth centuries. Starting in the ninth century, the number of sites begins to climb gradually, partly because of increased production at Chinese kilns, but more fundamentally because foreign merchants, and not just diplomats, were now coming to Japan. However, the total number of sites remains rela-

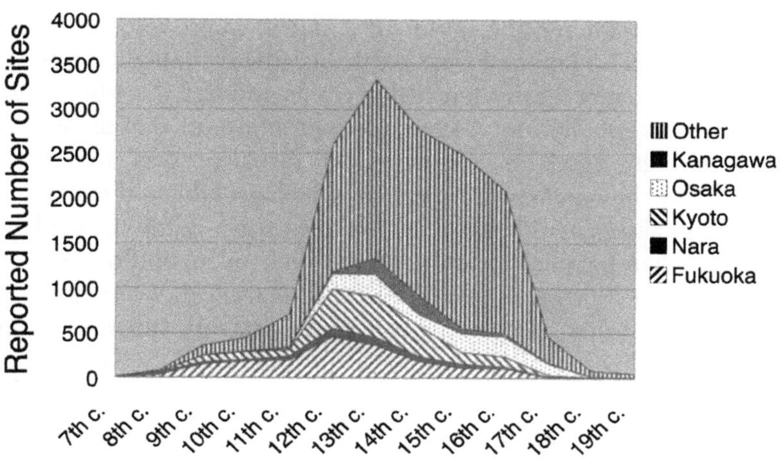

FIGURE 21. Reported number of sites yielding imported porcelain, 7th–19th c. *Source:* Compiled from data in Tsuchibashi Riko, "Nissō bōeki no shosō," p. 73 (table 2).

tively small through the eleventh century. Note also that most of the discoveries are from Fukuoka, the official port of entrance, and from political centers such as Nara and Kyoto. The number of sites grows rapidly from the twelfth century as political authorities lose their ability to control Japan's frontiers. Porcelain is now found in Osaka (medieval Sakai, the most important port on the Inland Sea) and Kanagawa, site of the capital of Kamakura—as well as at many other sites throughout the country. The growth in number of sites reflects improvements in domestic distribution—the economy was becoming increasingly commercialized—and also, of course, the fact that foreign merchants were visiting more and more ports. Interestingly, imports seem to drop off a bit during the Muromachi and Sengoku periods, possibly because the emergence of a domestic ceramic industry reduced demand for foreign wares. Then there is a very dramatic decrease from the seventeenth century, reflecting the reimposition of central controls over foreign contacts by the newly established Edo shogunate.

Another important point to be made here is that not just the total volume, but also the direction of cross-border traffic, varied systematically over time. In this book I have examined mostly inflows—foreigners arriving on Japanese shores. Inflows generally predominated over outflows during ancient times, partly because of technological disparities between Japan and the continent (Chinese ships were better built and navigated than Japanese) and partly because the Japanese court for the most part banned private travel overseas and had the wherewithal to enforce this prohibition. A similar situation prevailed in the Edo period (although here the technological disparity was maintained artificially by the Japanese government, which prohibited the manufacture of large ships capable of sailing the open seas). But in the medieval centuries, when Japan's borders were relatively open, outflows seem to have exceeded inflows by a considerable margin.[24] What does this mean? It means that, free from government controls, Japanese people have historically been curious about the outside world, and eager to go abroad. Of course, in the Sengoku era, many of these Japanese "ambassadors" were simply pirates. But that does not detract from the larger point: Japan may be an island country, but its people are not "naturally" insular.

Which brings us back to the importance of geography in Japan's history. Historically, Japan's geographic isolation made it relatively easy for rulers who wished—and many of them did, for reasons of personal power—to monopolize foreign contacts, making the country even more isolated than geography dictated. Isolation also led to ignorance of the outside world, which, coupled again with the lust for power, motivated some of these same governments to send their people overseas to fight doomed wars in Asia. Either way, Japanese governments over the ages have often been obstacles to international peace and understanding. For this, the country has its geography to blame.

But being an island country also had positive consequences. Specifically, it encouraged curiosity about other peoples and other places—witness the wholesale importation of Chinese culture in the ancient period, the outflow of Japanese adventurers during the relatively free medieval centuries, and the Westernization of the nineteenth and twentieth centuries. Today Japan again stands at a crossroads as it struggles to comprehend, and respond to, the forces of globalization. Will the Japanese people—or their leaders—resist, or will they embrace this opportunity to become part of the world, not apart from it? Is it possible, in today's global society, for Japan to overcome its historical ambivalence toward the outside world? Only time will tell.

Notes

INTRODUCTION

1. The history of research and excavation of the site has been recounted many times in the Japanese literature. An "official" summary can be found in Fukuoka shi kyōiku iinkai, *Kōrokan ato 14,* part 1, esp. pp. 1–7.
2. "Fukuoaka City Online," http://www.city.fukuoka.jp/asia/index-e.htm (accessed February 25, 2000).
3. See the official exhibition catalogue: Ajia Taiheiyō hakuran kyōkai, ed., *Michi, deai / Roads to Kyūshū, Communication in Kyūshū.*

CHAPTER 1: WAR

1. On Perry and the "black ships," see W. G. Beasley, "The Foreign Threat and the Opening of the Ports," and Andrew Gordon, *A Modern History of Japan,* pp. 46–50. For a revisionist view, downplaying the element of threat, see M. William Steele, *Alternative Narratives in Modern Japanese History.*
2. The name Tenji is posthumous; I follow scholarly convention in using it to refer to the king during his reign. The same convention is applied to the names of other Japanese rulers who appear in this book. Technically, Tenji's reign was 668–671: although he ruled the country from 661, he was not formally enthroned until 668.
3. For a balanced attempt to assess the genetic components of human behavior, see Edward O. Wilson, *On Human Nature.*
4. Donald Johanson and Blake Edgar, *From Lucy to Language,* pp. 93–96.
5. Or so it would seem. See the descriptions of early civilizations in J. R. McNeill and William H. McNeill, *The Human Web,* pp. 9–81, passim.
6. For an archaeological overview of the development of warfare in the Japanese islands, see the essays in Ōtsuka Hatsushige et al., eds., *Kōkogaku ni yoru Nihon rekishi 6 Sensō.*
7. This date represents a best guess as of the time of writing. In the 1980s and 1990s very early dates—up to 700,000 years ago—were advanced for the arrival of humans (or hominids) in Japan. It was discovered in November 2000 that many of these early "discoveries" were frauds

perpetrated by Fujimura Shin'ichi, an archaeologist based in Sendai. (For further information on the hoax, see the on-line "Index to materials on Japan's early Palaeolithic hoax" by Sophia University archaeologist Charles T. Keally: http://www.t-net.ne.jp/~keally/Hoax/hoax.html.) Following exposure of the hoax, many archaeologists seemed to settle on a conservative date of about 30,000 B.C.E. for the initial peopling of the islands. Lately, however, dates are being pushed back again. The date of 100,000 years was reported from a site in Hirado, Nagasaki, at the end of 2003: *Asahi shinbun,* December 20, 2003, p. 1. (Note, however, that if a date of 100,000 B.C.E. is correct, the first settlers are likely to have been *Homo erectus,* not *Homo sapiens.*) On the population history of the Japanese islands, see Kazuro Hanihara, "Dual Structure Model for the Population History of the Japanese"; Katayama Kazumichi, "The Japanese as an Asia-Pacific Population"; and Mark J. Hudson, *Ruins of Identity,* pp. 59–81. On prehistoric Japanese cultures in general, see Richard J. Pearson, Gina Lee Barnes, and Karl L. Hutterer, eds., *Windows on the Japanese Past;* Pearson, ed., *Ancient Japan;* and Keiji Imamura, *Prehistoric Japan.*

8. The date of 14,500 B.C.E. for the beginning of the Jōmon period comes from Junko Habu, *Ancient Jomon of Japan,* pp. 26–42. Most older works give a date of 10,000 B.C.E. or thereabouts, a figure based on uncalibrated (and thus incorrect) radiocarbon dates. If the calibrated dates cited by Habu are correct, the Jōmon culture actually predates the onset of climatic warming, which occurred between 13,000 and 11,000 B.C.E. and then more continuously after 9,500 B.C.E. On climatic trends in the Holocene (Recent) era, see Neil Roberts, *The Holocene,* pp. 55–86; Brian Fagan, *The Long Summer;* and Richard Alley, *The Two-Mile Time Machine.*
9. Suzuki Takao, *Hone kara mita Nihonjin,* pp. 55–69.
10. On this image, see Gavan McCormack, "Introduction," p. 2.
11. The beginning of the Yayoi period, formerly placed in the fourth century B.C.E. or thereabouts, has recently been pushed back as the result of more systematic application of radiocarbon dating (although not all workers yet accept the new dates). See the various articles in *Kikan kōkogaku* 88 (October 2004), an issue of this archaeological journal devoted to the dating of the initial Yayoi.
12. Suzuki, *Hone kara mita Nihonjin,* pp. 69–70.
13. The Kofun era was formerly thought to begin about 300 C.E. Again, advances in dating (this time using dendrochronology, or tree-ring dating) have caused a revision. Although the difference is only a century or so, it is highly significant because a date of 200 places the first historical description of "Wa," in the Chinese *Wei History,* within the Kofun period rather than the Yayoi period as was formerly thought. The description, relating to events in the mid-third century, features a "Queen Himiko"

of the "land of Yamatai," who was buried in a giant tomb mound (*Chūgoku seishi Nihon den 1,* pp. 39–54, translated in Wm. Theodore de Bary et al., eds. *Sources of Japanese Tradition,* vol. 1, pp. 6–8). A historiographical debate going back several centuries has focused on the location of Yamatai, with some scholars arguing for Kyushu and others for Yamato. Given the revised dating of the Yayoi-Kofun transition, the fact that the earliest and biggest tombs are in Yamato, and the similarity in pronunciation between Yamato and Yamatai, it now seems beyond question that Himiko was a ruler in Yamato, not Kyushu. For background on Yamatai, see William Wayne Farris, *Sacred Texts and Buried Treasures,* pp. 9–54, and Joan R. Piggott, *The Emergence of Japanese Kingship,* pp. 15–65.

14. On Iwai, see Oda Fujio, ed., *Kodai o kangaeru: Iwai no ran,* and Yamao Yukihisa, *Tsukushi no kimi Iwai no sensō.*
15. On the stele, see Farris, *Sacred Texts and Buried Treasures,* p. 115.
16. On Japanese imports from the peninsula—and Japanese-Korean relations in general—the best source in English is Farris, *Sacred Texts and Buried Treasures,* pp. 55–122. An older, but still useful, study is Hirano Kunio, "The Yamato State and Korea in the Fourth and Fifth Centuries."
17. Farris, *Sacred Texts and Buried Treasures,* pp. 109–122, passim.
18. For general background on state formation in East Asia, see the excellent account by Charles Holcombe, *The Genesis of East Asia: 221 B.C.–A.D. 907.* On "peer polities," see Colin Renfrew and John F. Cherry, eds., *Peer Polity Interaction and Socio-Political Change.*
19. *Chūgoku seishi Nihon den 1,* pp. 92–93, translated in de Bary et al., eds., *Sources of Japanese Tradition,* vol. 1, pp. 9–10. Bu had also asked for, but was not granted, authority over Paekche.
20. In Japanese, see Yoshimura Takehiko, "Wa no goō to wa dare ka," and Shinokawa Ken, *Ōkimi to chihō gōzoku;* in English, see Piggott, *Emergence of Japanese Kingship,* pp. 44–65.
21. In the period covered by the book, there were no "nations" in the modern sense, so "international" is an anachronism. However, the term is so convenient that I have decided to use it here and elsewhere as a synonym for the more correct "interstate."
22. On the Sui campaigns, see Woodridge Bingham, *The Founding of the T'ang Dynasty,* pp. 37–50; Arthur F. Wright, *The Sui Dynasty,* pp. 182–197; Wright, "The Sui Dynasty (581–617)," pp. 143–149; Joseph Wong, "Unfought Korean Wars"; and Ki-Baik Lee, *A New History of Korea,* p. 47.
23. On the Tang campaigns: C. P. Fitzgerald, *The Empress Wu,* pp. 51–75; R. W. L. Guisso, *Wu Tse-T'ien and the Politics of Legitimation in T'ang China,* pp. 107–125; Howard J. Wechsler, "T'ai-Tsung (Reign 626–49) the Consolidator," pp. 231–235; Denis Twitchett and Howard J. Wechsler, "Kao-Tsung (Reign 649–83) and the Empress

Wu," pp. 282–285; and Lee, *A New History of Korea,* pp. 48 and 66–71. The following paragraphs are also based on these works.

24. That account that follows is based mostly on primary sources. But there is an extensive secondary literature in Japanese on the subject, of which the reader should be aware. See in particular the following books: Kitō Kiyoaki, *Hakusuki-no-e;* Tōyama Mitsuo, *Hakusuki-no-e;* and Mori Kimiyuki, *"Hakusuki-no-e" igo.*
25. *Nihon shoki,* Saimei 6 (660) 10, Jomei 3 (631) 3/1. *Nihon shoki* (Chronicles of Japan) is an official history dating from 720. The earlier portions of the text, dealing with the divine origins of Japan and the activities of its early "emperors," are wholly mythical in nature, but entries from about 600 are generally considered to be factually reliable (although ideologically slanted, because the whole purpose of the text was to provide "historical" support for the legitimacy of the royal institution).
26. *Nihon shoki,* Saimei 7/1/6 and 3/25.
27. *Nihon shoki,* Saimei 7/7/24; ibid., Tenji sokui zenki, 7/7/24. According to *Nihon shoki,* Saimei 7/5/9, while the royal party was staying at a place called Asakura, trees at a local shrine were felled to construct a temporary "palace." This act angered the resident gods, who destroyed the "great hall." A "will-o'-the-wisp" *(onibi)* also appeared in the "palace," causing many of the queen's aides and attendants to "sicken and die." Perhaps the implication is that Saimei's death was also caused by supernatural forces.
28. *Nihon shoki,* Saimei 7/8/1; ibid., Tenji sokui zenki, Saimei 7/7 (entry for "this month"). The first of these two entries also states that on the night of Naka's departure for Hakata a "spirit" or "demon" *(oni)* wearing a "great cowl" gazed down upon the rites of mourning from the top of Mt. Asakura, causing people to "wonder."
29. Interment: *Nihon shoki,* Saimei 7/11/7; assumption of rulership: ibid., Tenji sokui zenki, Saimei 7/7/24; "attended to organization": ibid., Tenji sokui zenki, Saimei 7/7 (entry for "this month"). The translation is by W. G. Aston, *Nihongi,* vol. 2, p. 275.
30. *Nihon shoki,* Tenji sokui zenki, Saimei 7/8.
31. *Nihon shoki,* Tenji sokui zenki, Saimei 7/9.
32. *Nihon shoki,* Tenji sokui zenki, Tenji 1/1/27.
33. *Nihon shoki,* Tenji sokui zenki, Tenji 1/3/4.
34. *Nihon shoki,* Tenji 1 (662) 3 (entry for "this month").
35. *Nihon shoki,* Tenji 1/5.
36. *Nihon shoki,* Tenji 1 (entry for "this year").
37. *Nihon shoki,* Tenji 2/3.
38. Ikeuchi Hiroshi, *Mansenshi kenkyū jōsei,* vol. 2, pp. 141–152.
39. *Nihon shoki,* Saimei 6/10. Translation: Aston, *Nihongi,* vol. 2, pp. 268–269.
40. Indeed, after the war P'ung and his descendants continued to live in Japan under the name Kudaraō-shi or Paekche Royal Family, serving the

court as an internalized, "virtual" foreign dependency. Ishigami Eiichi, "Kodai Higashi Ajia chiiki to Nihon," pp. 264–270.

41. Details of the rout are given in *Nihon shoki,* Tenji 2/8/17 and 2/8/27.
42. Fitzgerald, *The Empress Wu,* p. 65; Guisso, *Wu Tse-T'ien and the Politics of Legitimation in T'ang China,* p. 116; Twitchett and Wechsler, "Kao-Tsung (Reign 649–83) and the Empress Wu," p. 282.
43. *Nihon shoki,* Tenji 2/9/24.
44. *Nihon shoki,* Jitō 4 (690) 10/22.
45. See sources in note 23, above.
46. Bruce Batten, "Foreign Threat and Domestic Reform." For better or for worse, this paper has received more citations than anything I have written since—in English, at least. The same situation applies in Japanese: my first historical article in any language (Batten, "Ritsuryō sei ka ni okeru Shiragi, Bokkaishi no settaihō") is a primitive undertaking by any standards, and yet for a long time it was the only work of mine consistently cited by Japanese scholars.
47. On political developments in the seventh century, see Inoue Mitsusada with Delmer M. Brown, "The Century of Reform," and Piggott, *The Emergence of Japanese Kingship,* pp. 66–166.
48. *Nihon shoki,* Keitai 23 (529) 12.
49. *Nihon shoki,* Senka 1 (536) 5/1.
50. On the history and archaeology of the Nanotsu Miyake, see Kurazumi Yasuhiko, *Kodai no Dazaifu,* pp. 1–14, and Tamura Enchō, *Dazaifu tankyū,* pp. 7–16.
51. The first historical reference to the Tsukushi Dazai is *Nihon shoki,* Suiko 17 (609) 4/4. On the early history of this institution, see Kurazumi, *Kodai no Dazaifu,* pp. 14–35, and Tamura, *Dazaifu tankyū,* pp. 17–30.
52. *Nihon shoki,* Tenji 3/5/17, 3/10/1, 3/10/4, and 3/12/12. Also see *Kaigaikoku ki,* quoted in Zuikei Shūhō, *Zenrin kokuhōki,* Tenji 3, pp. 40–43. This last source has been translated in Charlotte von Verschuer, "Japan's Foreign Relations 600 to 1200 A.D.," pp. 19–20.
53. *Nihon shoki,* Tenji 4/9/23, 4/10/11, 4/11/13, 4/12/14, 4/12 (entry for "this month"), and 4 (entry for "this year").
54. *Nihon shoki,* Tenji 6/11/9, 6/11/13.
55. *Nihon shoki,* Tenji 10/1/13, 10/7/11.
56. *Nihon shoki,* Tenji 10/11/10, Tenmu sokui zenki, Tenmu 1 (672) 3/18, 1/5/12, 1/5/30. The idea that 1,400 of the men were Japanese POWs comes from Naoki Kōrjirō, *Kodai Nihon to Chōsen, Chūgoku,* pp. 175–209. A report that Guo Wucong brought an embassy of 2,000 to Japan in 669 is thought to be a redundant account of the 671 mission: *Nihon shoki,* Tenji 8 (entry for "this year"), and Ikeuchi, *Mansenshi kenkyū jōsei,* vol. 2, pp. 209–210.
57. For a brief historiographical survey, see Kurazumi, *Kodai no Dazaifu,* pp. 97–109.

58. All quotations from *Nihon shoki,* dates as stated.
59. The gloss in *Nihon shoki* reads "Kanata," but today the name is usually read as stated.
60. *Nihon shoki,* Tenji 10/11/10.
61. On the archaeology of these fortresses, see Oda Fujio, *Nishi Nihon kodai yamajiro no kenkyū;* Oda, ed., *Kitakyūshū Setouchi no kodai yamajiro;* Kameda Hiroshi, "Chōsen shiki yamajiro wa naze tsukurareta ka"; and Nishitani Tadashi, "Chōsen shiki yamajiro."
62. On the institutional evolution of the Tsukushi Dazai/Dazaifu in the postwar years, see Kurazumi, *Kodai no Dazaifu,* pp. 110–138. Kurazumi dates the establishment of the Dazaifu bureaucracy per se to the promulgation of the Asuka Kiyomihara Code in the late 680s.
63. This is the term used by Aston, *Nihongi,* and also by Royall Tyler in his English rendition of Murasaki Shikibu's *The Tale of Genji.* "Governor-general" is a more literal, accurate translation of the original Japanese term, *sotsu.* "Viceroy" has a nice ring but carries the (incorrect) implication that the *sotsu* was something like a junior partner to the emperor.
64. *Nihon shoki,* Tenji 10/6 (entry for "this month"). In the text, the prince's name is glossed (by modern editors) as "Kurukuma," but I have chosen to stick with the more "commonsense" reading of the first character, "Kuri-."
65. *Nihon shoki,* Tenmu 1/6/26. This passage is perhaps not to be taken literally—but at the very least it shows how the early eighth-century editors of *Chronicles of Japan* viewed the role of Dazaifu.
66. Ibid.
67. *Nihon shoki,* Jitō 8/9/22.
68. Again, according to Naoki, *Kodai Nihon to Chōsen, Chūgoku,* pp. 175–209.
69. *Nihon shoki,* Tenmu 1/5/12. Pongee *(ashiginu)* is a type of coarse silk.
70. Before receiving these items Guo Wucong is said to have given his Japanese hosts a "letter box [i.e., an official diplomatic communication] and [a gift of] local products." *Nihon shoki,* Tenmu 1/3/21.
71. *Nihon shoki,* Tenji 4/10/11, mentions a military revue in Uji, evidently for the benefit of the Chinese visitors. The poetry collection *Kaifūsō,* in the introduction to "Ōmi chō Ōtomo no miko, nishu" (pp. 68, 70) also has one of the Tang envoys meeting with Prince Ōtomo, which can only have occurred at or near court.
72. Upon hearing the news, according to *Nihon shoki,* Tenmu 1/3/18, "Guo Wucong and party all donned mourning clothes and performed the rites of lamentation three times. They faced east and bowed in veneration."
73. On the archaeology of the Tsukushi Lodge/Kōrokan, the best sources are the original site reports. The report for 2004 is the most useful because it contains a summary of the results of all investigations to date: Fukuoka shi kyōiku iinkai, ed., *Kōrokan ato 14,* pp. 1–86. On the archaeology of

the Dazaifu headquarters, see Dazaifu shishi henshū iinkai, ed., *Dazaifu shishi kōko shiryō hen,* pp. 193–334, and Kyūshū rekishi shiryōkan, ed., *Dazaifu seichō ato.*

74. This claim is made so frequently that it is difficult to know whose idea it originally was. As an example, see Ishimatsu Yoshio and Kuwahara Shigeo, *Kodai Nihon o hakkutsu suru 4 Dazaifu to Tagajō,* pp. 4–5.
75. Kyūshū rekishi shiryōkan, ed., *Dazaifu fukugen,* p. 27. With apologies to the authors of all the learned texts cited elsewhere in these notes, this beautifully illustrated, easy-to-read, but completely obscure volume—the catalogue for a 1998 exhibition commemorating thirty years of excavation at Dazaifu—is probably the best single-volume introduction on Dazaifu available in any language.
76. Ibid., p. 9. More research of this type is needed, but for some reason few authors care to undertake it.
77. The concept of "centralized bureaucratic empires" comes from S. N. Eisenstadt, *The Political Systems of Empires.*
78. This is the traditional English translation of the Japanese term *tennō.* Joan R. Piggott has argued forcefully that "[t]erms such as *empire, emperor,* and *imperial* are not appropriate for the Japanese context" (Piggott, *The Emergence of Japanese Kingship,* p. 9). Her reasoning is as follows: (1) "Emperor" has been used to translate *tennō* because of the "assumption of strong parallels between Chinese and Japanese kingship," but in fact "structures of paramount leadership in the two societies have taken very different forms." (2) "[T]he translation of *tennō* as *emperor* is problematic because the term *empire* is strongly associated with a martial political formation founded on conquest—consider the imperial states of Rome, Persia, and China. In contrast, the *tennō* of eighth-century Nihon did not conquer his realm, he had no standing army save some frontier forces, and the realm remained significantly segmented rather than vertically subjugated" (p. 8). I respect Piggott's literal translation of *tennō* as "heavenly sovereign" (not to mention the more substantive aspects of her research). However, I do not think it necessary, or even desirable, to discard the term "emperor" and its cognates. This is not the place for a lengthy discussion, but in brief, my reasoning is as follows: (1) Although there were important differences between Japanese and Chinese structures of leadership, as Piggott herself acknowledges, "[t]hose who shaped the office of the *tennō* did take as their model structures of Chinese monarchy" (p. 9). In other words, the office was *intended* to be imperial. The second Chinese character in the two-character compound *tennō* very clearly signifies "emperor" rather than "king" or the plain-vanilla "sovereign." (2) Regarding Piggott's second point, that Japan was not really an "empire," there are many possible definitions of this word, but even taking hers at face value, the fact of the matter is that eighth-century Japan *was* a "martial political formation

founded on conquest." The Nara state conquered and incorporated tribal groups on its frontiers to the southwest (the Hayato in Kyushu) and northeast (the Emishi in Honshu). Although admittedly smaller in scale than Rome or China, Japan was indeed a multiethnic state based on conquest—an "empire," ruled by an "emperor."

79. Kawazoe Shōji et al., eds., *Kadokawa Nihon chimei daijiten 40 Fukuoka ken,* p. 1171.
80. On the geology of the area and changes in the coastline, see the essays in Kobayashi Shigeru et al., eds., *Fukuoka heiya no kokankyō to iseki ritchi.* The most egregious case of filling in the bay occurred in the early 2000s when the City of Fukuoka built an artificial island measuring 410 hectares in the eastern half of the bay. I am grateful to my friend Ikeda Manami for providing me with the background information on this case.
81. According to "defense procedures" codified in 732, "at least 100 ships are to be kept at Hakata Bay and at strategic points on Iki and Tsushima to prepare for the unexpected." *Shoku Nihongi,* Tenpyō Hōji 3 (759) 3/24.
82. Hino Takashi, "Saikaidō ni okeru ōji (San'yōdō) ni tsuite," esp. map on p. 191.
83. On roads in the area, see Hino Takashi, "Saikaidō," pp. 272–286.
84. On the archaeology of the various fortifications, see (in addition to the works cited in note 61, above) Dazaifu shishi henshū iinkai, ed., *Dazaifu shishi kōko shiryō hen,* pp. 395–436.
85. On Heijō-kyō, in particular, see Tsuboi Kiyotari and Tanaka Migaku, *The Historic City of Nara.*
86. On the archaeology of the Dazaifu city, see Kinda Akihiro, *Kodai Nihon no keikan,* pp. 185–249, and Dazaifu shishi henshū iinkai, ed., *Dazaifu shishi kōko shiryō hen,* pp. 335–394 and 733–746.
87. On the archaeology of the administrative offices, see the sources cited in note 73 above.
88. I.e., *Shoku Nihongi.*
89. On the Dazaifu and the Kyushu provinces, see Kurazumi, *Kodai no Dazaifu,* pp. 151–162.
90. For details, see ibid., pp. 139–151.
91. Indeed, contemporary sources refer to Dazaifu as the "hub of the nine provinces and two islands": *Ruijū sandai kyaku* 18, Tenchō 3 (826) 11/3 *Daijōkanpu,* p. 554.
92. On financial administration in Kyushu, see Hirano Kunio, "Dazaifu no chōzei kikō," and Okafuji Yoshitaka, "Dazaifu zaisei to kannai shokoku."
93. Some material collected from the six provinces was also funneled through Dazaifu to the frontier provinces of Iki, Tsushima, Ōsumi, and Satsuma, which were too poor to support their own operations. Hirano, "Dazaifu no chōzei kikō," and Okafuji, "Dazaifu zaisei to kannai shokoku."
94. *Nihon Montoku tennō jitsuroku,* Ninju 2 (852) 2/8.

95. *Shoku Nihongi,* Hōki 11 (780) 7/26, and *Ruijū sandai kyaku* 18, Hōki 11/7/26 *choku,* vol. 2, p. 547.
96. See sources cited in previous note.
97. On *sakimori,* see Kishi Toshio, *Nihon kodai seijishi kenkyū,* pp. 289–316; Naoki Kōjirō, *Asuka Nara jidai no kenkyū,* pp. 247–255; Noda Reishi, *Sakimori to eji;* Hōjō Hideki, *Nihon kodai kokka no chihō shihai,* pp. 171–196; and Chō Yōichi, "Sakimori o meguru mondai."
98. *Ryōnogige* 17, *Gunbōryō,* clause 55 *(Bōjin kōbō jō),* p. 198 (*Ritsuryō,* p. 336).
99. Translation by Paula Doe, *A Warbler's Song in the Dusk,* pp. 219–220.
100. *Nihon shoki,* Tenmu 14/12/4.
101. *Ryōnogige* 17, *Gunbōryō,* clause 59 *(Yokushi jō),* p. 199 (*Ritsuryō,* p. 336).
102. *Ryōnogige* 17, *Gunbōryō,* clause 62 *(Zaibō jō),* p. 200 (*Ritsuryō,* p. 337).
103. *Ryōnogige* 17, *Gunbōryō,* clause 63 *(Kyūka jō),* p. 200 (*Ritsuryō,* pp. 337–338).
104. There are many excellent books on Roman frontier defense; good starting points are Alan K. Bowman, *Life and Letters on the Roman Frontier;* Hugh Elton, *Frontiers of the Roman Empire;* and Steven K. Drummond and Lynn H. Nelson, *The Western Frontiers of Imperial Rome.*
105. *Ryōnogige* 17, *Gunbōryō,* clause 61 *(Bōjin bankan jō),* p. 199 (*Ritsuryō,* p. 337).
106. On which, see Batten, "State and Frontier in Early Japan," pp. 171–172.
107. A good introduction to Japanese foreign relations in the eighth and ninth centuries is Ishii Masatoshi, *Higashi Ajia sekai to kodai no Nihon.* (The notes to chapter 2 herein list references to other more-detailed, country-specific works.) Regarding Parhae, this is the Korean reading of the characters used to write the country's name; some works in English opt instead for the Chinese pronunciation, Bohai. The country itself was situated largely within modern Russia (Siberia) and northeast China, not Korea (either north or south). Although the general population consisted of proto-Manchu tribesmen, the ruling class was descended from the Koguryŏ elite. Since they presumably referred to their country by its Korean pronunciation, Parhae, I will do the same—with apologies to Sakayori Masashi, who tried to persuade me to use the Chinese reading, on grounds that this was a multiethnic state and that Chinese was the lingua franca of the period.
108. E.g., Kozo Yamamura, "The Decline of the *Ritsuryō* System."
109. On this topic, see William Wayne Farris, *Population, Disease, and Land in Early Japan, 645–900,* esp. pp. 141–149. Farris ignores the international context, but otherwise his analysis is sound.
110. For background information on changes in military administration in general, see Karl F. Friday, *Hired Swords,* and William Wayne Farris, *Heavenly Warriors.*

111. *Ruijū sandai kyaku* 18, Tenchō 3 (826) 1/3 *Daijōkanpu,* p. 554.
112. Unless you want to count the "Toi Invasion" of 1019, which is discussed in chapter 3 herein under the category of "piracy." Another example from modern history, of course, would be the terminal phase of the Pacific War and the subsequent American occupation of Japan.
113. In Japanese, see (for example) Amino Yoshihiko, *Mōko shūrai;* Saeki Kōji, *Mongoru shūrai no shōgeki;* and (for its excellent illustrations) Nishizono Reizō and Yanagida Sumitaka, *Genkō to Hakata.* In English, see Thomas D. Conlan, *In Little Need of Divine Intervention;* Kyotsu Hori, "The Economic and Political Effects of the Mongol Wars"; Ishii Susumu, "The Decline of the Kamakura Bakufu," pp. 131–148; Kawazoe Shōji, "Japan and East Asia," pp. 411–423; and Morris Rossabi, *Khubilai Khan,* pp. 99–103 and 207–213.
114. Conlan, *In Little Need of Divine Intervention,* pp. 266–267.
115. Ibid., p. 275.
116. On which, see Rossabi, *Khubilai Khan,* pp. 213–220.
117. See the works cited in note 113 above.

Chapter 2: Diplomacy

1. Even if authors do not explicitly state this bias, it is apparent from their research agendas. This is not to denigrate, of course, the excellent research that has been done on early Sino-Japanese relations. Three particularly important studies are Edwin O. Reischauer, *Ennin's Travels in T'ang China;* Charlotte von Verschuer, *Les relations officielles du Japon avec la Chine aux VIIIe et IXe siècles;* and Zhen-ping Wang, "Sino-Japanese Relations before the Eleventh Century."
2. A point argued strongly by Lee Sungsi, *Higashi Ajia no ōken to kōeki.* Although the bias is not as pronounced as in English-language scholarship, Japanese studies of ancient foreign relations also tend to favor China. It is interesting, although perhaps not surprising, to find this bias being criticized by Lee, a Korean resident of Japan.
3. Needless to say, there are many works on this subject in Japanese. In addition to the book by Lee cited in the previous note, the best one-volume studies of the past few decades include Suzuki Yasutami, *Kodai taigai kankei shi no kenkyū;* Hamada Kōsaku, *Shiragi kokushi no kenkyū;* and Ishii Masatoshi, *Higashi Ajia sekai to kodai no Nihon.* In English, not much has been written on the Japan-Silla relationship. Charlotte von Verschuer has, however, published an exceedingly valuable survey of Japanese research on foreign relations in general: "Looking from Within and Without: Ancient and Medieval External Relations."
4. This argument originates with Tamura Enchō. See Tamura, *Dazaifu tankyū,* pp. 73–74.
5. On early Japan as a ritual-centered "theater state" (a concept originating with Clifford Geertz), see Piggott, *The Emergence of Japanese Kingship.*

6. There was a vigorous, even somewhat acrimonious, debate in Japanese between Ishii Masatoshi (*Nihon Bokkai kankeishi no kenkyū,* pp. 576–653) and Nakanishi Masakazu ("Shiragishi, Bokkaishi no raichō to Dazaifu"; "Dazaifu to zonmon"; and "Bokkaishi no raichō to Tenchō gonen shōgatsu futsuka kanpu") regarding whether authority to open "state letters" was in fact vested with the central commissioners or with Dazaifu, with Ishii taking the former position and Nakanishi taking the latter. Ishii is correct, I believe, in arguing that the officials at Dazaifu did not have authority to open state letters on their own (see Bruce Batten, *Kokkyō no tanjō,* pp. 138–149). Although to the uninitiated this debate may seem arcane, it is important because it relates to the degree of centralization of the Nara state. How much authority, in other words, did central authorities delegate to local organs of government such as Dazaifu? The correct answer to this question, in my opinion, is "no more than absolutely necessary"—hence the dispatch of central commissioners to read diplomatic correspondence and perform other duties relating to the reception of foreign embassies in Kyushu.
7. *Shoku Nihongi,* Tenpyō Hōji 4 (760) 9/16.
8. This and other quotations regarding Kim T'aeryŏm's visit are from *Shoku Nihongi,* dates as noted, so I have not bothered to cite each one separately.
9. On the system of official highways in use in the eighth century, see Kinoshita Ryō, ed., *Kodai o kangaeru.*
10. The standard pronunciation of the name today is "Dejima," but it appears as "Deshima" in contemporary Dutch sources. See, for example, Englebert Kaempfer, *Kaempfer's Japan.*
11. *Nihon shoki,* Suiko 16 (608) 6/15, translated in Aston, *Nihongi,* vol. 2, p. 136.
12. *Engishiki* 21, *Genba-ryō,* p. 546.
13. Ibid.
14. See Hirano Takuji, "San'yōdō to kyakukan," for a detailed argument to this effect. Although from a slightly later period, *Nihon kōki,* Daidō 1 (806) 5/14, states that station houses along the San'yōdō had fallen into disrepair and that visiting envoys now made use of the sea route.
15. Greeting procedures at Naniwa are described in *Engishiki* 21, *Genba-ryō,* pp. 546–547. They closely match the description of the reception given to the above-mentioned Chinese envoys in 608. *Nihon shoki,* Suiko 16/6/15, translated in Aston, *Nihongi,* vol. 2, pp. 136–137. That rituals of this kind could remain virtually unchanged for three hundred years is a powerful reminder of the importance of tradition in ancient Japan.
16. *Shoku Nihongi,* Hōki 10 (779) 4/21, retroactively states, "Also, on the day Silla's tribute envoy Prince T'aeryŏm entered the capital, officials were ordered to go by horse to greet him. The guests drew their reins tight and gave their thanks from horseback."

17. On the guesthouse in Heijō-kyō, see Hirano Takuji, "Nihon kodai no kyakukan ni kansuru ichikōsatsu."
18. *Nihon shoki,* Shuchō 1 (685) 4/19 and Jitō 2 (688) 2/2.
19. *Engishiki* 30, *Ōkura-shō,* p. 739.
20. Wm. Theodore de Bary et al., eds., *Sources of Japanese Tradition,* vol. 1, p. 11. Original in *Chūgoku seishi Nihon den 1,* p. 100.
21. *Nihon shoki,* Suiko 16 (608) 6/15, translated in Aston, *Nihongi,* vol. 2, p. 137. This was no isolated incident, either; subsequent Chinese edicts to the Japanese sovereign, even when delivered, were conveniently filed away (possibly in the circular file?) without publicity. Tōno Haruyuki, "Japanese Embassies to T'ang China and Their Ships," pp. 51–52.
22. See Wang Zhen-ping, "Sino-Japanese Relations before the Eleventh Century," pp. 218–263, and Nishijima Sadao, "Kentōshi to kokusho."
23. E.g., Ishii Masatoshi, "8, 9 seiki no Nichi-Ra kankei." For discussion of other examples see Lee Sungsi, *Higashi Ajia no ōken to kōeki,* pp. 107–109.
24. For the definitive analysis of these documents see Tōno Haruyuki, *Shōsōin monjo to mokkan no kenkyū,* pp. 298–347.
25. In a later example, from 768, the government made outright gifts of huge quantities of silk floss from Dazaifu (Kyushu was a major producer of silk at this time) to members of the central aristocracy for use in purchasing goods from Silla. *Shoku Nihongi,* Jingo Keiun 2 (768) 10/24 and 30.
26. Even if the envoys were selling goods on their own (as most scholars assume), they were clearly doing so under official supervision. Both sellers and—particularly—buyers would have been clearly aware that these transactions only took place by imperial largesse. As Lee Sungsi has emphasized, the auctions thus served as a visible demonstration of the empress's monopoly on foreign relations and the nobility's dependency on her for access to much-desired foreign exotica. Lee, *Higashi Ajia no ōken to kōeki,* pp. 107–129.
27. Ibid. I should note that Lee's arguments in this regard have been subjected to excoriating criticism by Ishii Masatoshi, *Nihon Bokkai kankei shi no kenkyū,* pp. 42–58. Ishii does, I believe, successfully demonstrate the lack of solid evidence for Lee's contention that the embassy was sent because of Silla's troubles with Parhae. However, Ishii ignores Lee's larger (and in my view, correct) point that trade was inextricably linked with political considerations in this period.
28. *Shoku Nihongi,* Tenypō Shōhō 4 (752) 4/9.
29. These ideas come from Tamura Enchō, *Dazaifu tankyū,* pp. 159–177. Also see Tamura, *Higashi Ajia no kokka to Bukkyō,* pp. 265–266.
30. Actually, the situation may be a bit more complicated than this, since *Chronicles of Japan* mentions two other diplomatic facilities in this general period, a "Tsukushi Ōkōri" (*Nihon shoki,* Tenmu 2 [673] 11/21)

and a "Tsukushi Ogōri" (ibid., Jitō 3 [689] 6/24). The relationship of these facilities (which make no further appearances in the historical record) to the Tsukushi Lodge is unclear. The first reference to the Tsukushi Lodge is from 688 (ibid., Jitō 2/2/10).

31. Similarly, and for the same reasons, Japanese regimes tended to place bans on foreign travel by private Japanese individuals. The ban enforced by the Edo shogunate is well-known, but a similar situation applied in the Nara and Heian eras. Enomoto Jun'ichi, "'Shōyūki' ni mieru 'tokai kinsei' ni tsuite." Again, the exception was the Sengoku period, when many Japanese traveled overseas.
32. *Nihon sandai jitsuroku,* Jōgan 12 (870) 2/20.
33. Murai Shōsuke, *Ajia no naka no chūsei Nihon,* p. 111, and Murai, "The Boundaries of Medieval Japan," p. 73.
34. Hotate Michihisa, *Ōgon kokka,* pp. 231–238.
35. *Nihon sandai jitsuroku,* Jōgan 8 (866) 7/15.
36. *Nihon sandai jitsuroku,* Jōgan 12/11/13 and 17.
37. This point is also made by W. J. Boot, "Maxims of Foreign Policy," with regard to the Edo period.
38. A point first made by William H. McNeill, *Plagues and Peoples,* p. 124.
39. On this epidemic, see Farris, *Population, Disease, and Land in Early Japan,* pp. 50–73.
40. *Nihon sandai jitsuroku,* Jōgan 14/1/20.
41. *Shoku Nihongi,* Tenpyō 5 (735) 8/12.
42. *Engishiki* 3, *Jingi* 3, p. 66.
43. Ōba Kōji, personal communication, March 23, 2004. One also has to consider the lodging requirements for Japanese administrative personnel (Dazaifu officials) and border guards, or *sakimori,* who would have been responsible for keeping tabs on the visitors. Would some of these also have stayed in the Tsukushi Lodge? If so, the facilities would have been even more crowded. My own guess is that the lodge was probably reserved for foreign visitors and that Japanese personnel either camped out or stayed in another (as yet undiscovered) facility nearby.
44. Another possibility is that the dock was at Aratsu just west of the promontory atop which the lodge was located.
45. *Ryōnogige* 1, *Shokuinryō, Dazaifu jō,* p. 60 (*Ritsuryō,* pp. 191–192).
46. Itakusu Kazuko, "Shuchūshi kō." See *Engishiki* 24, *Shukei jō,* pp. 619–622, for a detailed (indeed, presumably complete) list of foodstuffs and other tax goods sent to Dazaifu from the Kyushu provinces.
47. Kanehara Masaaki and Kanehara Masako, "Kōrokan ato no dokō (benjo ikō) ni okeru kiseichūran, kafun, shujitsu no dōtei bunseki." Unless otherwise noted, all information given in this paragraph about the contents of the latrines is taken from this article.
48. Ibid., pp. 30 and 37.
49. Ōta kuritsu kyōdo hakubutsukan, ed., *Toire no kōkogaku,* pp. 34–35. I

am grateful to Ikezaki Jōji of the Fukuoka City Board of Education for calling my attention to this work.

50. *Ryōnogige* 1, *Shokuinryō, Dazaifu jō*, p. 60 (*Ritsuryō*, pp. 190–191). The term *ban*, which I have rendered as "vassal states," is sometimes incorrectly translated as "barbarian." (There is another character with the same pronunciation that *does* mean "barbarian," which is perhaps the source of this particular confusion.) Technically, the *ban* in question refers to foreign dependencies. Of course, Japan had no actual dependencies overseas, but for the reasons described in this chapter, countries such as Silla and Parhae were whenever possible treated as subordinate.
51. For an excellent description of diplomatic receptions in early Japan (for guests from Parhae, not Silla, and held at the capital, not Dazaifu), see Robert Borgen, *Sugawara no Michizane and the Early Heian Court*, pp. 228–240.
52. *Shoku Nihongi*, Hōki 1 (770) 3/4. The purpose of Kim Ch'ojŏng's visit was to deliver letters from Fujiwara Kiyokawa and Abe Nakamaro, two Japanese diplomats stranded in China after their ships had been wrecked. The letters had found their way to Silla via a Korean prince who met the two Japanese while the prince was serving in the Tang imperial guard.
53. Unless, of course, Nakano's hypothesis about toilets segregated by sex is correct, in which case it is possible that the envoys were entertained by wine, women, and song. However, as noted, there is no substantiating evidence for this idea.
54. On Michizane, see Borgen, *Sugawara no Michizane and the Early Heian Court*. Michizane's role in ending the missions to Tang is described on pp. 240–253.
55. On Japanese relations with Parhae, see Ueda Takashi, *Bokkai koku no nazo;* Ueda Takashi and Song Yongong, *Nihon Bokkai kōshōshi;* Sakayori Masashi, *Bokkai to kodai no Nihon;* Ishii Masatoshi, *Nihon Bokkai kankeishi no kenkyū;* and Satō Makoto, ed., *Nihon to Bokkai no kodaishi*. In English, see Borgen, *Sugawara no Michizane and the Early Heian Court*, pp. 228–240.
56. See *Shoku Nihongi*, Hōki 4/6/24 and Hōki 8/1/24.
57. On which, see Kōjiya Yoshiaki, ed., *Matsubara kyakukan no nazo ni semaru*.
58. A detailed discussion of these various envoys and their reception in Japan appears in Ishigami Eiichi, "Nihon kodai 10 seiki no gaikō," pp. 118–134.
59. On medieval foreign relations, probably the best source in English is Kawazoe, "Japan and East Asia."

Chapter 3: Piracy

1. Enomoto Jun'ichi, "'Shōyūki' ni mieru 'tokai kinsei' ni tsuite."
2. *Tosōki*, Eihō 2 (1082) 9/5, p. 50. Clerics who wished to study abroad could apply for a special "exit visa," although these seem to have been

difficult to obtain. For an example of such a visa, see Ninju 3 (853) 2/11 *Dazaifu chō,* in *Heian ibun,* vol. 1, p. 89 (doc. #102). This document was issued by Dazaifu to the priest Enchin.

3. Yamauchi Shinji, *Nara Heian ki no Nihon to Ajia,* pp. 111–112; Ki-baik Lee, *A New History of Korea,* pp. 92–98.
4. *Nihon kōki,* Kōnin 3 (812) 1/5.
5. Largely, one suspects, because there had been little direct contact between Tsushima and Korea since the emergence of the international boundary in the late seventh century.
6. *Nihon kiryaku,* Kōnin 4/3/18.
7. *Ruijū sandai kyaku* 5, Kōnin 4/9/29 *Daijōkanpu,* p. 217.
8. On Chang Pogo, see Reischauer, *Ennin's Travels in T'ang China,* pp. 272–294, and Hamada Kōsaku, "Sovereignty and Maritime Power."
9. *Shoku Nihon kōki,* Jōwa 8 (841) 2/27.
10. *Ruijū sandai kyaku* 18, Hōki 5 (774) 5/17 *Daijōkanpu,* p. 569. On the treatment of castaways, see Yamauchi, *Nara Heian ki no Nihon to Ajia,* pp. 67–108.
11. The story that follows is taken in its entirety from *Shoku Nihon kōki,* Jōwa 9/1/10.
12. *Ruijū sandai kyaku* 18, Jōwa 9/8/15 *Daijōkanpu,* p. 570; *Shoku Nihon kōki,* Jōwa 9/8/15.
13. See sources cited in previous note. Korean merchants were also prohibited at this time from staying in the Kōrokan—the old Tsukushi Lodge; presumably this meant that they had to stay aboard their ships anchored in Hakata bay, unless of course, they could manage to convince Dazaifu officials that they were Chinese, rather than Korean.
14. Again, on immigration and castaways, see Yamauchi, *Nara Heian ki no Nihon to Ajia,* pp. 67–108.
15. *Nihon sandai jitsuroku,* Jōgan 11/6/15.
16. Ibid., Jōgan 11/7/2.
17. Ibid.
18. *Fusō ryakki,* Kanpyō 6 (894) 9/5.
19. At any rate, this is one possible reading of a difficult passage. For discussion, see Yamauchi, *Nara Heian ki no Nihon to Ajia,* p. 112 and pp. 125–126, n. 1.
20. *Ruijū sandai kyaku* 16, Enryaku 15 (796) 11/21 *Daijōkanpu,* pp. 495–496.
21. *Sumitomo tsuitōki,* quoted in *Fusō ryakki,* Tengyō 3 (941) 11.
22. Ibid. Among other things, this passage raises the interesting question of why women were aboard the pirate vessels; unfortunately, no further information is available on this point.
23. *Honchō seiki,* Tengyō 4/11/5, reports that Tōyasu killed Sumitomo and his son and sent their heads to court.
24. On the archaeology of the Dazaifu headquarters, see Kyūshū rekishi

shiryōkan, ed., *Dazaifu seichō ato,* and Dazaifu shishi henshū iinkai, ed., *Dazaifu shishi kōko shiryō hen,* pp. 175–746. The layer of scorched earth and its implications are discussed, respectively, on p. 56 and p. 202 of these publications.

25. *Shōyūki,* Chōtoku 3 (997) 10/1. Other sources on these and similar raids: *Nihon kiryaku,* Chōtoku 3/10/1, Chōtoku 3/11/2, Chōtoku 4/9/14, and Chōhō 1 (999) 8/19; and *Hyakurenshō,* Chōtoku 3/10/1 and Chōtoku 4/2.
26. Except where otherwise noted, all information and quotations relating to the Toi invasion are taken from *Chōya gunsai* 20, Kannin 3 (1019) 4/16 *Dazaifu ge,* pp. 459–461.
27. *Shōyūki,* Kannin 3/6/29.
28. From the letter by Takaie quoted in *Shōyūki,* Kannin 3/4/25. The following two paragraphs are also based on this source.
29. *Shōyūki,* Kannin 3/4/17, 3/4/18; *Nihon kiryaku,* Kannin 3/4/17, 3/4/18; *Fusō ryakki,* Kannin 3/4/18.
30. Details are given in *Shōyūki,* Kannin 3/6/29.
31. On the general political background, see Ki-baik Lee, *A New History of Korea,* pp. 124–126.
32. *Koryŏ sa* 4, Hyŏnjong 10 (1019) 4/29, *Koryŏ sa chŏryo,* Hyŏnjong 10/4/29.
33. *Shōyūki,* Kannin 3/9/19, 3/9/22, 3/9/23, and 3/9/24; *Sakeiki,* Kannin 3/9/22; *Nihon kiryaku,* Kannin 3/9/22.
34. *Shōyūki,* Kannin 3/8/3.
35. The traditional figures for the Mongol invasions are 32,000 men in 1274 and 142,000 men (42,000 via Korea and 100,000 from China) in 1281. Conlan, *In Little Need of Divine Intervention,* pp. 261–264, casts doubt on these numbers, arguing for forces of 2,000–3,000 and perhaps 10,000, respectively. The Toi forces can be estimated by multiplying the fifty ships that attacked Tsushima by the 50–60 men per ship seen at Hakata, for a total of 2,500–3,000. Of course, these figures may be inflated as well, but at least they are based on eyewitness accounts.
36. In a sense, the Kamakura government did a better job of coastal defense than the Heian court: it responded to the Mongol attacks by building a wall around Hakata Bay and creating a permanent defense system, whereas the court took no such actions following the Toi attack—either because the latter was correctly perceived as a onetime event or, equally likely, because the court was too weak to implement such a scheme.
37. Conlan, *In Little Need of Divine Intervention,* pp. 271–275.

Chapter 4: Trade

1. On Wu Yue, see Worthy, "Diplomacy for Survival." On the country's diplomatic initiatives vis-à-vis Japan, see Ishigami, "Nihon kodai 10 seiki no gaikō," pp. 125–130.

2. Two other important ports, Fuzhou and Quanzhou, did not become part of Wu Yue's territory until 947.
3. Except where otherwise noted, my discussion of the ship and its arrival in Japan is based on the following report by Dazaifu: Tengyō 8 (945) 6/25 *Dazaifu ge,* quoted in *Honchō seiki,* entry for Tengyō 8/7/26.
4. Tajima Isao's chronology of foreign relations states that three ships arrived in Hizen, not one, an interpretation apparently based on the fact that three "captains" are listed in the original source: Tajima, "Nihon, Chūgoku, Chōsen taigai kōryū nenpyō," p. 464. This interpretation is also followed by Hotate, *Ōgon kokka,* p. 244. The presence of multiple "captains" is admittedly confusing, but the original source, cited in the previous note, clearly states that there was only one ship.
5. For details of ship construction, see Shiba Yoshinobu, *Commerce and Society in Sung China,* pp. 6–10, and Writing Group Reporting on the Excavation of a Sung Dynasty Seagoing Vessel at Ch'üan-chou Bay, "A Brief Report on the Excavation of a Sung Dynasty Seagoing Vessel at Ch'üan-chou Bay." The vessel in question was discovered in 1973 and excavated the following year. Apparently dating from the late thirteenth century, the hulk contained a cargo of lakawood, sandalwood, gharuwood, pepper, betel nuts, frankincense, ambergris, cinnabar, mercury, tortoiseshell, and other goods from Southeast Asia, Africa, and the Arabian Peninsula.
6. On labor and management in the Chinese shipping business, see Shiba, *Commerce and Society in Sung China,* pp. 15–40.
7. Tōno Haruyuki, *Kentōshisen,* p. 90.
8. The reading "Himosaki" is a guess; this place-name no longer exists. Yūgen gaisha Heibonsha chihō shiryō sentā, ed., *Nagasaki ken no chimei,* p. 257, equates "Himosaki" with "Hinomisaki," placing it in the Nomo region at the southern tip of Nagasaki Peninsula.
9. Although use of the alternate character *sho* (place) may be significant. Recall that Dazaifu was burned down in 941 by the pirate leader Fujiwara Sumitomo. It is by no means impossible that the Kōrokan and other facilities along Hakata Bay suffered a similar fate. If so, "Kōrosho" could mean "[former] location of the Kōro[-kan]."
10. *Teishinkōkishō,* Tengyō 8/7/29, in *Teishinkōki,* p. 219.
11. *Honchō seiki,* Tengyō 8/8/5.
12. According to *Chōya gunsai* 5, Ōtoku 2 (1085) 10/29 *jin no sadame,* p. 131, weather conditions for the crossing were best in the second and eighth months. For a brief description of how seasonal winds affected travel across the East China Sea, see Tōno, *Kentōshisen,* p. 90.
13. *Honchō seiki,* Tengyō 8/10/20. Another source indicates that two trade commissioners were sent. They came from the emperor's private secretariat, known as the Kurōdodokoro or Chamberlains' Office. See *Shingishiki, Daitō shōkyaku no koto,* p. 76.

14. In addition to the goods offered for sale, Chinese merchants also seem to have brought presents (oddly, referred to as *kamotsu* or "freight") for the Japanese court. These can be interpreted as bribes to obtain permission to trade, or they can be viewed as a kind of "tribute." The latter view is taken by Yamauchi, *Nara Heian ki no Nihon to Ajia*, pp. 177–181.
15. *Shingishiki, Daitō shōkyaku no koto*, p. 76.
16. *Teishinkōkishō*, Tengyō 8/2/23, in *Teishinkōki*, p. 227.
17. An important book on Japanese external commerce from its origins to the sixteenth century is Charlotte von Verschuer, *Le commerce extérieur du Japon*. Although I will not be citing this work regarding individual points (mainly because of my linguistic inadequacies), it is a pioneering work relevant to this entire chapter.
18. George F. Hourani, *Arab Seafaring*, pp. 46–50, 61–79; Wang Gungwu, *The Nanhai Trade*, pp. 52–53, 72–73, 75, and 96–98; Tansen Sen, *Buddhism, Diplomacy, and Trade*, pp. 142–196. As all of these works make clear, the origins of maritime trade in Asia are very ancient. Nonetheless, as indicated, the seventh and eighth centuries saw a very significant increase in the scale of commercial activity.
19. Edwin O. Reischauer, "Notes on T'ang Dynasty Sea Routes."
20. On whom, see Reischauer, *Ennin's Travels in T'ang China*, pp. 272–294, and Hamada, "Sovereignty and Maritime Power."
21. By Hamada, "Sovereignty and Maritime Power," p. 134.
22. *Ruijū sandai kyaku* 18, Tenchō 8 (831) 9/7 *Daijōkanpu*, pp. 569–570. Some scholars believe that merchants from Silla began coming to Japan in the late eighth century. Evidence for this consists of archaeological finds of pottery from Silla (which could have been brought by diplomatic embassies and thus do not constitute proof of anything) and two historical sources. (1) The first, *Shoku Nihongi*, Jingo Keiun 2 (768) 10/24 and 30, records the disbursement of silk floss to central nobles for the purpose of purchasing "Silla trade goods." Hotate, *Ōgon kokka*, pp. 72–74, takes these entries as prima facie evidence for the presence of Korean merchants. I think it is just as likely that the floss was intended to be used to purchase goods brought by diplomatic envoys. Admittedly, no embassy from Silla was in Japan at this time (the next one arrived the following year, in 769), but as Tamura, *Dazaifu tankyū*, pp. 191–192, notes, the disbursement could have been made in advance, on the expectation that envoys would be arriving soon. Alternatively, the floss could have been used to purchase goods previously brought by Korean emissaries that were now in the possession of Dazaifu or some other organ of government. (2) The second source, *Ruijū sandai kyaku* 18, Hōki 5 (774) 5/7 *Daijōkanpu*, p. 569, also contained in *Shoku Nihongi*, same date, is a state council order regarding the repatriation of men from Silla who have "drifted" to Japan. Tanaka Fumio, *Nihon kodai kokka no minzoku shihai to toraijin*, pp. 210–255, thinks that

many of these "castaways" were in fact merchants. Hotate, *Ōgon kokka,* pp. 97–99, citing Tanaka, goes one step further and proposes that this document created a legal framework for the "immigration control" of merchants. Not only is there no direct evidence that the "castaways" referred to in 774 were merchants, but the document in question specifically states that these men "do not come of their own will." In short, while it is theoretically possible that Korean merchants were visiting Japan in the late eighth century, there is no solid evidence, either archaeological or historical, to support this claim.

23. Jōgan 13 (871) 8/17 *Anshōji garan engi shizaichō,* in *Heian ibun,* vol. 1, p. 141 (doc. #164).
24. *Ruijū sandai kyaku* 18, Tenchō 8/9/7 *Daijōkanpu,* p. 570.
25. *Chōya gunsai,* Enkyū 2 (1070) 12/7 *jin no sadame,* pp. 130–131.
26. *Ruijū sandai kyaku* 18, Tenchō 8/9/7 *Daijōkanpu,* pp. 569–570.
27. These institutional changes are discussed in more detail in Bruce Batten, "Cross-Border Traffic on the Kyushu Coast, 794–1086." In Japanese some of the major studies are Mori Katsumi, *Shintei Nissō bōeki no kenkyū;* Ishigami, "Nihon kodai 10 seiki no gaikō," pp. 109–118; Inagawa Yayoi, "'Tokai-sei' to 'karamono-no-tsukai' no kentō"; and Ishii Masatoshi, "10 seiki no kokusai hendō to Nissō bōeki."
28. *Ruijū sandai kyaku* 18, Jōwa 9 (842) 8/15 *Daijōkanpu,* p. 570; *Shoku Nihon kōki,* Jōwa 9/8/15.
29. The first example of a centrally dispatched trade commissioner seems to be from 862. Matsubara Hironobu, "Chin Taishin no shojō to karamono-kōeki-shi no seiritsu."
30. At the same time, the shift toward silk and porcelain may also reflect economic factors, specifically the explosive growth of these industries under the Song dynasty.
31. On which, see Ethan Segal, "Economic Growth and Changes in Elite Power Structures in Medieval Japan, 1150–1500," pp. 25–62.
32. On sulfur, see Yamauchi, *Nara Heian ki no Nihon to Ajia,* pp. 249–257. Yamauchi also argues that Kyushu rice *(Chinzeimai)* may also have been exported, partly again for use as ballast. Ibid., pp. 246–248.
33. For discussion of several important exports—swords, Japanese paper or *washi,* mother-of-pearl work and lacquerware, and handheld fans—see von Verschuer, "Across the Sea," pp. 20–26.
34. *Midō kanpakuki,* Chōwa 4 (1015) 7/15, vol. 3, pp. 18–20.
35. Bruce Batten, "An Open and Shut Case?"
36. *Chōya gunsai* 20, Chōji 2 (1105) 8/5 *keigosho ge,* pp. 450–451; Chōji 2/8/22 *zonmonki,* pp. 451–452; Chongning 4 (1105) 6 *kōhyō,* pp. 452–455.
37. *Chōya gunsai* 5, Enkyū 2/12/7 *jin no sadame,* pp. 130–131.
38. This is not to say that the government was omniscient or omnipotent. Recall that in 945 Jiang Gun's ship was apparently not detected by

authorities until it left the Gotō Archipelago for mainland Kyushu. There are also several known cases of Japanese monks secretly (more or less) boarding Chinese merchant vessels. One example mentioned in the previous chapter is Kaikaku, who traveled to China in 1082. Another, more famous, example is Jōjin, who went to China in 1072 and spent the rest of his life (ending in 1081) there. Regarding Jōjin, see Robert Borgen, "The Case of the Plagiaristic Journal"; "Japanese Nationalism"; "Jōjin's Travels from Center to Center (With Some Periphery in Between)"; "*San Tendai Godai sanki* as a Source for the Study of Sung History"; and "Through Several Glasses Brightly."

39. The following is based on the much more detailed analysis in Batten, "An Open and Shut Case?"
40. Actually not just Heian times but the entire premodern period. Taigai kankei shi sōgō nenpyō henshū iinkai, ed., *Taigai kankei shi sōgō nenpyō*. Tajima, "Nihon, Chūgoku, Chōsen taigai kōryū nenpyō," provides a much greater level of detail for the Nara and Heian periods.
41. Nihon jinkō gakkai, ed. *Jinkō daijiten,* pp. 91–92.
42. For up-to-date figures see the home page of the Government of Japan's Statistics Bureau: http://www.stat.go.jp/data/nihon/02.htm.
43. Even this could be debated since that reference is to a "Kōrosho" rather than "Kōrokan" per se (see note 9, above). "Kōrokan" as a term is last seen (with reference to Hakata) in 873; see *Nihon sandai jitsuroku* Jōgan 15/9/25. On the demise of the Kōrokan as seen from historical sources, see Tajima Isao, "Dazaifu Kōrokan no shūen." The main point of Tajima's article is that a source from 1091 refers not to the Kōrokan in Hakata, as previously thought, but to a guesthouse in Kyoto (which had similarly long outlived its original function).
44. *Fusō ryakki,* Eishō 2 (1047) 11/9, and *Hyakurenshō,* Eishō 2/11.
45. No artifact related to the Kōrokan, that is. As described in the Introduction, the site was later used for a seventeenth-century castle, a nineteenth-century military barracks, and a twentieth-century baseball stadium. A convenient summary of the results of the first seventeen years (1987–2003) of excavation at the Kōrokan site can be found in Fukuoka shi kyōiku iinkai, *Kōrokan ato 14,* pt. 1 (pp. 1–86).
46. See the various essays in Kobayashi Shigeru et al., eds., *Fukuoka heiya no kokankyō to iseki ritchi.* This book represents a unique, cross-disciplinary effort by geologists, archaeologists, and historians, most of them based at Kyushu University in Fukuoka, to unravel the historical evolution of Hakata.
47. For general background on the history of Hakata the best single-volume reference is Kawazoe Shōji, ed., *Yomigaeru chūsei 1 Higashi Ajia no kokusai toshi Hakata.* On more specific aspects of Hakata's history, see the following articles by Saeki Kōji and Ōba Kōji: Saeki, "Hakata" and "Trade between Japan and Sung China and the *Hakata Gōshu*";

Ōba, "Shūsanchi iseki to shite no Hakata"; "Hakata gōshu no jidai"; and "Fukuoka shinai kenshutsu no kodai, chūsei dōro ikō ni tsuite."

48. On this point, see the analysis by von Verschuer, "Across the Sea," pp. 14–19. The chart on p. 19 summarizes von Verschuer's principal conclusions. An earlier version of the chart appears in von Verschuer's French-language book, *Le commerce extérieur du Japon,* p. 178.
49. On the rise of the Taira family in general, see Takahashi Masaaki, *Kiyomori izen.* On the Taira in Kyushu, see Shimada Jirō, "Horon."
50. Shimada, "Horon."

Chapter 5: Medieval Hakata

1. On medieval Hakata, see the sources cited in notes 46 and 47 to chapter 4, as well as the following popular books by Takeno Yōko: *Hakata no gōshō* and *Hakata: Chōnin ga sodadeta kokusai toshi.*
2. The following is based loosely on a walking tour I took of the area with Professor Saeki Kōji of Kyushu University on March 24, 2004. We were accompanied by Professor Sakaue Yasutoshi (who also appears in the Introduction to the present volume) and several graduate students from the same university. I am deeply indebted to Professor Saeki both for arranging the tour and for all the information he provided orally and in written form, much of which is reflected in the following paragraphs.
3. Saeki, *Mongoru shūrai no shōgeki,* pp. 45–46.
4. Hakata kenkyūkai, ed., *Hakata isekigun shutsudo bokusho shiryō shūsei,* and Ōba, "Hakata iseki shutsudo bokusho shiryō shūsei 2."
5. See the various articles by Ōba cited in note 47 to chapter 4.
6. For more information on the historical events described in this paragraph and below, see Kawazoe, ed., *Yomigaeru chūsei 1 Higashi Ajia no kokusai toshi Hakata,* and Saeki, *Mongoru shūrai no shōgeki.*
7. Regarding the invasions, see Mary Elizabeth Berry, *Hideyoshi,* pp. 207–217, and Jurgis Elisonas, "The Inseparable Trinity," pp. 265–293. In Japanese, Kitajima Manji, *Hideyoshi no Chōsen shinryaku,* is a good, readable introduction to the topic.
8. On Japanese communities abroad, see Thomas Nelson, "Southeast Asian Polities and Society as Seen through Japanese Communities," and Ishii Yoneo, "Siam and Japan in Pre-Modern Times."
9. Much has been written on Japan's so-called Christian Century, but probably the best introduction is Jurgis Elisonas, "Christianity and the Daimyo." Some of the more important writings by Western missionaries to Japan have been translated in Michael Cooper, ed., *They Came to Japan.*
10. John Saris, quoted in Cooper, ed., *They Came to Japan,* pp. 287–288.
11. *Gūji enji shō, Hakozaki zōei no koto,* in *Dazaifu, Dazaifu Tenmangū shiryō,* vol. 6, pp. 439–440.

12. Shin Sukchu, *Haedong chegukki,* p. 164.
13. *Zoku fudoki* and *Hakata tsu yōroku,* cited in Kawazoe Shōji et al., eds., *Kadokawa Nihon chimei daijiten 40 Fukuoka ken,* p. 1065.
14. Song Hŭigyŏng, *Nosongdang Ilbon haengnok,* pp. 57–72 and 165–179.
15. Ibid., p. 63.
16. The Dutch mission was moved to Deshima in 1641; before that it was at Hirado, also in Nagasaki Prefecture.
17. On foreign relations in the Edo period, the best single-volume work in English remains Ronald P. Toby, *State and Diplomacy in Early Modern Japan.* Also see the bibliographic review by Brett Walker, "Foreign Affairs and Frontiers in Early Modern Japan," and the recent books by Reinier H. Hesselink, *Prisoners from Nambu,* and James B. Lewis, *Frontier Contact between Chosŏn Korea and Tokugawa Japan.* The last book focuses on the "Japan House" maintained for Japanese representatives in Pusan. In many ways the "Japan House" would make a good comparison with the Kōrokan in Hakata. Unfortunately, I came across Lewis's book too late to incorporate its arguments into the present work.
18. Several of Edwin O. Reischauer's (generally excellent) books start out with a discussion of the twin phenomena of isolation and homogeneity. See, for example, Reischauer, *The Japanese Today,* pp. 31–36.
19. For example, see the various essays by Australian and Japanese scholars in Donald Denoon, Mark Hudson, Gavan McCormack, and Tessa Morris-Suzuki, eds., *Multicultural Japan.*
20. Von Verschuer, "Across the Sea," pp. 14–18, and graph on p. 19.
21. E.g., Amino Yoshihiko, "Emperor, Rice, and Commoners."
22. On foreign imports, especially technological imports, see the important but neglected book by Masayoshi Sugimoto and David L. Swain, *Science and Culture in Traditional Japan.*
23. On the *wakō,* see Kawazoe, "Japan and East Asia," pp. 405–408 and 423–432, and Elisonas, "The Inseparable Trinity," pp. 239–265.
24. See von Verschuer, "Across the Sea," pp. 14–18 and chart on p. 19.

Works Cited

All Japanese-language works were published in Tokyo unless otherwise stated.

Primary Sources

Chōya gunsai. Shintei zōho kokushi taikei, vol. 29, pt. 1. Ed. Kuroita Katsumi and Kokushi taikei henshūkai. Yoshikawa kōbunkan, 1938.

Chūgoku seishi Nihon den 1: Weizhi Woren zhuan, Hou Han shu Wozhuan, Sung shu Woguo zhuan, Sui shu Woguo zhuan (J. *Gishi Wakokuden, Gokanjo Waden, Sōsho Wakokuden, Zuisho Wakokuden*). Iwanami bunko 33-401-1. Ed. Ishihara Michihiro. Iwanami shoten, 1985.

Dazaifu, Dazaifu Tenmangū shiryō. 17 vols. to date. Ed. Takeuchi Rizō and Kawazoe Shōji. Dazaifu: Dazaifu Tenmangū, 1964–.

Engishiki. Shintei zōho kokushi taikei, vol. 26. Ed. Kuroita Katsumi and Kokushi taikei henshūkai. Yoshikawa kōbunkan, 1973.

Fujiwara Akihira. *Shinsarugakuki.* Tōyō bunko 424. Ed. Kawaguchi Hisao. Heibonsha, 1983.

Fusō ryakki. Shintei zōho kokushi taikei, vol. 12. Ed. Kuroita Katsumi and Kokushi taikei henshūkai. Yoshikawa kōbunkan, 1932.

Heian ibun. 13 vols. Ed. Takeuchi Rizō. Tōkyōdō, 1965.

Hokuzanshō. Teihon Tankaku sōsho, vols. 26–28. Ed. Asakura Haruhiko. Taikūsha, 1998.

Honchō seiki. Shintei zōho kokushi taikei, vol. 9. Ed. Kuroita Katsumi and Kokushi taikei henshūkai. Yoshikawa kōbunkan, 1933.

Hyakurenshō. Shintei zōho kokushi taikei, vol. 11. Ed. Kuroita Katsumi and Kokushi taikei henshūkai. Yoshikawa kōbunkan, 1929.

Kaifūsō. Nihon koten bungaku taikei, vol. 69. Ed. Kojima Noriyuki. Iwanami shoten, 1964.

Koryŏ sa (J. *Kōrai shi*). 3 vols. Kokusho kankōkai, 1977.

Koryŏ sa chŏryo (J. *Kōrai shi setsuyō*). Gakutō sōsho, vol. 3. Gakushūin Tōyō bunka kenkyūsho, 1960.

Midō kanpakuki. 3 vols. Dainihon kokiroku. Ed. Tōkyō daigaku shiryō hensanjo. Iwanami shoten, 1952–1954.

Nihon kiryaku. Shintei zōho kokushi taikei, vols. 10–11. Ed. Kuroita Katsumi and Kokushi taikei henshūkai. Yoshikawa kōbunkan, 1929.

Nihon kōki. Yakuchū Nihon shiryō. Ed. Kuroita Nobuo and Morita Tei. Shūeisha, 2003.

Nihon Montoku tennō jitsuroku. Shintei zōho kokushi taikei, vol. 3. Ed. Kuroita Katsumi and Kokushi taikei henshūkai. Yoshikawa kōbunkan, 1934.

Nihon sandai jitsuroku. Shintei zōho kokushi taikei, vol. 4. Ed. Kuroita Katsumi and Kokushi taikei henshūkai. Yoshikawa kōbunkan, 1934.

Nihon shoki. 2 vols. Nihon koten bungaku taikei, vols. 67–68. Ed. Sakamoto Tarō, Ienaga Saburō, Inoue Mitsusada, and Ōno Susumu. Iwanami shoten, 1965–1967.

Ritsuryō. Nihon shisō taikei, vol. 3. Ed. Inoue Mitsusada, Seki Akira, Tsuchida Naoshige, and Aoki Kazuo. Iwanami shoten, 1976.

Ruijū kokushi. Shintei zōho kokushi taikei, vols. 5–6. Ed. Kuroita Katsumi and Kokushi taikei henshūkai. Yoshikawa kōbunkan, 1933–1934.

Ruijū sandai kyaku. Shintei zōho kokushi taikei, vol. 25. Ed. Kuroita Katsumi and Kokushi taikei henshūkai. Yoshikawa kōbunkan, 1936.

Ryōnogige. Shintei zōho kokushi taikei, vol. 22. Ed. Kuroita Katsumi and Kokushi taikei henshūkai. Yoshikawa kōbunkan, 1939.

Sakeiki. Shiryō taisei, vol. 4. Naigai shoseki, 1936.

Shin Sukchu. *Haedong chegukk* (J. *Tōkai shokoku ki*). Iwanami bunko 33-458-1. Ed. Tanaka Takeo. Iwanami shoten, 1991.

Shingishiki. In Gunsho ruijū, vol. 5, pp. 35–78. Ed. Hanawa Hokiichi. Keizai zasshi sha, 1898.

Shoku Nihon kōki. Shintei zōho kokushi taikei, vol. 3. Ed. Kuroita Katsumi and Kokushi taikei henshūkai. Yoshikawa kōbunkan, 1934.

Shoku Nihongi. 5 vols. Shin Nihon koten bungaku taikei, vols. 12–16. Ed. Aoki Kazuo, Inaoka Kōji, Sasayama Haruo, and Shirafuji Noriyuki. Iwanami shoten, 1989–1998.

Shōyūki. 11 vols. Dainihon kokiroku. Ed. Tōkyō daigaku shiryō hensanjo. Iwanami shoten, 1959–1986.

Song Hŭigyŏng. *Nosongdang Ilbon haengnok* (J. *Rōshōdō Nihon kōroku*). Iwanami bunko 33-454-1. Ed. Murai Shōsuke. Iwanami shoten, 1987.

Teishinkōki. Dainihon kokiroku. Ed. Tōkyō daigaku shiryō hensanjo. Iwanami shoten, 1956.

Tosōki. In "'Tosōki': Mikkō sō Kaikaku no nikki," by Hashimoto Yoshihiko. *Asahi hyakka Nihon no rekishi, bessatsu: Rekishi no yomikata,* pt. 4. *Bunken shiryō o yomu: Kodai,* pp. 46–53. Ed. Asahi shinbunsha. Asahi shinbunsha, 1992.

Zuikei Shūhō. *Zenrin kokuhōki*. Yakuchū Nihon shiryō. Ed. Tanaka Takeo. Shūeisha, 1995.

Secondary Sources and Translations

Ajia Taiheiyō hakuran kyōkai, ed. *Michi, deai / Roads to Kyūshū, Communication in Kyūshū.* Fukuoka: Ajia Taiheiyō hakuran kyōkai, 1989.

Alley, Richard. *The Two-Mile Time Machine: Ice Cores, Abrupt Climate Change, and Our Future.* Princeton, N.J.: Princeton University Press, 2003.

Amino Yoshihiko. "Emperor, Rice, and Commoners." In *Multicultural Japan: Palaeolithic to Postmodern,* ed. Donald Denoon, Mark Hudson, Gavan McCormack, and Tessa Morris-Suzuki, pp. 235–244. Cambridge: Cambridge University Press, 1996.

———. *Mōko shūrai.* Shōgakukan bunko. Shōgakukan, 2001.

Asao Naohiro, Uno Shun'ichi, and Tanaka Migaku, eds. *Kadokawa shinpan Nihonshi jiten.* Kadokawa shoten, 1996.

Aston, W. G., trans. *Nihongi: Chronicles of Japan from the Earliest Times to A.D. 697.* 2 vols. in 1. Rutland, Vt.: Tuttle, 1972.

Batten, Bruce L. "Cross-Border Traffic on the Kyushu Coast, 794–1086." In *Centers and Peripheries in Heian Japan,* ed. Mikael Adolphson, Edward Kamens, and Stacie Matsumoto. Honolulu: University of Hawai'i Press, forthcoming.

———. "Foreign Threat and Domestic Reform: The Emergence of the *Ritsuryō* State." *Monumenta Nipponica* 41.2 (1986): 199–219.

———. *Kokkyō no tanjō: Dazaifu kara mita Nihon no genkei.* NHK bukkusu 922. Nihon hōsō shuppan kyōkai, 2001.

———. "An Open and Shut Case?: Some Thoughts on Late Heian Foreign Trade." Jeffrey P. Mass Memorial Symposium. Stanford University. May 5, 2001.

———. "Ritsuryō sei ka ni okeru Shiragi, Bokkaishi no settaihō." *Kyūshū shigaku* 83 (1985): 1–22.

———. "State and Frontier in Early Japan: The Imperial Court and Northern Kyushu, 645–1185." Ph.D. dissertation, Stanford University, 1989.

———. *To the Ends of Japan: Premodern Frontiers, Boundaries, and Interactions.* Honolulu: University of Hawai'i Press, 2003.

Beasley, W. G. "The Foreign Threat and the Opening of the Ports." In *The Cambridge History of Japan.* Vol. 5: *The Nineteenth Century,* ed. Marius B. Jansen, pp. 259–307. Cambridge: Cambridge University Press, 1989.

Berry, Mary Elizabeth. *Hideyoshi.* Harvard East Asian Series, 97. Cambridge: Harvard University Press, 1982.

Bingham, Woodridge. *The Founding of the T'ang Dynasty.* Baltimore: Waverly Press, 1941.

Boot, W. J. "Maxims of Foreign Policy." In *Shifting Communities and Identity Formation in Early Modern Asia,* ed. Leonard Blussé and Felipe Fernández-Armesto, pp. 7–23. Leiden: Research School of Asian, African, and Amerindian Studies (CNWS), Leiden University, 2003.

Borgen, Robert. "The Case of the Plagiaristic Journal: A Curious Passage from

Jōjin's Diary." In *New Leaves: Studies and Translations of Japanese Literature in Honor of Edward Seidensticker,* ed. Aileen Gatten and Anthony Hood Chambers, pp. 63–74. Ann Arbor: Center for Japanese Studies, University of Michigan, 1993.

———. "Japanese Nationalism: Ancient and Modern." *Meiji gakuin daigaku kokusai gakubu fuzoku kenkyūjo kenkyūjo nenpō* 1 (1998): 49–59.

———. "Jōjin's Travels from Center to Center (With Some Periphery in Between)." In *Centers and Peripheries in Heian Japan,* ed. Mikael Adolphson, Edward Kamens, and Stacie Matsumoto. Honolulu: University of Hawai'i Press, forthcoming.

———. "*San Tendai Godai sanki* as a Source for the Study of Sung History." *Bulletin of Sung Yuan Studies* 19 (1987): 1–16.

———. *Sugawara no Michizane and the Early Heian Court.* Cambridge: Harvard University Press, 1986.

———. "Through Several Glasses Brightly: A Japanese Copy of a Chinese Account of Japan." *Sino-Japanese Studies* 2.2 (1990): 5–19.

Bowman, Alan K. *Life and Letters on the Roman Frontier.* New York: Routledge, 1994.

Chō Yōichi. "Sakimori o meguru mondai." *Tofurō* 25 (1998): 2–21.

Conlan, Thomas D. *In Little Need of Divine Intervention: Takezaki Suenaga's Scrolls of the Mongol Invasions of Japan.* Cornell East Asia Series, no. 113. Ithaca, N.Y.: Cornell University East Asia Program, 2001.

Cooper, Michael, ed. *They Came to Japan: An Anthology of European Reports on Japan, 1543–1640.* Michigan Classics in Japanese Studies, no. 15. Ann Arbor: Center for Japanese Studies, University of Michigan, 1995 [1965].

Dazaifu shishi henshū iinkai, ed. *Dazaifu shishi kōko shiryō hen.* Dazaifu, 1992.

de Bary, Wm. Theodore; Donald Keene; George Tanabe; and Paul Varley, eds. *Sources of Japanese Tradition.* Vol. 1: *From Earliest Times to 1600.* 2d ed. New York: Columbia University Press, 2001.

Denoon, Donald; Mark Hudson; Gavan McCormack; and Tessa Morris-Suzuki, eds. *Multicultural Japan: Palaeolithic to Postmodern.* Cambridge: Cambridge University Press, 1996.

Doe, Paula. *A Warbler's Song in the Dusk: The Life and Work of Ōtomo Yakamochi (718–785).* Berkeley: University of California Press, 1982.

Drummond, Steven K., and Lynn H. Nelson. *The Western Frontiers of Imperial Rome.* Armonk, N.Y.: M. E. Sharpe, 1994.

Eisenstadt, S. N. *The Political Systems of Empires.* London: Free Press of Glencoe, 1963.

Elisonas, Jurgis. "Christianity and the Daimyo." In *The Cambridge History of Japan.* Vol. 4: *Early Modern Japan,* ed. John Whitney Hall, pp. 301–372. Cambridge: Cambridge University Press, 1991.

———. "The Inseparable Trinity: Japan's Relations with China and Korea."

In *The Cambridge History of Japan*. Vol. 4: *Early Modern Japan*, ed. John Whitney Hall, pp. 235–300. Cambridge: Cambridge University Press, 1991.

Elton, Hugh. *Frontiers of the Roman Empire*. Bloomington and Indianapolis: Indiana University Press, 1996.

Enomoto Jun'ichi. " 'Shōyūki' ni mieru 'tokai kinsei' ni tsuite: Ritsuryō kokka no taigai hōshin to sono henshitsu." In *Sekkan jidai to kokiroku*, ed. Yamanaka Yutaka, pp. 162–189. Yoshikawa kōbunkan, 1991.

Fagan, Brian. *The Long Summer: How Climate Changed Civilization*. New York: Basic Books, 2004.

Farris, William Wayne. *Heavenly Warriors: The Evolution of Japan's Military, 500–1300*. Harvard East Asian Monographs 157. Cambridge: Council on East Asian Studies, Harvard University, 1992.

———. *Population, Disease, and Land in Early Japan, 645–900*. Harvard-Yenching Institute Monograph Series, 24. Cambridge: Council on East Asian Studies, Harvard University, 1985.

———. *Sacred Texts and Buried Treasures: Issues in the Historical Archaeology of Ancient Japan*. Honolulu: University of Hawai'i Press, 1998.

Fitzgerald, C. P. *The Empress Wu*. London: Cresset Press, 1968.

Friday, Karl F. *Hired Swords: The Rise of Private Warrior Power in Early Japan*. Stanford, Calif.: Stanford University Press, 1992.

Fukuoka shi kyōiku iinkai, ed. *Kōrokan ato 14: Heisei 11, 12 nendo hakkutsu chōsa hōkokusho*. Fukuoka shi maizō bunkazai chōsa hōkokusho dai 783 shū. Fukuoka: Fukuoka shi kyōiku iinkai, 2004.

Gordon, Andrew. *A Modern History of Japan: From Tokugawa Times to the Present*. New York: Oxford University Press, 2003.

Guisso, R. W. L. *Wu Tse-T'ien and the Politics of Legitimation in T'ang China*. Bellingham: Western Washington University, 1978.

Habu, Junko. *Ancient Jomon of Japan*. Case Studies in Early Societies. Cambridge: Cambridge University Press, 2004.

Hakata kenkyūkai, ed. *Hakata isekigun shutsudo bokusho shiryō shūsei*. Fukuoka: Hakata kenkyūkai, 1996.

Hamada Kōsaku. *Shiragi kokushi no kenkyū: Higashi Ajia shi no shiten kara*. Yoshikawa kōbunkan, 2002.

———. "Sovereignty and Maritime Power: Chang Pogo's Ch'ŏnghae Garrison and Pirates." *Interaction and Transformations, Bulletin of Japan Society for the Promotion of Science 21st Century COE Program (Humanities), East Asia and Japan: Interaction and Transformations, Kyushu University* 1 (2003): 131–145.

Hanihara Kazuro. "Dual Structure Model for the Population History of the Japanese." *Japan Review* 2 (1991): 1–33.

Hesselink, Reinier H. *Prisoners from Nambu: Reality and Make-Believe in 17th-Century Japanese Diplomacy*. Honolulu: University of Hawai'i Press, 2002.

Hino Takashi. "Saikaidō." In *Kodai o kangaeru: Kodai dōro,* ed. Kinoshita Ryō, pp. 251–288. Yoshikawa kōbunkan, 1996.

———. "Saikaidō ni okeru ōji (San'yōdō) ni tsuite." *Kyūshū bunkashi kenkyūjo kiyō* 3 (1987): 187-224.

Hirano Kunio. "Dazaifu no chōzei kikō." In *Ritsuryō kokka to shakai,* ed. Takeuchi Rizō hakase kanreki kinenkai, pp. 319–360. Yoshikawa kōbunkan, 1969.

———. "The Yamato State and Korea in the Fourth and Fifth Centuries." *Acta Asiatica* 31 (1977): 51–82.

Hirano Takuji. "Nihon kodai no kyakukan ni kansuru ichikōsatsu." *Kokugakuin zasshi* 89.3 (1988): 38–53.

———. "San'yōdō to kyakukan." *Kokushigaku* 135 (1988): 25–50.

Hirth, Friedrich, and W. W. Rockhill. *Chau Ju-Kua: His Work on the Chinese and Arab Trade in the Twelfth and Thirteenth Centuries, Entitled Chu-Fan-Chï.* Reprint ed. Taipei: Ch'eng-Wen, 1967 [1911].

Hōjō Hideki. *Nihon kodai kokka no chihō shihai.* Yoshikawa kōbunkan, 2000.

Holcombe, Charles. *The Genesis of East Asia: 221 B.C.–A.D. 907.* Asian Interactions and Comparisons. Honolulu: Association for Asian Studies and University of Hawai'i Press, 2001.

Hori, Kyotsu. "The Economic and Political Effects of the Mongol Wars." In *Medieval Japan,* ed. John W. Hall and Jeffrey P. Mass, pp. 184–198. New Haven, Conn.: Yale University Press, 1974.

Hotate Michihisa. *Ōgon kokka: Higashi Ajia to Heian Nihon.* Shiriizu minzoku o tou 3. Aoki shoten, 2004.

Hourani, George F. *Arab Seafaring: In the Indian Ocean in Ancient and Early Medieval Times.* Expanded ed. Princeton, N.J.: Princeton University Press, 1995 [1951].

Hu, Shiu-ying. *An Enumeration of Chinese Materia Medica.* Hong Kong: Chinese University Press, 1980.

Hudson, Mark J. *Ruins of Identity: Ethnogenesis in the Japanese Islands.* Honolulu: University of Hawai'i Press, 1999.

Ikeuchi Hiroshi. *Mansenshi kenykū jōsei.* 6 vols. Yoshikawa kōbunkan, 1933–1972.

Imamura, Keiji. *Prehistoric Japan: New Perspectives on Insular East Asia.* Honolulu: University of Hawai'i Press, 1996.

Inagawa Yayoi. " 'Tokai-sei' to 'karamono-no-tsukai' no kentō." *Shiron* 44 (1991): 94–112.

Inoue Mitsusada with Delmer M. Brown. "The Century of Reform." In *The Cambridge History of Japan.* Vol. 1: *Ancient Japan,* ed. Delmer M. Brown, pp. 163–220. Cambridge: Cambridge University Press, 1993.

Ishigami Eiichi. "Kodai Higashi Ajia chiiki to Nihon." In *Nihon no shakaishi 1 Rettō naigai no kōtsū to kokka,* pp. 55–96. Iwanami shoten, 1987.

———. "Nihon kodai 10 seiki no gaikō." In *Higashi Ajia sekai ni okeru*

Nihon kodaishi kōza 7 Higashi Ajia no hensen to Nihon ritsuryō kokka, pp. 97–143. Gakuseisha, 1982.

Ishii Masatoshi. "8, 9 seiki no Nichi-Ra kankei." In *Nihon zenkindai no kokka to taigai kankei,* ed. Tanaka Takeo, pp. 273–315. Yoshikawa kōbunkan, 1987.

———. *Higashi Ajia sekai to kodai no Nihon.* Nihonshi riburetto 14. Yamakawa shuppansha, 2003.

———. *Nihon Bokkai kankeishi no kenkyū.* Yoshikawa kōbunkan, 2001.

———. "10 seiki no kokusai hendō to Nissō bōeki." In *Shinpan kodai no Nihon 2 Ajia kara mita Nihon,* ed. Tamura Kōichi and Suzuki Yasutami, pp. 339–362. Kadokawa shoten, 1992.

Ishii Susumu. "The Decline of the Kamakura Bakufu." In *The Cambridge History of Japan.* Vol. 3: *Medieval Japan,* ed. Kozo Yamamura, pp. 128–174. Cambridge: Cambridge University Press, 1990.

Ishii Yoneo. "Siam and Japan in Pre-Modern Times: A Note on Mutual Images." In *Multicultural Japan: Palaeolithic to Postmodern,* ed. Donald Denoon, Mark Hudson, Gavan McCormack, and Tessa Morris-Suzuki, pp. 153–159. Cambridge: Cambridge University Press, 1996.

Ishimatsu Yoshio and Kuwahara Shigeo. *Kodai Nihon o hakkutsu suru 4 Dazaifu to Tagajō.* Iwanami shoten, 1985.

Itakusu Kazuko. "Shuchūshi kō." In *Dazaifu kobunka ronsō,* ed. Kyūshū rekishi shiryōkan, vol. 1, pp. 473–505. Yoshikawa kōbunkan, 1983.

Johanson, Donald, and Blake Edgar. *From Lucy to Language.* New York: Simon and Schuster, 1996.

Kaempfer, Englebert. *Kaempfer's Japan: Tokugawa Culture Observed.* Trans., ed., and annotated Beatrice M. Bodart-Bailey. Honolulu: University of Hawai'i Press, 1999.

Kameda Hiroshi. "Chōsen shiki yamajiro wa naze tsukurareta ka." In *Shinshiten Nihon no rekishi 2 Kodai hen I,* ed. Shiraishi Taichirō and Yoshimura Takehiko, pp. 338–345. Shinjinbutsu ōraisha, 1993.

Kanehara Masaaki and Kanehara Masako. "Kōrokan ato no dokō (benjo ikō) ni okeru kiseichūran, kafun, shujitsu no dōtei bunseki." In *Kōrokan ato 4: Heisei 4 nendo hakkutsu chōsa gaiyō hōkoku,* ed. Fukuoka shi kyōiku iinkai, pp. 25–38. Fukuoka shi maizō bunkazai chōsa hōkokusho dai 372 shū. Fukuoka: Fukuoka shi kyōiku iinkai, 1994.

Kaneko Hiromasa, Konishi Masayasu, Sasaki Kiyomitsu, and Chiba Tokuji. *Nihonshi no naka no dōbutsu jiten.* Tōkyōdō shuppan, 1992.

Katayama Kazumichi. "The Japanese as an Asia-Pacific Population." In *Multicultural Japan: Palaeolithic to Postmodern,* ed. Donald Denoon, Mark Hudson, Gavan McCormack, and Tessa Morris-Suzuki, pp. 19–30. Cambridge: Cambridge University Press, 1996.

Kawazoe Shōji. "Japan and East Asia." In *The Cambridge History of Japan.* Vol. 3: *Medieval Japan,* ed. Kozo Yamamura, pp. 396–446. Cambridge: Cambridge University Press, 1990.

———, ed. *Yomigaeru chūsei 1 Higashi Ajia no kokusai toshi Hakata.* Heibonsha, 1988.

———, Chō Yōichi, Tsutsumi Keijirō, Doi Senkichi, and Noguchi Kikuo, eds. *Kadokawa Nihon chimei daijiten 40 Fukuoka ken.* Kadokawa shoten, 1988.

———, Takesue Jun'ichi, Okafuji Yoshitaka, Nishitani Masahiro, Kajiwara Yoshinori, and Orita Etsurō, eds. *Fukuoka ken no rekishi.* Kenshi 40. Yamakawa shuppansha, 1997.

Kinda Akihiro. *Kodai Nihon no keikan.* Yoshikawa kōbunkan, 1993.

Kinoshita Ryō, ed. *Kodai o kangaeru: Kodai dōro.* Yoshikawa kōbunkan, 1996.

Kishi Toshio. *Nihon kodai seijishi kenkyū.* Hanawa shobō, 1966.

Kitajima Manji. *Hideyoshi no Chōsen shinryaku.* Nihonshi riburetto 34. Yamakawa shuppansha, 2002.

Kitō Kiyoaki. *Hakusuki-no-e: Higashi Ajia no dōran to Nihon.* Rekishi shinsho, Nihonshi 33. Kyōikusha, 1981.

Kobayashi Shigeru, Iso Nozomi, Saeki Kōji, and Takakura Hiroaki, eds. *Fukuoka heiya no kokankyō to iseki ritchi: Kankyō to shite no iseki to no kyōzon no tame ni.* Fukuoka: Kyūshū daigaku shuppankai, 1998.

Kōjiya Yoshiaki, ed. *Matsubara kyakukan no nazo ni semaru.* Tsugaru: Kehi shigakukai, 1994.

Kurazumi Yasuhiko. *Kodai no Dazaifu.* Nihon kodaishi kenkyū sensho. Yoshikawa kōbunkan, 1985.

Kyūshū rekishi shiryōkan, ed. *Dazaifu fukugen.* Dazaifu: Kyūshū rekishi shiryōkan, 1998.

———, ed. *Dazaifu seichō ato.* Dazaifu: Kyūshū rekishi shiryōkan, 2002.

Lee, Ki-baik. *A New History of Korea.* Trans. Edward W. Wagner and Edward J. Schultz. Cambridge: Harvard University Press, 1984.

Lee Sungsi (Ri Sonshi). *Higashi Ajia no ōken to kōeki: Shōsōin no hōmotsu ga kita mō hitotsu no michi.* Aoki Library Nihon no rekishi. Aoki shoten, 1997.

Lewis, James B. *Frontier Contact between Chosŏn Korea and Tokugawa Japan.* London: RoutledgeCurzon, 2003.

Matsubara Hironobu. "Chin Taishin no shojō to karamono-kōeki-shi no seiritsu." *Shoku Nihongi kenkyū* 317 (1998): 22–34.

McCormack, Gavan. "Introduction." In *Multicultural Japan: Palaeolithic to Postmodern,* ed. Donald Denoon, Mark Hudson, Gavan McCormack, and Tessa Morris-Suzuki, pp. 1–15. Cambridge: Cambridge University Press, 1996.

McNeill, J. R., and William H. McNeill. *The Human Web: A Bird's-Eye View of World History.* New York: W. W. Norton and Company, 2003.

McNeill, William H. *Plagues and Peoples.* Garden City, N.Y.: Anchor Press, 1976.

Mori Katsumi. *Shintei Nissō bōeki no kenkyū.* Mori Katsumi chosakushū, vol. 1. Kokusho kankōkai, 1975.

Mori Kimiyuki, *"Hakusuki-no-e" igo: Kokka kiki to Higashi Ajia gaikō*. Kōdansha sensho mechie 132. Kōdansha, 1998.

Murai Shōsuke. *Ajia no naka no chūsei Nihon*. Azekura shobō, 1988.

———. "The Boundaries of Medieval Japan." *Acta Asiatica* 81 (2001): 72–91.

Murasaki Shikibu. *The Tale of Genji*. Trans. Royall Tyler. New York: Penguin, 2002.

Nakanishi Masakazu. "Bokkaishi no raichō to Tenchō gonen shōgatsu futsuka kanpu." *Hisutoria* 159 (1998): 30–77.

———. "Dazaifu to zonmon." In *Nihon shoki kenkyū 21*, ed. Yokota Ken'ichi, pp. 109–133. Hanawa shobō, 1997.

———. "Shiragishi, Bokkaishi no raichō to Dazaifu." *Kodaishi no kenkyū* 8 (1990): 13–30.

Naoki Kōjirō. *Asuka Nara jidai no kenkyū*. Hanawa shobō, 1975.

———. *Kodai Nihon to Chōsen, Chūgoku*. Kōdansha gakujutsu bunko. Kōdansha, 1988.

Nelson, Thomas. "Southeast Asian Polities and Society as Seen through Japanese Communities." In *Japan Memory Project Conference Proceedings, Academic Year 2001–2002*, ed. Japan Memory Project (COE, Historiographical Institute, University of Tokyo), pp. 296–309. University of Tokyo, 2003.

Nihon jinkō gakkai, ed. *Jinkō daijiten*. Baifūkan, 2002.

Nishijima Sadao. "Kentōshi to kokusho." In *Kentōshi kenkyū to sono shiryō*, ed. Mozai Torao, Nishijima Sado, Tanaka Takeo, and Ishii Masatoshi, pp. 45–96. Tōkai daigaku shuppankai, 1987.

Nishitani Tadashi. "Chōsen shiki yamajiro." In *Iwanami kōza Nihon tsūshi 3 Kodai 2*, pp. 283–302. Iwanami shoten, 1994.

Nishizono Reizō and Yanagida Sumitaka. *Genkō to Hakata: Shashin de yomu Mōko shūrai*. Fukuoka: Nishi Nihon shinbunsha, 2001.

Noda Reishi. *Sakimori to eji*. Rekishi shinsho. Kyōikusha, 1980.

Ōba Kōji. "Fukuoka shinai kenshutsu no kodai, chūsei dōro ikō ni tsuite." *Hakata iseki kenkyūkai shi (Hakata)* 9 (2001): 21–31.

———. "Hakata gōshu no jidai." *Rekishigaku kenkyū* 756 (2001): 2–11, 74.

———. "Hakata iseki shutsudo bokusho shiryō shūsei 2." *Hakata kenkyūkai shi* 11 (2003): 83–136.

———. "Shūsanchi iseki to shite no Hakata." *Nihonshi kenkyū* 448 (1999): 67–101.

Oda Fujio. *Nishi Nihon kodai yamajiro no kenkyū*. Meicho shuppan, 1985.

———, ed. *Kitakyūshū Setouchi no kodai yamajiro*. Meicho shuppan, 1983.

———, ed. *Kodai o kangaeru: Iwai no ran*. Yoshikawa kōbunkan, 1991.

Okafuji Yoshitaka. "Dazaifu zaisei to kannai shokoku." In *Shinpan kodai no Nihon 3 Kyūshū, Okinawa*, ed. Shimojō Nobuyuki, Hirano Hiroyuki, Chinen Isamu, and Takara Kurayoshi, pp. 297–324. Kadokawa shoten, 1991.

Ōta kuritsu kyōdo hakubutsukan, ed. *Toire no kōkogaku*. Tōkyō bijutsu, 1997.

Ōtsuka Hatsushige, Shiraishi Taichirō, Nishitani Tadashi, and Machida Akira, eds. *Kōkogaku ni yoru Nihon rekishi 6 Sensō*. Yūzankaku, 2000.

Pearson, Richard, ed. *Ancient Japan*. New York: George Braziller, 1992.

———; Gina Lee Barnes; and Karl L. Hutterer, eds. *Windows on the Japanese Past: Studies in Archaeology and Prehistory*. Ann Arbor: Center for Japanese Studies, University of Michigan, 1986.

Piggott, Joan R. *The Emergence of Japanese Kingship*. Stanford, Calif.: Stanford University Press, 1997.

Reischauer, Edwin O. *Ennin's Travels in T'ang China*. New York: Ronald Press, 1955.

———. *The Japanese Today: Change and Continuity*. Cambridge: Belknap Press of Harvard University Press, 1980.

———. "Notes on T'ang Dynasty Sea Routes." *Harvard Journal of Asiatic Studies* 5 (1940–1941): 142–164.

Renfrew, Colin, and John F. Cherry, eds. *Peer Polity Interaction and Socio-Political Change*. Cambridge: Cambridge University Press, 1986.

Roberts, Neil. *The Holocene: An Environmental History*. 2nd ed. Oxford: Blackwell, 1998 [1989].

Rossabi, Morris. *Khubilai Khan: His Life and Times*. Berkeley and Los Angeles: University of California Press, 1988.

Saeki Kōji. "Hakata." In *Iwanami kōza Nihon tsūshi 10 Chūsei 4*, pp. 283–300. Iwanami shoten, 1994.

———. *Mongoru shūrai no shōgeki*. Nihon no chūsei 9. Chūō kōronsha, 2003.

———. "Trade between Japan and Sung China and the *Hakata Gōshu*." *Transactions of the International Conference of Eastern Studies* 48 (2003): 39–50.

Sakayori Masashi. *Bokkai to kodai no Nihon*. Rekishi kagaku sōsho. Azekura shobō, 2001.

Satō Makoto, ed. *Nihon to Bokkai no kodaishi*. Yamakawa shuppansha, 2003.

Schafer, Edward H. *The Golden Peaches of Samarkand: A Study of T'ang Exotics*. Berkeley and Los Angeles: University of California Press, 1963.

———. *The Vermilion Bird: T'ang Images of the South*. Berkeley and Los Angeles: University of California Press, 1967.

Segal, Ethan. "Economic Growth and Changes in Elite Power Structures in Medieval Japan, 1150–1500." Ph.D. dissertation, Stanford University, 2003.

Sen, Tansen. *Buddhism, Diplomacy, and Trade: The Realignment of Sino-Indian Relations, 600–1400*. Asian Interactions and Comparisons. Honolulu: University of Hawai'i Press, 2003.

Shiba Yoshinobu. *Commerce and Society in Sung China*. Trans. Mark Elvin. Michigan Abstracts of Chinese and Japanese Works on Chinese History. Ann Arbor: University of Michigan Center for Chinese Studies, 1970.

Shibata Shōji and Kunaichō Shōsōin jimusho, eds. *Zusetsu Shōsōin yakubutsu*. Chūō kōronsha, 2002.

Shimada Jirō. "Horon: Heishi seiken no tai-Sō bōeki no rekishiteki zentei to sono tenkai." In *Rekishi kenkyū to kokusaiteki keiki,* ed. Chūō daigaku keizai kenkyūjo, pp. 233–271. Chūō daigaku shuppanbu, 1974.

Shimojō Nobuyuki, Hirano Hiroyuki, Chinen Isamu, and Takara Kurayoshi, eds. *Shinpan kodai no Nihon 3 Kyūshū, Okinawa.* Kadokawa shoten, 1991.

Shinokawa Ken. *Ōkimi to chihō gōzoku.* Nihonshi riburetto 5. Yamakawa shuppansha, 2001.

Steele, M. William. *Alternative Narratives in Modern Japanese History.* London: Curzon, 2003.

Sugimoto, Masayoshi, and David L. Swain. *Science and Culture in Traditional Japan.* MIT East Asian Science Series 6. Rutland, Vt.: Charles E. Tuttle, 1989.

Suzuki Takao. *Hone kara mita Nihonjin: Kobyōrigaku ga kataru rekishi.* Kōdansha sensho mechie 142. Kōdansha, 1998.

Suzuki Yasutami. *Kodai taigai kankei shi no kenkyū.* Yoshikawa kōbunkan, 1985.

Taigai kankei shi sōgō nenpyō henshū iinkai, ed. *Taigai kankei shi sōgō nenpyō.* Yoshikawa kōbunkan, 1999.

Tajima Isao. "Dazaifu Kōrokan no shūen." *Nihonshi kenkyū* 389 (1995): 1–29.

———. "Nihon, Chūgoku, Chōsen taigai kōryū nenpyō: Taihō gannen—Bunji gannen." In *Bōeki tōji: Nara Heian no Chūgoku tōji,* ed. Nara kenritsu Kashihara kōkogaku kenkyūjo fuzoku hakubutsukan, pp. 417–540. Kyoto: Rinsen shoten, 1993.

Takahashi Masaaki. *Kiyomori izen: Ise Heishi no kōryū.* Heibonsha sensho 85. Heibonsha, 1984.

Takeno Yōko. *Hakata: Chōnin ga sodadeta kokusai toshi.* Iwanami shinsho 704. Iwanami shoten, 2000.

———. *Hakata no gōshō.* Parirusu bunko 10. Fukuoka: Ashi shobō, 1980.

Tamura Enchō. *Dazaifu tankyū.* Yoshikawa kōbunkan, 1990.

———. *Higashi Ajia no kokka to Bukkyō.* Yoshikawa kōbunkan, 2002.

Tanaka Fumio. *Nihon kodai kokka no minzoku shihai to toraijin.* Rekishi kagaku sōsho. Azekura shobō, 1997.

Toby, Ronald P. *State and Diplomacy in Early Modern Japan: Asia in the Development of the Tokugawa Bakufu.* Reprint ed. Stanford, Calif.: Stanford University Press, 1992 [1984].

Tōno Haruyuki. "Japanese Embassies to T'ang China and Their Ships." *Acta Asiatica* 69 (1995): 39–62.

———. *Kentōshisen: Higashi Ajia no naka de.* Asahi sensho 634. Asahi shinbunsha, 1999.

———. *Shōsōin monjo to mokkan no kenkyū.* Hanawa shobō, 1977.

Tōyama Mitsuo. *Hakusuki-no-e: Kodai Higashi Ajia taisen no nazo.* Kōdansha gendai shinsho 1379. Kōdansha, 1996.

Tsuboi Kiyotari and Tanaka Migaku. *The Historic City of Nara: An Archaeological Approach.* Trans. David W. Hughes and Gina L. Barnes. Tokyo: Centre for East Asian Cultural Studies, 1991.

Tsuchibashi Riko. "Nissō bōeki no shosō." In *Kōkogaku ni yoru Nihon rekishi 10 Taigai kōshō,* ed. Ōtsuka Hatsushige, Shiraishi Taichirō, Nishitani Tadashi, and Machida Akira, pp. 61–76. Yūzankaku, 1997.

Twitchett, Denis, and Howard J. Wechsler. "Kao-Tsung (Reign 649–83) and the Empress Wu: The Inheritor and the Usurper." In *The Cambridge History of China.* Vol. 3: *Sui and T'ang China, 589–906, Part 1,* ed. Denis Twitchett, pp. 242–289. Cambridge: Cambridge University Press, 1979.

Ueda Takashi. *Bokkai koku no nazo.* Kōdansha gendai shinsho 1104. Kōdansha, 1992.

——— and Song Yongong (Son Eiken). *Nihon Bokkai kōshōshi.* Rokkō shuppan, 1990.

von Verschuer, Charlotte. "Across the Sea: Intercourse of People, Know-How, and Goods in East Asia." In *8–17 seiki no Higashi Ajia chiiki ni okeru hito, mono, jōhō no kōryū: Kaiiki to kōshi no keisei, minzoku, chiiki kan no sōgo ninshiki o chūshin ni,* ed. Murai Shōsuke, vol. 1, pp. 13–28. Tōkyō daigaku daigakuin jinbun shakai kei kenkyūka, 2004.

———. *Le commerce extérieur du Japon: Des origenes au XVIe siècle.* Paris: Maisonneuve and Larose, 1988.

———. "Japan's Foreign Relations 600 to 1200 A.D.: A Translation from *Zenrin Kokuhōki.*" *Monumenta Nipponica* 54.1 (1999): 1–39.

———. "Looking from Within and Without: Ancient and Medieval External Relations." *Monumenta Nipponica* 55.4 (2000): 537–566.

———. *Les relations officielles du Japon avec la Chine aux VIIIe et IXe siècles.* Geneva: Droz, 1985.

Walker, Brett L. "Foreign Affairs and Frontiers in Early Modern Japan." *Early Modern Japan* 10.2 (2002): 44–62, 124–128.

Wang, Gungwu. *The Nanhai Trade: The Early History of Chinese Trade in the South China Sea.* Reprint ed. Singapore: Times Academic Press, 1998 [1958].

Wang, Zhen-ping. "Sino-Japanese Relations before the Eleventh Century: Modes of Diplomatic Communication Reexamined in Terms of the Concept of Reciprocity." Ph.D. dissertation, Princeton University, 1989.

Wechsler, Howard J. "T'ai-Tsung (Reign 626–49) the Consolidator." In *The Cambridge History of China.* Vol. 3: *Sui and T'ang China, 589–906, Part 1,* ed. Denis Twitchett, pp. 188–241. Cambridge: Cambridge University Press, 1979.

Wilson, Edward O. *On Human Nature.* Cambridge: Harvard University Press, 1988.

Wong, Joseph. "Unfought Korean Wars: Prelude to the Korean Wars of the Seventh Century." *Papers in Far Eastern History* 22 (1980): 123–142.

Worthy, Edmund H., Jr. "Diplomacy for Survival: Domestic and Foreign Relations of Wu Yüeh, 907–978." In *China among Equals: The Middle Kingdom and Its Neighbors, 10th–14th Centuries*, ed. Morris Rossabi, pp. 17–44. Berkeley and Los Angeles: University of California Press, 1983.

Wright, Arthur F. *The Sui Dynasty*. New York: Alfred A. Knopf, 1978.

———. "The Sui Dynasty (581–617)." In *The Cambridge History of China*. Vol. 3: *Sui and T'ang China, 589–906, Part 1*, ed. Denis Twitchett, pp. 48–149. Cambridge: Cambridge University Press, 1979.

Writing Group Reporting on the Excavation of a Sung Dynasty Seagoing Vessel at Ch'üan-chou Bay. "A Brief Report on the Excavation of a Sung Dynasty Seagoing Vessel at Ch'üan-Chou Bay." *Chinese Sociology and Anthropology* 9.3 (1977): 6–53.

Yamamura, Kozo. "The Decline of the *Ritsuryō* System: Hypotheses on Economic and Institutional Change." *Journal of Japanese Studies* 1.1 (1974): 3–37.

Yamao Yukihisa. *Tsukushi no kimi Iwai no sensō: Higashi Ajia no naka no kodai kokka*. Shin Nihon shuppansha, 1999.

Yamauchi Shinji. *Nara Heian ki no Nihon to Ajia*. Yoshikawa kōbunkan, 2003.

Yoshimura Takehiko. "Wa no goō to wa dare ka." In *Sōten Nihon no rekishi 2 Kodai hen 1*, ed. Shiraishi Taichirō and Yoshimura Takehiko, pp. 62–73. Shinjinbutsu ōraisha, 1990.

Yūgen gaisha Heibonsha chihō shiryō sentā, ed. *Nagasaki ken no chimei*. Nihon rekishi chimei taikei 43. Heibonsha, 2001.

Index

About the Author

BRUCE L. BATTEN was educated at the University of Oregon and Stanford University, where he received his Ph.D. in 1989. He has lived in Japan since the mid-1980s and is currently professor of Japanese history and director of the Center for International Studies at Ōbirin University in Tokyo. Professor Batten has published numerous articles and three previous books on Japanese history, including *To the Ends of Japan: Premodern Frontiers, Boundaries, and Interaction* (University of Hawai'i Press, 2003).

CPSIA information can be obtained
at www.ICGtesting.com
Printed in the USA
LVHW01s2216220118
563534LV00016B/1637/P

9 780824 830298